Leon Trotsky and World War One

Also by Ian D. Thatcher

ALEC NOVE ON ECONOMIC THEORY

ALEC NOVE ON COMMUNIST AND POSTCOMMUNIST COUNTRIES

MARKETS AND SOCIALISM (*with Alec Nove*)

* REGIME AND SOCIETY IN TWENTIETH-CENTURY RUSSIA

* *From the same publishers*

First published in Great Britain 2000 by
MACMILLAN PRESS LTD
Houndmills, Basingstoke, Hampshire RG21 6XS and London
Companies and representatives throughout the world

A catalogue record for this book is available from the British Library.

ISBN 0–333–91806–1

First published in the United States of America 2000 by
ST. MARTIN'S PRESS, INC.,
Scholarly and Reference Division,
175 Fifth Avenue, New York, N.Y. 10010

ISBN 0–312–23487–2

Library of Congress Cataloging-in-Publication Data
Thatcher, Ian D.
Leon Trotsky and World War One : August 1914–February 1917 / Ian D. Thatcher.
p.   cm.
Includes bibliographical references and index.
ISBN 0–312–23487–2 (cloth)
1. Trotsky, Leon, 1879–1940 — Views on World War, 1914–1918. 2. Trotsky, Leon,
1879–1940 — Contributions in literature. 3. World War, 1914–1918 — Press
coverage — Russia. I. Title: Leon Trotsky and World War I. II. Title.

DK254.T6 T49   2000
947.084'092 — dc21

00–027151

This book is printed on paper suitable for recycling and made from fully managed and sustained
forest sources.

10   9   8   7   6   5   4   3   2   1
09 08 07 06 05 04 03 02 01 00

Printed and bound in Great Britain by
Antony Rowe Ltd, Chippenham, Wiltshire

Leon Trotsky and World War One

August 1914–February 1917

Ian D. Thatcher
Lecturer in the History of Soviet Russia
Department of History
University of Leicester

Contents

Preface

Leon Trotsky is perhaps most famous for his leading role in the Russian Revolution and Civil War and for his analysis of Stalin's USSR. It would be wrong though to dismiss his pre-1917 biography. It was in the pre-Revolutionary era that he developed his famous theory of permanent revolution. Indeed, one could argue that Trotsky had written his finest political texts by 1917. As a historical figure, Trotsky developed his theory very much in the fire of events, most importantly in journalistic essays. Journalism also contributed towards covering living expenses; one of Trotsky's chief sources of income was the articles he wrote for newspapers. They are thus an important source both for tracing the evolution of Trotsky's views and for evaluating his effectiveness as a revolutionary. It is no surprise that they are the main source for this study, although relevant archives have also been consulted.

Trotsky is acknowledged to have been a successful journalist. His command of language combined with a clear framework through which events could be analysed with confidence enabled him to produce incisive and effective copy. Doubt is rarely present; biting and humorous criticism prevails. Given that his journalism of the Balkan Wars has been translated and published in English, it is surprising that his output of World War One has not received similar treatment. After all, the impact of the First World War was far greater than that of the Balkan Wars, including for Trotsky's own intellectual development. It is precisely between 1914 and 1917, for example, that Trotsky himself located the convergence of his thought and Lenin's, making the alliance of 1917 the natural outcome of a longer-term process. Upon examination this claim, like so many others, turns out to be false. But this has not prevented it from making a deep impact on the historiography to date. Only by reading Trotsky's writings of the time can his main concerns as a thinker and a publicist be illustrated. This book has set itself the task of being the first full account of Trotsky's writings of World War One. It will therefore in the first instance be a work of exposition.

Readers should also expect to discover why, for example, Trotsky sought subsequently to rewrite his intellectual biography of these years. They should also leave this study with an appreciation of how much previous historians left out of their accounts. Isaac Deutscher's standard biography is shown to be deficient in its version of several aspects of Trotsky's activities, from the impact of the Parisian censor to the nature of Trotsky's essays for the Ukrainian newspaper *Kievskaya Mysl.* Israel Getzler's standard biography of Martov is criticised for not mentioning the dilemmas faced by Martov in dealing with differences in the Menshevik camp, and how this complicated his relations with Trotsky. Finally, the conclusion addresses the issue of what is lasting in Trotsky's output as the war to end all wars was being fought. It is interesting to note that in many respects Trotsky's journalism of the century's beginning still has strong echoes in that of the century's end.

Thanks are due to Paul Dukes and James D. White for their help during the book's research and writing. Any errors are my own.

Ian D. Thatcher
Leicester, July 1999

1
Switzerland

On 19 July 1914, when Germany declared war on Russia, Trotsky was in Vienna. The following day he questioned socialist deputies on the likely position of Russian émigrés. He met Fritz Adler who informed him that the Austrian government had just counselled its citizens to be on the look-out for suspicious foreigners who should then be reported to the police. Along with Fritz's father, Victor, Trotsky then sought the advice of the head of the Austrian political police. He was informed that an order for the arrest and internment of all Serbs and Russians living in Austria would possibly be issued on the next day:

It follows then that you recommend departure?
Certainly, and the quicker the better.
All right ... tomorrow I'll go to Switzerland with my family.
Well, it would be better to do this today.[1]

The above conversation took place at three o'clock in the afternoon. At 6.10 p.m. Trotsky and his family were on a train bound for Switzerland, that 'temporary political watchtower from which several Russian Marxists reviewed the development of those unprecedented events'.[2]

Safe in Zurich Trotsky noted his first reactions to the events immediately following the outbreak of the World War One in his dairy; a literary form he often employed when in difficult circumstances:

after two to three weeks, when the French and German newspapers in Zurich gave a complete picture of the total political and moral catastrophe of official socialism, the diary was a substitute for a critical and political pamphlet.[3]

In the 1914 diary Trotsky did not concern himself with elaborating an explanation of the causes for the outbreak of the war. At this point he focused on the collapse of the Second International.

Referring to the 'collapse' of internationalism Trotsky stressed that this did not spring out of a vacuum. In the entry for the 10th of August he noted that the question of the danger of war was raised in the Second International every three years. During discussions war was roundly condemned, disagreements surfaced only around the problems of how to hinder war efforts and, if war actually started, how to prevent 'backward' elements from obeying mobilisation orders and how to break the war 'with the heads of the ruling classes.' However, when war looked likely the German Social-Democrat Party had entered into secret negotiations with its government; the French establishment had convinced its Socialist Party of its peaceloving nature; and Austrian Social-Democrats had announced Austro-Hungary's ultimatum to Serbia as justified. When the hostilities began German socialists in the Reichstag voted for an extra five million in war credits and Austro-Hungarian comrades became intoxicated with nationalism. For Trotsky,

> It is absolutely clear that what happened was not simply mistakes, or isolated opportunistic steps, or 'awkward' declarations from the floors of parliaments, or the votes of the Grand-Duchy Social-Democrats for the budget, or the experiments of French ministerism, or the degeneracy of several leaders – what took place was the collapse of the International in the most crucial epoch, *a collapse prepared by all its previous work*.[4]

Elaborating upon this theme on the 12th of August Trotsky highlighted Austrian Social-Democracy to illustrate his general point that national contradictions were long ago evident in the Second International. He cited Victor Adler as describing the International Department in Brussels as 'decorative', and remembered an earlier article against the chauvinistic tendencies of the Austrian Social-Democratic newspaper *Arbeiter-Zeitung*, which he had felt compelled to write and publish in the *Neue Zeitung*. He labelled Adler's statement 'short-sighted' in that in a multi-national country such as Austria, the external policy of the Austro-German Social-Democrats would always have internal repercussions:

> One cannot separate the 'German idea' and the 'German spirit'

from the 'Slav' idea as the *Arbeiter Zeitung* did everywhere and at the same time unite the German workers with the Slavs. One cannot day-in day-out slight the Serbs as 'horsethieves' and expect to unite the German workers with the Austrian South-Slavs.[5]

It was precisely such instances of nationalism which, for Trotsky, had directly led to socialists backing the war efforts of their home governments:

> The Social-Democratic deputy Ellenbogen said at a mass meeting in Vienna: 'We are faithful to the German nation in good times and bad, in peace and in war' ... As a result of this policy the party split into different national groupings, and at the moment of war the German Social-Democrats of Austria appeared as a subsidiary detachment of the monarchy.[6]

For Trotsky, what was true of Austrian Social-Democracy also held true for West European Social-Democracy. Thus, for instance, Bebel of the German Social-Democratic Party 'at some point promised to put a gun on his shoulder for the defence of the fatherland against tsarism'.[7] And, according to Trotsky, the only distinguishing feature of German Social-Democracy was that it kept its formal affiliation to internationalism hidden better than any other Western Social-Democratic party.[8]

However, forever the revolutionary optimist, Trotsky did not fall into a mood of absolute despair. Indeed, he viewed the generally positive reactions to the outbreak of war and the collapse of the Second International as temporary phenomena.

Trotsky explained initial feelings of joy by reference to the fact that, for the workers, war arrives as a break from a routine of life which is one of insufferable hell. Moreover, war brings with it promises of change for the better. However, for Trotsky, the moods of the masses would go through the following general pattern of rise and fall: the first months of the war are a period of hope; this stage is soon concluded and followed by worry as the material hardships imposed by war begin to be felt; then news of the first 'blessed victories' renews hopes and spirits; this tide of joy is then dissipated by a return of the hardships of war. The accumulative effect of dashed hopes and privations can then create a situation which leads to a revolution:

> War often brings about revolution. This is not so much because the

war was unsuccessful in a state sense, as because the war did not satisfy all expectations.[9]

Furthermore, Trotsky noted several developments which put the prospects for socialist revolution into a healthy light.

First, with reference to Germany, in the entry for 15 August, Trotsky reacted to the unconfirmed news that Liebknecht had been killed in an anti-war demonstration in Berlin by writing that Liebknecht had saved the honour and pride of German Social-Democracy. Then, on 17 August, Mol'kenbur told Trotsky that in the discussions on tactics to be adopted in the Reichstag during the vote on the war credits, 36, one-third of those present, had voted for a rejection and 15 had abstained. Hence, the decision to go to the Reichstag and support the government had been passed by a few votes only. For Trotsky, the 'shameful character' of the German SPD's war vote of 4 August had not been removed by the objections of the 36. But, he said,

> the figures for the groups inside the fraction are in themselves very suggestive for the future: what upset could the vote [for war credits] have brought forth among the masses if, even within the fraction, the most opportunistic part of the party, almost half of the members were against it.[10]

Furthermore, according to Trotsky, the war would break the link between the German proletariat on the one side, and its Social-Democratic organisations on the other. This was a positive development since the latter had become contamintaed with bourgeois opinion. According to the diarist, bourgeois influence had stemmed from the nature of German Social-Democratic parliamentarianism, i.e., the creation of a bureaucracy which had daily contact with the leading representatives of bourgeois society. This, in turn, had created an atmosphere of compromise which had inevitably influenced the thinking of the workers' representatives, making them susceptible to bourgeois policy. For Trotsky, the consequence of this process was that in the epoch leading-up to World War One the German proletariat had received neither an international perspective, nor a revolutionary temper, from its representatives. However, mobilisation

> mechanically and moreover at one blow tears the workers from productive and organisational cages: from foremen, trade unions,

political organisations and so on ... placing and uniting them in the new fiery and iron cages of regiments, brigades, divisions ...[11]

Second, in a discussion of his homeland's prospects Trotsky predicted that Russia would not withstand the pressures of war for long. Dismissing the notion that the Russian army had put itself to rights after the Russo-Japanese War of 1905, Trotsky turned to an evaluation of the current condition of the constituent parts of Russia's armed forces. To begin with he noted that the Russian peasant had broken with patriarchal passivity. The events of the 1905 revolution had, he said, awakened a new personality in the Russian peasant: a personality which, given continual economic growth in the countryside could have taken an individualistic bent, thus providing a support for a bourgeois order; but, under the reality of economic uncertainty and 'depressions', was still far from bourgeois norms and, as such, not a reliable ally. Furthermore, the growing weight of workers and national minority groups as a percentage of the army provided a further force for instability. In particular, Trotsky pointed to the strikes in St. Petersburg on the eve of the war, mentioning their 'revolutionary character', and argued that the workers would carry their hatred of the Russian ruling classes into the army. And, once there, he predicted that the proletariat would recognise its class enemy in the officer corps; a group which, he said, had become an integral part of Russia's ruling elite, distinguished for its 'embezzlement, nepotism and terrible indifference.' For Trotsky, this had all the makings of an explosive situation:

> From all of this there flows an inevitable, awful disintegration which, in its turn, unleashes the revolutionary energy of the people. Hence one cannot exclude the possibility that we will be returning to the homeland before the year is out.[12]

Third, Trotsky thought that socialist planning would grow out of the economic dislocation caused by the war. He reached this conclusion through an analysis of a debate taking place in Switzerland over how to guarantee the supply of essential foodstuffs for the duration of the hostilities. Switzerland was not self-sufficient, supplying only one quarter of its domestic consumer market. On 12 August 1914 the Zurich Social-Democratic newspaper *Volksrecht* proposed the requisition of all grain and potatoes. These would then be distributed through canton and communal organs. Finance was to come from the state bank, which would act as a mediator between the state and the agricultural sector. Describing this as only one step towards the distribution of essentials Trotsky continued,

> The more war introduces chaos into international economic relations, the more it disorganises production and the means of communication, the more one has to distribute the available staple foodstuffs ahead of time and wisely. But one can only produce and distribute in a wise and economic manner on a socialist basis ... Humanity will not be destroyed under the smoke of militarism's wreckage. It scrambles out of this and discovers the real road. Beginning with a concern about the planned distribution of potatoes, it moves toward a socialist organisation of production.[13]

Finally, Trotsky retained his revolutionary optimism, derived from his belief in Marxism and the proletariat. This is best illustrated by the following spirited, polemical entry of 11 August 1914:

> One cannot doubt that even in the course of the next few months the European proletariat will raise its head and show that the European revolution lives under European militarism. Only the awakening of the revolutionary socialist movement, which should immediately take-on a very energetic form, can lay the basis for a new International. This will be created through profound internal struggles, which will not only throw off many old elements from socialism but will also widen its base, recasting its political appearance. In any case, socialism will not be forced to begin from the beginning. The Third International will, in a principled sense, mark a return to the First International, but from the springboard of the organisational-educational conquests of the Second International.
>
> The coming years will be an epoch of socialist revolution. Only the revolutionary awakening of the proletariat can stop this war, otherwise it ... will last until the total exhaustion of the world, throwing our civilisation back by several decades ...[14]

The Zurich diary also served as a notebook for the writing of Trotsky's first pamphlet of the war, *The War and the International*. Despite some overlap between the two texts, the latter is distinguished from the former in that the focus is less upon the death of the Second International and more upon the war-aims of the Great Powers. Indeed, for Trotsky, 'The exposure of diplomatic trickery, cheating and knavery is one of the most important functions of socialist political agitation.'[15]

In a discussion of perceptions of the war as one of 'liberation' or 'defence', Trotsky argued that each of the belligerents viewed the hostilities from the standpoint of the power interests of the state. Thus, for example, for Austria-Hungary the war was necessary as a way of preserving a multi-national state threatened by ethnic nationalism:

> Austria-Hungary [as] a state organisation ... is identical with the Hapsburg monarchy ... Since Austria-Hungary is surrounded on all sides by states composed of the same races as within its borders ... [it] is compelled to extinguish the hearthfire that kindles their political leanings – the independent kingdom of Serbia.[16]

In turn, Austrian action was sanctioned by Germany which, for several reasons, needed to preserve the Austro-Hungarian monarchy. Most notably, the Austro-Hungarian monarchy provided an ideological support to a German society dominated by the Junker class. Added to this, the Austro-Hungarian army acted as a reserve military contingent to Germany's disputes with the Entente.

Trotsky highlighted Germany's anti-democratic political structures to ridicule a notion, employed by pro-war German socialists, that Germany was waging a war of liberation against Russian despotism. Trotsky countered that, for political and ideological reasons, Russia's autocracy would be preserved by a German victory:

> the existence of tsarism strengthens the Hohenzollern monarchy and the Junker oligarchy since, if there were no tsarism, German absolutism would face Europe as the last mainstay of feudal barbarism.[17]

German imperialists also had one more reason for propping-up Nicholas II: since tsarism was inefficient in carrying-out its administrative and governmental tasks, Russia was prevented from developing into a real rival to German expansion. Thus, reasoned Trotsky, in swallowing the 'liberation myth' German Social-Democracy had been totally fooled into accepting the claims of German war propaganda. It was, he stated, Germany's intention to retain tsarism as a political structure after German economic hegemony had been established through victory in battle. The real targets of German aggression were the more developed and dangerous competitors – France and Britain.

A successful conclusion to the war for the Central Powers would, according to Trotsky, pave the way for an alliance of the anti-democratic forces of Germany, Austria-Hungary and Russia; an alliance which would 'mean a period of the darkest reaction in Europe and the whole world'.[18]

Locating the causes of World War One in state-power interests followed from Trotsky's general analysis of why hostilities had broken out. He traced the origins of the war to 'imperialist antagonisms between the capitalist states'.[19] By 'imperialist antagonisms' Trotsky meant a situation in which colonies were necessary for the further capitalist development of the advanced nations, but there were no more areas remaining 'free' for colonisation. Thus, 'there was nothing left for these states except to grab colonies from each other'.[20] He cited from the recently published works of Arthur Dix and George Irmer as evidence of Germany's imperialist ambition to become the dominant world state power. In order to achieve this Germany had to destroy the British economy. In turn, Britain had entered the war not so much out of principle over Belgium neutrality, but because a 'German Belgium' would threaten British domination of the sea.[21]

Trotsky presented his most theoretical exposition of the underpinnings of imperialist rivalry in the Preface to *War and the International*. This was Trotsky's first formulation of the causes of the war in terms of 'a revolt of the forces of production against the political form of nation and state'.[22] According to Trotsky, capitalism had transformed the world economy into 'one economic workshop'.[23] This, in turn, demanded international political structures to reflect the nature of the economic base. One can see how this approach is in harmony with the base/superstructure model of society outlined by Marx in his Preface to *A Contribution to a Critique of Political Economy*.[24] But, Trotsky objected, capitalism could not resolve this task by peaceful, organised cooperation across national boundaries. Rather, the capitalist response was to wage a struggle for hegemony on the world market. Hence, the current imperialist rivalry in which the key question was: 'which country is by this war to be transformed from a Great Power into the World Power [?]'[25] However, for Trotsky, it was already impossible for a single capitalist country to establish a hegemonic position over the world's productive forces. In short, the war was a last gamble on behalf of a system which could not resolve its own internal contradictions which had developed to the full.[26] The destruction and chaos introduced by the war would, he predicted, lead to economic collapse:

The economic rivalry under the banner of militarism is accompanied by robbery and destruction which violate the elementary principles of human economy. World production revolts not only against the confusion produced by national and state divisions but also against the capitalist economic organisations, which has now turned into barbarous disorganisation and chaos.[27]

For Trotsky, the only solution to the current crisis was proletarian revolution and socialism. Above all, there had to be a socialist organisation of the world economy. In order to attain this the international proletariat would have to establish what the national capitalist state could not; namely, a harmonisation of political forms with productive forces, i.e., an international political order. To this end, Trotsky advanced the idea of a 'republican United States of Europe, as the foundation of the United States of the World'.[28] At this point Trotsky did not say why Europe should be the foundation rather than Africa, America or Australasia and so on, but he did stress that the Russian revolution would be 'an integral part' of the European revolution. Of course, Trotsky had emphasised that the Russian revolution could only survive if a wider European revolution came to its aid as early as 1906, in the work *Results and Prospects*. However, in *Results and Prospects* this point was made through an argument based on necessity, i.e., the contradictions facing a workers' government in a predominantly peasant country could only be overcome if help was received from the victorious proletariat of the advanced West. Now Trotsky related the link between revolution in Russia and in France, Britain and Germany to the creation of a republican United States of Europe, the urgency of which flowed out of the revolt of the productive forces against the limitations of national boundaries.

A final point of note in the *War and the International* is that imperialism is viewed as a source both of working-class support for the imperialist state and of eventual working-class rebellion. Initially the workers back their home government in its imperialist designs as this meets the immediate needs of their economic position: the more successful the imperialist ambitions of the capitalist state, the more wealth in that society; some of which would go to the workers. When the imperialist state engages in war, however, the chance arises that the workers will revolt because of the hardships imposed by the military situation. Most notably, the violent behaviour of the imperialist competitors acts as lesson to the working-class. Any former allegiance to bourgeois legality would, Trotsky stated, be smashed:

Is it not clear that all these circumstances must bring about a profound change in the mental attitude of the working class, curing them radically of the hypnosis of legality in which a period of political stagnation expresses itself? ... the terrible poverty that prevails during this War and will continue after its close, will be of a sort to force the masses to violate many a bourgeois law.[29]

So that socialists would win over the workers during the then current hostilities Trotsky recommended the adoption of the slogan of Peace.[30]

*

Trotsky's stay in Switzerland was brought to a close by an invitation from the Ukrainian newspaper *Kievskaya Mysl* to work as its war correspondent in France. Although he spent less than three months in neutral Switzerland Trotsky could leave for Paris feeling that he had accomplished something of worth. He had formulated his response to three very important questions: why had the Second International collapsed? what had caused the war? and, finally, what slogans should socialists advance to reunite the proletariat around a revolutionary programme of action? Most importantly, he had arranged for his pamphlet *War and the International* to be translated and published in German.[31] Trotsky thought this to be of supreme importance given that the German Social-Democratic movement had been the most powerful section of the Second International. In later years Trotsky remained proud of the fact that he had been sentenced by a German court for the contents of his Zurich pamphlet.[32] The ideas expressed in it will also feature in subsequent chapters, which examine the articles penned by Trotsky while a resident of Paris during World War One.

2
Kievskaya Mysl

On 19 November 1914 Trotsky crossed the French border as war correspondent for the newspaper *Kievskaya Mysl*. He subsequently
summarised his initial impressions of the situation he found in Paris
in several texts: first, in 1917 in a series of articles taken 'from a notebook' and published in the Russian émigré newspaper *Novyi Mir*. These
articles were then reprinted by Trotsky, with some additions, in *War
and the Revolution* (1922). Finally, Trotsky included a brief account of
his arrival in Paris in his autobiography of the late 1920s, *My Life*.
These sources are interesting when juxtaposed, as Trotsky took some
sections from the 1917 and 1922 texts and placed them unaltered in
his autobiography. Other parts were changed or omitted altogether.
One can illustrate this process with the example of Trotsky's explana-
tions of why he accepted the job offer from *Kievskaya Mysl*. In *War and
Revolution* he wrote: 'I accepted *Kievskaya Mysl*'s offer the more willingly as it gave me the possibility to become better acquainted with
France's political life in that critical epoch.'[1] Later, in *My Life*, Trotsky
changed the account of his motivation to a 'chance to get closer to
war'.[2]

Whatever the real reason for his acceptance, Trotsky, according to
his reminiscences, discovered a subdued Paris:

> Paris was sad. The hotels stood empty ... Women in black were
> everywhere ... Children played at war, many of them dressed in
> military uniforms by their mothers. Wounded convalescents,
> recently decorated, walked the streets. Old men ... talked respect-
> fully and ingratiatingly with them. There were many
> uncompromising supporters of 'war to the finish' walking the
> streets: too young for military service in 1870 and now too old ...[3]

Trotsky describes the mood in his hotel during a Zeppelin attack. Arriving there after walking through the streets during a black-out, in which he had witnessed a searchlight pointing to the sky from the Eiffel Tower, he found the guests sitting by candles reading, talking, or playing cards. Later the alarm bells rang to signal that the raid was over. Those who had bothered to go to the cellars returned to their floor. Trotsky laconically recounts that, 'on the next day the newspapers stated on which parts of the town the bombs had fallen and how many people had died'.[4]

However, even when painting such a sombre picture Trotsky did not permit the possibility of workers' unrest to slip totally from view:

> the cafes closed towards eight o'clock on an evening. 'What explains this?,' I asked people in the know, – 'It's very simple: General Gallieni, the Governor of Paris, does not want the public to congregate in them. In times such as ours cafes, for the working class who are busy during the day, can on evenings easily become centres of criticism and dissatisfaction.[5]

Trotsky was, though, particularly pessimistic about the state of French politics. He spoke of the possibility of a Bonapartist coup d'état when Joffre's authority stood on high after a German attack had been repulsed at Marne. However, for a Bonapartist uprising one needs a Bonapart and, according to Trotsky, 'never had mediocrity reigned so brightly in the Third Republic as at that tragic time'.[6] For Trotsky, the most prominent politician was Aristide Briand, an 'instigator of bribery and corruption, the clearest mockery of a "great", "national", "liberating war"'.[7] Among the Russian émigrés Trotsky witnessed the light of patriotism shining brightly. The Russian workers in Paris were 'disorientated and confused'.[8] In his summary of these impressions we find Trotsky at his bleakest:

> Isolated opposition was scattered about here and there, but it showed almost no signs of life. It seemed as if there were no gleams of a better future.[9]

In this bleak environment Trotsky may have hoped that he could continue the critical stance typical of his previous correspondence for *Kievskaya Mysl* during the Balkan wars:

> At the time of the Balkan Wars, when the imperialist mood had still

not overtaken the whole of the petty-bourgeoisie, including the intelligentsia, I was able on the pages of *Kievskaya Mysl* to conduct an open struggle against the raids and crimes ... in the Balkans and against the neo-Slav imperialism on which the Kadet opposition reached agreement with the third of June monarchy.[10]

In *The Prophet Armed* Isaac Deutscher pointed out that Trotsky's writings have either been ignored or given attention depending upon the extent to which they were bound up with his political fortunes.[11] He further claimed that if this had not been so, Trotsky would have been given a place in literature on the basis of his contributions for the newspaper *Kievskaya Mysl* during World War One.[12] However, although Deutscher was right to draw attention to the *Kievskaya Mysl* articles, he provided only a brief exposition of these writings.[13] Moreover, Deutscher's evaluation of the nature of these texts is at variance with that given by Trotsky himself. This difference of opinion has, not surprisingly, been ignored by subsequent Trotsky biographers. After all, Deutscher himself did not realise that his own interpretation was at variance with Trotsky's.[14] Trotsky's own view of his writings for the newspaper *Kievskaya Mysl* during World War One has been overlooked in scholarly accounts of his life; Deutscher's version standing alone as 'orthodoxy'. The rest of this chapter has two aims. First, to fill the lacuna left by Deutscher's exposition. Second, to evaluate the conflicting interpretations of author and biographer.

In the 1922 introduction to *War and Revolution* Trotsky explained why the non-Marxist *Kievskaya Mysl* should have hired a Marxist by refering to the social, political and economic structure of Kiev.[15] According to Trotsky, Kiev had a weak industry which had retarded the class struggle in comparison with Petrograd. This, in turn, resulted in a gentry and intelligentsia-led democratic opposition movement. This movement acquired a radical element in response to Tsarist political oppression which, in the Kievan context, had the additional burden of measures directed against nationalities:

> This explains the general policy of the editors, who associated themselves neither with Social-Democracy nor with the working class, to set aside a lot of room for Marxist contributors and allow them to explain events, especially foreign, even from a social-revolutionary point of view.[16]

From November 1914 to December 1916 Trotsky wrote a total of 16 articles for *Kievskaya Mysl*. By the end of this period the newspaper had, according to Trotsky, 'under the pressure of bourgeois social opinion and the prods of social-patriotic contributors gone over to patriotism, aspiring only to preserve "allusions of the great home-land"'.[17]

One thus learns that Trotsky was able to continue to work for the newspaper, which had previously hired him at the time of the Balkan Wars, until it changed its character. This would mean, of course, that it became even more patriotic just before the monarchy's collapse, when critical voices were raised as never before.

Isaac Deutscher, however, makes no such distinction in the nature of the newspaper as it developed over time. Deutscher highlights two particular constraints which Trotsky had placed upon his reportage by becoming an employee of *Kievskaya Mysl*. First, the newspaper supported the war and this meant that,

> Trotsky could tell his readers in Russia only half the truth as he saw it, that half which somehow fitted in with official Russian policy. He tried on occasion to tell it in such a manner that the shrewd reader should guess the suppressed half of the story.[18]

This view could be used to explain Trotsky's later reluctance to elaborate on his contributions for *Kievskaya Mysl* in *My Life*. In his autobiography Trotsky focused exclusively upon his work for the political newspapers *Golos* and *Nashe Slovo*.[19] If Deutscher's view is correct then Trotsky's omission would be understandable. After all, why bother with a series of articles, written for a newspaper over which one had no editorial control, which did not reflect the full range of one's views?[20]

However, Deutscher's commentary is true of only a tiny proportion of Trotsky's articles. For example, 'The Bosnian Volunteer' does end on an enigmatic note: 'You say that the war has deeper reasons? Certainly, one does not doubt this.'[21] But on other occasions there is no room for doubt on the author's exact intended meaning. Thus, for example, 'The Seventh Infantry Regiment in the Belgium Epic' argues that the positions of the pro- and anti-German sections of the Belgian bourgeoisie had nothing to do with the rights of nations, but every-thing to do with the rights of property:

> Could one allow the Germans through Belgium? Nobody permitted this, apart from small commercial and industrial circles who were

directly dependent upon German capital. For the peasantry and for the petty-bourgeoisie the issue was absolutely clear: one could not allow the Germans. Certainly this was not because it was contrary to international law but because a German army entering Belgium would not want to leave it. Moreover, an army on the march grabs and ruins everything that it comes across. One had to fight.[22]

The economic interests underpinning military action were further illustrated in 'Two Armies'. Here Trotsky argued that, initially, Germany did not want to attack France and Belgium. These countries posed no economic threat to Germany. Germans could even admire certain aspects of the French 'character'. However, 'sad necessity' dictated the military defeat of France and Belgium in the struggle against 'the deadly enemy of German imperialism, England ... one had to defeat France to get to England, and the shortest path to the heart of France was through Belgium.'[23]

Moreover, if Trotsky did not always engage in explicit Marxist analysis, he was still able to bring Marxist conclusions to a reader's attention. For example, 'From whence it came' highlights the futility of individual terrorism in the struggle to liberate a nation.[24] The division between mental and manual labour under capitalism is criticised in 'War and Technology'. Trotsky pointed out that the development of the machinery of war takes place in the intellectual atmosphere of laboratories, depriving research of the actual and real physical test of action, something which happens comparatively rarely:

If the exclusiveness of the division between mental and manual labour has a negative effect in all contemporary production, it is fatal in the military sphere in which weapons are utilised only in the comparatively short period of war.[25]

According to Trotsky, the beginning of a campaign is characterised by the failure of technology going through its first real test. In the course of the war technical problems are continually solved until near total success rates are achieved by its conclusion. A new period of peace then condemns military inventiveness to the laboratory where it is once again subject to the limitations of the division between mental and manual labour. The smooth operation of the best developed technology by the end of one war is totally outdated by the time of the next. Indeed, the article ends by suggesting that the nature of modern technology would like wars to occur more frequently: 'Is one not brought to the conclusion that war happens too rarely for present-day technology?'[26]

'All Roads Lead to Rome' serves to illustrate the futility of religious belief. The article outlines the desires of Catholics of various countries to receive the Pope's blessing for their campaign of national defence. However, the Pope's response is shown to be a series of political manoeuvres with two basic 'unholy' intentions. First, to secure the role of broker for the Pope in any future peace negotiations. Second, to attain maximum advantage in such negotiations for the Papacy: 'in this way universal neutrality becomes a means of political bargaining.'[27]

The primacy of social conflict was the subject of Trotsky's first article for *Kievskaya Mysl* of November 1914. This discussed the war as a political moratorium; a temporary suspension of national contradictions which would once again resurface. Trotsky presented this thought through an analysis of Austria-Hungary, although his underlying idea could easily be generalised. He begins by describing a patriotic demonstration outside the War Ministry in Vienna on 2nd August and asking what motivated the demonstrators. After all, Austria-Hungary, unlike Switzerland and the United States, had not successfully solved the problem of nationality in a multi-national state. The Swiss population might be split in loyalty towards France and Germany, but if either country attacked Switzerland all cantons would rush to its defence. For Trotsky, this was because life in Switzerland offered so many advantages. The same could not be said of Austria-Hungary. Formed as a central-European defence against Turkey, the Austro-Hungarian state had not yet fallen prey to the centrifugal tendencies that had destroyed Turkey for two *negative* reasons: the weaknesses of the various nationalities and the strength of reactionary forces. Furthermore, this situation also prevented Austria-Hungary from becoming another Switzerland:

It is true that capitalism brings about a meeting of tendencies to economic unification. But the capitalist development of Austria, exhausted by landowners and militarism, developed very slowly. Progress for the Danube peoples would be the reconstruction of their state structure on the Swiss model: not only would this make Austria-Hungary invulnerable, it would also make it overwhelmingly attractive for all the national fragments spread along its periphery. But cultural backwardness of a large sections of the population, and especially the reactionary historical forces which still head the Austro-Hungarian state, are obstacles to the path of regeneration. Hence the national chaos which forms the internal life of the Danube monarchy.[28]

In the absence of positive feelings towards the state Trotsky focused on two factors to explain the rise of patriotic feelings. First, war breaks the normal routines of life. In such a worrying situation the state – armed from head to foot – seems to be the most stable institution to which one can turn for comfort. Second, the state becomes the repository of hopes for improvements raised by the war. However, Trotsky made it clear that this harmony between the population and the state would only be temporary. His warning to patriots and to any supporters of the existing order was clear, national and social contradictions would return:

> In the first moments of the war one could not expect too much of radical, national and social movements ... for the government, even while reeling from centrifugal forces which it had only just managed to suppress, immediately became master of the situation ... Mobilisation and the declaration of war appear to wipe all national and social contradictions from the face of the earth. But this is only an historical adjournment, a political moratorium. The promissory note has been rewritten for a new time, but they will still have to pay for it ... [29]

In the biographical essay 'Jean Jaurès' Trotsky clearly delineated reformist and revolutionary approaches to the solution of social conflict. Reformism is shown to be a compromise with the bourgeoisie which had prevented neither the exploitation of the workers nor the outbreak of war. However, according to Trotsky, the war amounted to a break with the previous era of conservatism and reform. The future belonged to revolution:

> The working classes, in the last decades grasping the idea of socialism, are only now in the terrible ordeals of war acquiring a revolutionary temper. We are entering a period of unprecedented revolutionary tremors. New organisations will be advanced by the masses and new leaders will emerge ... When the European revolution ends the war the truth about Jaurès's death will also be revealed.[30]

Even in seemingly neutral, factual accounts Trotsky managed to include something related to Marxism. For instance, the problem of class is raised in the short biography of the commander-in-chief of the British forces, Sir John French. Ireland, French's place of birth, is referred to as a place where 'landlords rule over an emaciated country like demi-gods, where in the ruling strata there reigns an atmosphere very conducive for raising military leaders of the old "heroic" type'.[31]

In 'Two Armies' Trotsky compared the economic and social origins of the German and French armies and how this affected their respective strategies. For Trotsky, the German army possessed the mightier technology, a reflection of Germany's higher level of capitalist development: 'in the last analysis military techniques are dependent upon a country's general technical-industrial development.'[32] However, militarism is not only technology, but also the level of human skills. According to Trotsky, Germany also had an advantage in the field of human resources in two senses. First, again as a result of its industrial development, Germany had a greater quantity of workers who, as a class, were 'not only more intelligent and more able to adapt to conditions than peasants, but had greater powers of endurance.'[33] A second, and more important factor, was the German officer class, a homogenous group dedicated to war. German social development had, for Trotsky, been characterised by a lack of revolutionary traditions and the late development of a strong and independent bourgeoisie. The tasks of capitalist development had therefore been handed to the Junkers:

> The liberal bourgeoisie did not step beyond the boundaries of a 'loyal opposition', forever commissioning the Junkers to introduce order into the capitalist society and spread their military might. Finally, when capitalist development placed new tasks of a world character before the German bourgeoisie it, as before, commissioned the Junkers united around the monarchy to lead the military nation.[34]

This, in turn, led to the development of an offensive strategy:

> All German strategy was built on attack. This corresponds to the basic conditions of Germany's social development: to the rapid growth of the population and national wealth on the one hand and to the backward state structure on the other. The German Junkers

have a 'will to power' and in directing this will the nation provides the highest technology and qualified labour.[35]

France, according to Trotsky, had a totally different tradition and had thus developed a different strategy. Formed through a series of revolutionary periods France's petty-bourgeois republican régimé did not consider a standing army to be compatible with it. However, the petty-bourgeois radicals thought an army of some sort necessary to guarantee order. So, an army was retained, but there were endless disputes over how it should be organised and it never had the German army's status. Thus, there arose what Jaurès called 'the bastard regime', in which old and new forms collided and neutralised each other. The former French major Drian is cited as comparing a German army united in the spirit of attack and a French army whose officers were split in a struggle between monarchists and masons. Furthermore, Drian declared that the masons had separated the state and the church and had thus deprived the French army of the psychological cement of religion. For Trotsky, all of this had the consequence that France developed a defensive strategy which corresponded to its social structure:

> The country's petty-bourgeois and strongly conservative economic structure did not permit imperialist desires on a world scale. A halting population growth brought forth caution in relation to the supply of labour.[36]

In this and in the other articles examined thus far it is clear that Trotsky was not limited to half-truths as suggested by Deutscher. Nevertheless, the second constraint which Deutscher pinpoints follows on from the first. As *Kievskaya Mysl* supported official Russian policy Trotsky was forced to focus upon a critique of Germany:

> in his articles he had to tack about cautiously to avoid a breach with the paper. The Kievan editor was only too glad to publish the Paris correspondent's denunciations of German imperialism, but his criticisms of the Entente were unwelcome.[37]

However, Trotsky did write about the problems of the Entente and in such a way that could not have been particularly reassuring for those who supported it. Moreover, the newspaper did publish these contributions. For instance, the 'Japanese Question' portrays a desperate

France in dispute over whether it should enlist Japanese help in the immense task of forcing German troops from its territory. The problems facing the French government were not only related to how much compensation they would have to give to Japan and if they could afford it, but also concerned the fact that they did not have total control over this issue. Apart from inability to meet any demands that Japan might set, there existed only two routes for any Japanese forces travelling to Europe: by land across Russia and by sea under British protection. However, 'Japan has formal ties only with Britain and ... it is precisely Britain who is less than others interested in speeding-up military operations.'[38] Moreover, if Trotsky did have a bias, then he also gave an explicit warning to his readers to be wary of war reports for this very reason:

> The correspondent himself is not objective. He is a passionate agent in this drama: a national wire between the war and society. He aims to cheer up his own people and to terrorise the enemy. Correspondents paint their judgements, conclusions and factual accounts in certain colours.[39]

Furthermore, if the role of the World War One correspondents was to boost national morale, then Trotsky certainly did not fulfil his duties. Morale could hardly have been increased by the following description of a war-weary Europe after 12 months of hostilities:

> I remembered clearly that cold autumn morning when I came to France from Switzerland. Then the war was still new ... people were a lot more generous than they are now. In the past months everybody has become poorer in money, enthusiasm and hopes – the rich mourn. Then, in that autumn ... everyone spoke anxiously about the winter campaign and of hopes for a great spring offensive ... Winter and spring came and now summer is already rushing towards autumn. Once again people in wagons and in families talk anxiously about the coming winter.[40]

In several articles Trotsky wrote moving accounts of the horrors of war, both for civilians and for soldiers. In, for example, 'The Seventh Infantry Regiment in the Belgium Epic' the military career of a Belgian law student, De Baer, provides the background against which Trotsky presents a brilliant exposition of human lives thrown into turmoil by the fall of Belgium. The article begins by portraying the university town of Leuven – small, quiet, provincial. There the happy, moderately hard-working De Baer studied law. The war caught him totally unawares, procrastinating over whether to join the ruling clerics or the liberal opposition. However, at this stage confidence was high that, together with the French, the Belgians would reach Berlin in several weeks. These illusions were soon shattered in the face of rapid German victories. In depicting De Baer's first taste of battle and a defeated army in retreat, Trotsky vividly illustrates the cruelties of war. During the hostilities around the town of Aerskot, De Baer stumbles across a dead woman: 'both breasts were cut off, below the stomach was a gaping wound.'[41] Over the next months the regiment retreated, engaged on several occasions with the enemy, was promised rest and then immediately recalled to battle, and was even once victorious. The army retreats in confusion, ashamed of what they were leaving behind:

> A stream of retreating soldiers mixed with a whirlpool of desperate people ... Women roamed the town carrying children ... An old woman, wailing loudly, pushed an armchair with a paralysed, old man in it ... Children ran in-between the soldiers, crying and searching for their parents ... 'Colonel!', cried a grey clean-shaven old man ..., 'you are leaving us to the tyranny of the Germans!' The colonel ... moved on in silence.[42]

For De Baer his personal downfall had come with that of his country. What use would a knowledge of Belgian law be in a country dominated by Germany? However, this mood was soon to be replaced by one of self-preservation. Surviving while his comrades fell De Baer was tortured by the thought of whether he would be one of the lucky ones who survive the war without a scratch: his life was ruled by this 'law of statistics.' This turned out to be the case but, in the meantime, he was a witness to the dehumanising experience of war. As a law-student De Baer was twice called-upon to defend soldiers accused of a breach of discipline. One of those he defended (Ekkhaut) was acquitted and later befriended De Baer in the trenches. At night it was cold and while the soldiers slept, anxiously awaiting a German attack, Ekkhaut would carefully cover De Baer with half of his clothes. On the dawn of their last day in the trenches in Izer, De Baer was suddenly awoken by the familiar sound of attack. He sensed a movement to his right and he recoiled in horror: 'under the shared clothes lay Ekkhaut's motionless body: the bullet had entered right between his eyes leaving a small accurate hole.'[43] The craters left by enemy shells would be modified into graves by the same shovels that had dug the trenches. When the Germans attacked De Baer shot mechanically at a seemingly mechanical procession of bodies moving towards him: 'it did not have anything tragic in itself because there was already nothing human in it.'[44] After losing his spectacles in battle De Baer was sent to a military hospital. It was discovered that he was too short-sighted for military service and he was discharged. The dead bodies, danger and filth of the trenches were behind him. Trotsky stressed the futility of war in reporting De Baer's reward for his courage: 'A new life started for De Baer. He roamed without connections, almost dishev-elled and always hungry . . .'[45]

Trench warfare was a new phenomenon and Trotsky devoted several (negative) articles to this subject. 'Fortresses or Trenches?' asks whether the trenches had replaced the medieval fortresses of old. Reviewing opinions both for and against, Trotsky argued that modern warfare had rendered fortresses anachronistic in two ways. First, as witnessed in Northern France and Belgium, it reduced them to rubble. Second, large stocks of shells were needed to protect a fortress. Trenches also demanded huge quantities of shells, but for the attack-ing side only. Trotsky painted a picture of future wars in which underground defences would play an even greater role: 'a refuge, ware-houses, workshops, electrical stations . . . spread along a wide space . . . not penetrable to heavy enemy artillery fire'.[46] In the meantime, the triumph of the trenches was so clear that both militarists and pacifists worshipped them:

> One [pacifist], apparently Swiss, came to the happy conclusion that war could be abolished if state borders were surrounded by trenches protected by massive electrical currents. The poor golden pacifist who seeks refuge in the trenches![47]

In 'The Trenches' Trotsky moved from a macro-analysis of the general role of trenches in war to a micro-view of the everyday life of the soldiers in them. This experience is portrayed as one of physical and mental monstrosity. The trenches are described as 'decisive boundaries, the smallest crossing of which by either side is paid for with countless victims.'[48] Constructed from whatever material at hand ('tree trunks . . . haversacks filled with earth, greatcoats of dead Germans'[49]) the trenches become an underground 'temporary sanctu-ary'.[50] Trotsky answered the cries of the French press that the

Germans had forced the French into 'disgusting dumps' by stressing that soldiers from all nations shared a similar experience: 'the originality of the national genius is still safeguarded in one field: the French sit in the trenches like the Germans, like the Russians, like the Italians'.[51] Arriving at the trenches the soldier enters the zone of military danger, his closest contact with the enemy. This in itself induces order into the ranks; all thoughts are of self-preservation:

> in the trenches there is very little consideration of general war aims and, although this may seem paradoxical, even less about the enemy. Certainly the enemy trenches which threaten death ... are always utmost in the soldier's mind. But he thinks not about Germany, not about the Emperor's plans, not of German exports, not of the historical enemy – but of the bullets and shrapnel which one has to avoid while returning the compliment to the enemy trenches ... The enemy lives the same life, experiences common events with similar feelings ... In incessant struggle they imitate one another: raising periscope against periscope, grenade against grenade ... Equally uncertain whom destiny promises to blow-up first.[52]

The trenches and the war become so intertwined that the removal of the former leads to the cessation of the latter. For example, Trotsky quotes from a Russian volunteer's letter – written during the July floods – which reports how all soldiers, as if in silent agreement, did not fire at each other. It was only after the common task of pumping out the water and returning to the trenches had been completed that the war resumed.

The trenches are also the means by which the soldier orientates himself. With increasing familiarity the soldier looks upon the trench 'not only as a defence, but also as a home.'[53] If enemy fire is not too heavy then one company can occupy the same trench for a long period and life becomes regulated. For each soldier this underground life induces feelings of isolation. According to Trotsky, these feelings are expressed in two ways. First, a process already observed in barracks, prisons and boarding-houses. The soldiers develop their own language to describe old and new phenomena as they appear to them from the point of view of their own trench. Soldiers from the latest levy are called 'Marie-Louise', the biggest enemy shells are labelled 'pots', and so on. Second, the soldiers become self-centred and feel themselves cut off from civilian life. Letters from home awaken half-forgotten thoughts and anxieties. However, the trenches soon recapture attention, domestic concerns are blotted out. Trotsky follows a group of soldiers home on leave to illustrate the extent of the psychological effects of trench warfare on the soldier:

> In the family, in the home village ... despite the joy of safety they do not feel settled. There is no longer that former equanimity between themselves and home. Psychological contact is not immediately renewed ... The four days soon pass ... the returning soldiers meet their comrades. They chatter about leave but the trenches have already captured their minds. They talk about them, remember and foresee. Isolation absorbs them more psychologically than they are physically entrapped in the trenches.[54]

Trotsky often focused upon the psychological effects of war. 'The Psychological Mysteries of the War' is perhaps his strongest attack on the futility of the hostilities. He argues that noone had had control over the conflict's origins. Indeed, people had struggled to come to terms with a reality thrust upon them:

> ... great events do not spring from the mind but, on the contrary, events emerge from the combinations, mutual actions and intersections of great objective historical forces, only later forcing our inert, lazy psychology ... to accommodate itself to them. The united chorus of guns and rifles cry out this fact in the fate of contemporary culture and nations ... The war occured without their knowledge and against their will: it revealed itself to them and subordinated to itself not only material-social life in all of its complexity but also the nation's spirit of survival ...[55]

According to Trotsky, this amounted to nothing less than the waste of a whole generation of creative talent:

> Current events have ... placed the question of losses ... in the psychological light of the European nations. Its most lively and artistic generation which is presently entrapped in ... divisions ... and through barracks, depots, camps, and trenches goes through all the stages which bring it closer to the focus of contemporary events: to physical clashes with the enemy, attacks, defence, retreat, so that some can be crossed-out from the books of the

living and others, via field hospitals and convalescent homes, return to society blinded, armless and legless ...[56]

*

Trotsky's articles for *Kievskaya Mysl* not only covered a wide range of topics – war and technology, religion, psychology, biography, the origins of history etc. – but were rich in anti-war sentiment. Moreover, he was able to write from a Marxist perspective. It is true that Trotsky published his more overtly political and polemical writings on, for example, social-patriotism among 'Left' groupings in *Golos* and *Nashe Slovo*; but then such articles were more suited to the nature of those newspapers. A survey of his contributions published in *Kievskaya Mysl* support Trotsky's own claim that he was able to write freely for the newspaper until it went totally over to the side of patriotism, rather than Deutscher's account of a Trotsky continually forced into half-truths. The next chapter will examine what effect, if any, the censor in Paris had upon Trotsky's writings for the Russian internationalist press published in the French capital.

However, before moving on, it is worth noting that Trotsky's work as war reporter for *Kievskaya Mysl* was also significant for his future career as military commander. It is true that Trotsky's first stint as war correspondent for the Ukrainian newspaper of 1912–13 afforded him better opportunities to become acquainted with war; in 1914 *Kievskaya Mysl* did not demand that he accompany the army to the front, nor were war correspondents permitted to do so by the authorities. However, he was able to visit Marseilles, Menton, Boulogne and Calais where he spoke with British and Belgian soldiers about their experiences of battle.[57] It was this knowledge of war and its participants which was later used by the founder and leader of the Red Army in the Russian Civil War.

3
The Censor in Paris

Although Trotsky was in France as war correspondent for *Kievskaya Mysl*, the vast majority of his journalistic writings during his stay in Paris did not appear in the Ukrainian publication, but in *Golos* and its successors, *Nashe Slovo* and *Nachalo*, socialist newspapers produced by Russian émigrés residing in the French capital. *Nashe Slovo* contains the richest store of Trotsky's writings of this period. It survived longer than its predecessor and successor, and its production coincided with Trotsky's time in Paris.

In *The Prophet Armed* Trotsky's most famous and most influential biographer gave the following account of *Nashe Slovo*:

> *Nashe Slovo* began to appear on 29 January 1915. This was a modest sheet of two, rarely four, pages abundantly strewn with white spaces marking the censor's deletions, and yet packed with news and comment. The paper was constantly in danger of being killed off by the censor and by its own poverty.[1]

Deutscher's emphasis upon the censor's far from helpful interference followed Trotsky's own interpretation. In the introduction to *War and Revolution*, for example, Trotsky mentioned two particular difficulties in the production of a radical Russian newspaper in war time France; first fiscal and second the censor:

> The newspaper was published under great financial and technical difficulties. Before the first number was printed there was about 30 francs in Antonov's and Manuil'skii's 'cash register'. Obviously no-one with any common sense could have believed that one could have published a daily revolutionary newspaper with this basic

'capital', especially in war-time, with chauvinist fury and the censor's brutality.[2]

In turn, when Trotsky came to write his autobiography at the end of the 1920s he said of *Nashe Slovo*, 'under the blows of deficit and the censor, disappearing and soon appearing under a new name, the newspaper survived in the course of 2 years, i.e., until the 1917 February Revolution'.[3] And thus the matter has stood until this day. Deutscher's and Trotsky's claims about the censor have not been examined.

However, some of the articles which were completely or partly censored when they were sent for approval were later published in fuller form when the two volume *War and Revolution* was issued in Moscow and Petrograd between 1922–1924. When Trotsky gathered his writings of the World War One period he obviously checked their contents for suitability of publication. It was most likely during this task that he seized the opportunity of filling in some of the gaps left by the censor's white marks. This was probably a hit-and-miss process. Trotsky was proud of his excellent memory,[4] but even he could not reconstruct all of the censored articles as exact reproductions of their original. When one compares the versions published in *War and Revolution* against *Nashe Slovo* one can see that the text subsequently inserted by Trotsky is not equal to that removed by the censor.

However, despite the fact that Trotsky's reconstructions are not as accurate as one would like, his efforts do enable us to do several things. First, we learn what Trotsky wanted to say to his readership at the time but was prevented from doing so. Second, we can check whether the censor cut certain themes consistently. We thus enter the mind of the censor and discover what he considered to be 'sensitive' subjects. Third, because Trotsky left some articles in their cut versions, we can see if we can make any sense of what remains. This should lead us to draw some conclusions about the overall effectiveness of the censor, and thus test Deutscher's and Trotsky's 'orthodoxy'.

The governments of warring nations not surprisingly like to ensure that only the most optimistic reports of military operations reach the civilian population and soldiers in combat. The fact that this consideration ranked high on the censor's list of sensitive subjects can be deduced from the alterations made to several of Trotsky's pessimistic evaluations of the state of the war.

In, 'The Key to the Position', for example, the censor cut the statement that the Russian assault on the Galician front would not alter the general stalemate.[5] Moreover, the censor was so keen to avoid any recognition that Europe had fallen into a hopeless situation that he deleted sentences expressing this thought, even when their absence did not prevent the essential point from being made. Thus, in the same contribution, Trotsky discussed the possibility of American intervention as the deciding factor, guaranteeing the victory of one side over the other. At the outset of this section the censor cut the thought that the European powers were turning to America in self-recognition of their own powerlessness:

> [Aware of the terrible dead-end of the military situation], in the past few months the ruling groups and parties of Europe have again turned their gaze on America.[6]

Trotsky then explained why America would not involve itself in the war by reference to the profits American capital was making: 'Europe is breaking-up and America is enriching itself.'[7] However when, in the concluding sentences, he summarised this argument by linking it to a Europe floundering in a hopeless bloodbath, the censor once again reached for his eraser:

> [while the American bourgeoisie has the opportunity of warming its hands on Europe's bones it will not alter its attitude. 'The key to the position' in America? But in the meanwhile America thinks that the most advantageous position for it is supporting the bloody European dead-end.][8]

In other instances the censor seemed more perturbed by the *strength* of the language employed than by the message Trotsky was attempting to express. In 'A Year of War' the censor revealed his sensitiveness to harsh critiques of capitalism's responsibility for Europe's hopeless military situation. It was the use of the word dead-end (*tupik*) that the censor most objected to:

> On the Gallipili peninsula, as on the new Austro-Italian front, the line of the trenches was immediately designated [as a line of military hopelessness] ... In this picture [brought about by the blind automatism of capitalist forces and the conscious dishonourable-ness of the ruling classes] ... [The European strategic situation gives a mechanical expression of that historical dead-end into which capitalist forces have driven themselves].[9]

Nevertheless, despite these cuts, Trotsky was still able to put across his less than optimistic appraisal of the state of the war and his moral condemnation of the ruling class:

> there are no trump cards which, from the military point of view, would give either of the warring sides reasonable hope of a rapid, decisive victory. Even if the European ruling forces possessed as much historical good will as they do evil, even then they would be powerless to resolve by their means problems which led to war.[10]

If the censor was unreceptive to overtly harsh condemnations of the war situation, he was also careful to avoid allowing discussion of the likely spoils of the war to appear in print. This applied at a general as well as at a specific level. Thus, in an appraisal of the group centred around the newspaper *Nasha Zarya*, the censor cut Trotsky's sarcastic response to the claim that the Entente was fighting for the most worthy aims:

> One has to find the coalition whose victory would be more benefi-cial for world development. So judge the authors of the document analysed by us. [The answer turns out, by a fortuitous concurrence of circumstances, to be the 'Western democracies' in struggle with the 'Junker monarchies.' Tsarism? It acts as a subsidiary force of democracy] ... This ... is the official French point of view ... Theoretically and politically this is the most banal ideological democratism – without social flesh, without historical perspectives, and without a trace of the materialist dialectic.[11]

A reader of this passage would not have known what view Trotsky was criticising. In a report of Milyukov's visit to Paris of May 1916 Trotsky was prevented from referring to negotiations between the Entente powers concerning Russia's claims to Constantinople, the Bosporus and the Dardanelles:

> [April 1915 remains as a memorable date in Russian history, for in this month our relations with the allies about the Straits were precisely regulated: in the world struggle the East was put aside as Russia's sphere of influence (nous a été assign comme domaine)][12]

The fact that France was allied to Russia and Great Britain also had consequences for what the censor would look for when he checked an article for publication. The French censor was keen to expunge any remarks which may have caused embarrassment to people holding leading posts in the Allied governments. In 'Wonders the Wise did not dream of' an accusation that the Russian ambassador in Paris had had a hand in the appearance of an announcement in *Intransigent* attacking *Nashe Slovo* was appropriately cut.[13] On other occasions the censor removed references to the '[ungovernable appetite of Tsarist diplomacy]';[14] and while the censor was happy to see Trotsky criticise the imperialism of the Central Powers, he did not permit similar remarks about Russia: 'If Austro-Germany seizes Poland, this is imperialism; [if Russia seizes Galacia or Armenia, this is national liberation of the oppressed]'.[15]

The censor's alterations did not protect only Russia. On two occasions Trotsky's remarks concerning Lloyd-George did not appear in print. The first time Trotsky was discussing accusations that the Russian socialists in Paris were pan-Germanists: '[... see we are not for Syria and we are not for Constantinople ... we do not support Lloyd-George and we do not agree with Plekhanov]'.[16] On the second occasion Trotsky's prognosis of the overthrow of Lloyd-George in the wake of the Dublin Uprising was deleted:

> The historical role of the Irish proletariat is only beginning ... [This rebellion will not fade away. On the contrary, it echoes across the whole of Great Britain ... Lloyd-George's executions will be severely revenged by the same workers whom Henderson is currently attempting to chain to the bloody wheels of imperialism.][17]

This, of course, left France itself and the censor's patriotism was an undoubted criterion for resolving what to erase. The censor twice deleted uncomplimentary references to 'bourgeois France' helping Tsarism to crush the 1905 Russian revolution.[18] However, the censor objected most of all to any critique of the French government during the war. Thus, for instance, in 'A Convent of Confusion and Hopelessness' the censor removed the following appraisal of the sorry state of French democracy:

> [... historical development of the last decades has finally undermined the social foundation of democracy. Imperialism is not compatible with democracy ... because imperialism is stronger than democracy, it has ravaged it. Universal general rights give us

a parliament, parliament gives us a ministry, but the ministry has now fallen into the mess of secret diplomatic obligations. The banks and finance capital ... reign. Clemenceau is not happy with the powerless parliament.][19]

But in the light of Clemenceau's then opposition to the French government for its poor conduct of war policy, Trotsky's portrayal of Clemenceau as an opportunist was allowed to appear in *Nashe Slovo*:

The utopian thought that capitalist imperialism should subordinate itself to the democratic regime is, however, completely alien to the 'Jacobin' Clemenceau. He wants to preserve only a democratic shell, the shedding of which would be too risky an experiment for the French bourgeoisie. At the same time he attempts to use the parliamentary mechanism for a struggle with the excesses or deficiencies of militarism.[20]

The censor's desire to protect the French government's image as a government of national unity impinged upon Trotsky's account of Longuetism. The Longuetists derived their name from Jean Longue (1876–1938), son of Charles Longue and Jenny Marx, editor of *Le Populaire* and leader of the pacifist minority of the French Socialist Party. The censor was quite content for Trotsky's critique of Longuetism to see the light of day, but the Longuetist's demand for French Socialist Party leaders to resign from their ministerial portfolios was kept in the dark:

Hence the necessity for the Longuetists to advance a new programme. [Now they insist – with their natural indecisiveness – that socialists resign from the French government. However] undoubtedly logic and thoroughness is not on the side of the Longuetists; a party which supports the war and participates in the union sacrée has no principles to refuse government service.[21]

In making the above alteration the censor managed to publicise the view of the French Socialist Party leadership without affording a similar service to the Longuetists; work he must have been proud of.

During World War One contact between citizens of the warring nations was outlawed. Any socialist in Paris who wanted to report efforts to retain links with comrades in the Central Powers would most likely collide with restrictions to be imposed by the censor. This was certainly behind the prohibition placed upon any immediate reference to the Zimmerwald Conference of September 1915, while one of Trotsky's reports on the proceedings of the Second Zimmerwald Conference was also censored.[22] Although it was possible to mention Zimmerwald by name by October 1915, in the summer of 1916 the censor was still attempting to ensure that only negative accounts of Zimmerwald appeared in *Nashe Slovo*. He did this by cutting any specific piece of information Trotsky might want to pass on to the reader while leaving Trotsky's general position intact. Thus, Trotsky's use of Karl Liebknecht's campaign against social-patriotism on both sides of the Rhine was cut from his rejoinder of August 1916 to representations of Zimmerwald as 'Pan-German intrigue'.[23] This did not discourage Trotsky from submitting further articles in which he continued to struggle against patriotic misrepresentations of Zimmerwald, but the censor once again deleted direct reference to Liebknecht as supporting evidence:

> As soon as Liebknecht was locked-up ... the servile Entente socialists decided that the hour had come to use Liebknecht's name for a struggle against his ideas ... [How they lie about the jailed as about the dead ... Is this really not clear? Liebknecht himself struggles with the enemy above all in his own country. Liebknecht is ours and not yours.][24]

Thus the censor consistently cut several themes from Trotsky's writings. The list contains no real surprises: the Entente in a hopeless military situation, negotiations between Entente diplomats on what they expected from a successful conclusion to the war, unflattering accounts of high politics in the Entente countries, and the activities of a united international marxist leadership. However, the fact that the censor often deleted only the most outspoken of Trotsky's statements, while overlooking others which expressed the same thought in a more restrained language, suggests that the censor's regime was not as harsh as it could have been. Moreover, the censor's alterations were probably made less effective by the fact that the readership knew that he checked the paper. On several occasions Trotsky wrote accounts of his battles with the censor.

For instance, in an article of August 1915 Trotsky began by declaring that now Russian setbacks in Galicia, Poland and the Baltic had become general knowledge, perhaps the censor would permit him to explain why the Russians had not been so successful. After all, he pointed out that he had predicted this outcome but had been silenced by the censor: 'the privilege of free judgement is available only to those who foresaw nothing and understood nothing.'[25]

In an (admittedly censored) contribution of October 1915, Trotsky argued that the censor's work could not blot-out the significance of the Zimmerwald Conference.[26] In any case, Trotsky's reports from Zimmerwald had already appeared in *Nashe Slovo* under the cloaked heading of 'From a Notebook'.[27] In January 1916 the censor kept only his protection of the French Socialist Party from Trotsky's pen secret when Trotsky listed his grievances against the censor's deletions:

> We have been prevented from distressing not only French ministers but also Russian governors. [Moreover: the censor took the French Socialist Party under his protection], and only recently we were not allowed to speak of the ideological banality of the socialism which Pierre Renaudel heads. We are nearly always not able to print the Social-Democratic deputies' speeches in the Duma, in the course of several weeks we could not mention the name Zimmerwald, and now we are not able to publish the resolutions of the Foreign Section of our party ... In all cases when the censor may have had doubts he decided against us: what is the sense of standing on ceremony with an émigré newspaper published in the Russian language![28]

At least the reader could become very well acquainted with most of the topics he was not supposed to know of!

Furthermore, Trotsky twice published articles under the rubric of censorship. In 'There is still a censor in Paris!' he reported that the French government liked to profess that there was no censorship in Paris, only a 'special regime' for the press. He conceded that there may have been some justification for this view. After all, pieces had been published which contained such revelations as Russian bureaucrats taking bribes, the fact that Russian Jews were not living in heaven on earth, that Alexander III was not a republican and so on. However, the censor had only just rejected two large articles and this should serve as warning to all that, 'under a special regime things are just the same as under a censor.'[29] Trotsky enjoyed the freedom not only to complain of his lack of freedom, he was also permitted to write a critical account of the arbitrariness of the censor's judgement. In an article of September 1916 the censor was teased with the following questions:

Can one say that the All-General Conference of Labour is 'dizzy with nationalism'? We have written this dozens of times. Now we are suddenly prevented from mentioning this. What happened? *Le Temps* which, it seems, should be sufficiently loyal writes of the necessity to renew the political struggle – in particular the struggle against royalism, conducting during the war endless agitation 'for the phantom of the past'. Can one in view of this say that the struggle of *Bonnet Rouge* against *Action Francaise* is the forerunner to the battle of a new republican 'concentration' against a royalist reaction? It seems one can. But yesterday we were not allowed to do so. What does this mean? What happened, Mr Censor![30]

Trotsky was quite right to point out that the censor sometimes objected to material which he had previously passed. Occasionally the censor's apparent arbitrariness could be explained by the wider context in which Trotsky submitted his articles. In the light of heightened attention on the working class during the 1 May celebrations, for example, the censor became more sensitive to revolutionary appeals to the masses. Thus, Trotsky's article '1st May 1916' is full of white spaces inserted by the censor, with Zimmerwald again falling victim to the censor's prejudices:

[The Zimmerwald conference was held. This was made possible only thanks to an awakening of revolutionary indignation on the left-wing of the official parties, who raised banners and organised Zimmerwald ... The publicists and theoreticians of the Second International put all their efforts to degrading socialist thought to the level of its political role.] The previous May 1st [was the lowest point in this process of decline, fall and betrayal ... bourgeois society was able to hold the proletariat's class organisations captive as never before ... For socialist leaders frightened by events pacifism is a self-imposed exile and a procrastinating passivism. For the masses pacifism means a moments reflection, a stage on the path from slavish patriotism to international action ... We have become stronger. In the coming year we will be stronger than we are now. Nothing and nobody can delay the growth of our strength.][31]

Perhaps the most telling evidence for evaluating the effect the censor had on distorting the meaning of Trotsky's writings is an examination of the articles censored in *Nashe Slovo*, which appeared in their censored form when they were reprinted in later publications.

Can one make any sense of these articles? Are they devoid of any material which might have hurt the sensibilities of a patriot supporting the war? The answer to the first question is 'yes' and to the second 'no'.

In several censored pieces Trotsky's critique of the ruling classes as cynical and hypocritical manages to reach the reader. In 'On the beginnings of Reciprocity' Trotsky began by recounting Wilhelm II's offer to Nicholas II: Russian prisoners held in German camps would be allowed to celebrate their monarch's name-day if a reciprocal right were bestowed upon German prisoners in Russian camps. The censor deleted Trotsky's concluding sentences, but the Russian revolutionary's disgust at the niceties of the monarchical club while their respective subjects suffered remained:

> On the beginnings of reciprocity! German and Russian cannon fodder is blown up and destroyed by shells, frozen in cold filth and falling to pieces; but the holy flame of monarchical enthusiasm, despite everything, is carefully upheld in the hearts of the armoured priests in Berlin and in Petrograd.[32]

The censor removed 20 lines of text from 'A Law of Mechanics'.[33] However, it would be hard to claim that the missing sentences would have made any radical difference to the article's meaning. In the context of a relatively small contribution, Trotsky makes his point. At the outset he reminds the reader that press censorship during the Balkan War had led many to doubt the apparent war aim of 'peasant democracy'. Clemenceau is then presented as a man who objected to press censorship – he changed the name of his newspaper from *L'Homme libre* to *L'Homme enchaîné* as a protest against censorship – while remaining silent when *Golos* was closed. Clemenceau's apparent hypocrisy is explained by his position as a politician: eventually he wants to gain power to silence others so cannot afford the luxury of general principles. However, even when acting under dubious political motivations Clemenceau could still be perspicacious. Thus, in a recent article he had raised the issue of the likely reaction of returning soldiers, discovering what the state of affairs had been at home while they had been fighting for freedom. Clemenceau warned of the law of mechanics which states that resistance grows as applied pressure increases. Trotsky pointed out that Clemenceau was hoping that this 'law of mechanics' would one day transfer power into his hands; but he had provided a useful service in foreseeing a 'catastrophic upheaval in the mood of the people'.[34] The implication was clear; the prerequisites for revolution were in the offing.

Twenty sentences were also cut from 'Stages', but Trotsky was still able to express his views on a number of sensitive issues, including, the hopelessness of the present war and of the incompatibility of social-patriotism with the interests of the working class. The rest of the article was devoted to a review of the growing successes gained by the revolutionary section of the international proletarian movement; from the first to the second Zimmerwald Conferences and onwards to the establishment of a Third International.[35]

In 'On What the French Press Is Silent About' Trotsky discussed Stürmer's programme for Poland.[36] Although the censor cut over 35 sentences from this two-column article, Trotsky's rejection of the Russian Foreign Minister's plans for a united Poland under Russian protection is clear.

Finally, despite censorship in 'Wager on the Strong' this article stands as an open assault on notions of the First World War as a war of liberation. The fate of small nations (Belgium, Serbia, Turkey, Bulgaria, Roumania, Greece and Portugal) is likened to the fate of small businesses crushed in the competition between large trusts:

> In the field of international relations capitalism carries-over those methods by which it 'regulates' the internal economic life of an individual nation. Competition is the systematic destruction of small and middle enterprises and the domination of large capital. World capitalist competition entails the systematic subordination of small, middle and backward nations to the large and largest capitalist powers ... The 'liberation' of Belgium is not an end-in-itself. In the further course of the war, as after it, Belgium will become an integral and subordinate pawn of the great play of the capitalist giants.[37]

Hardly an inspiring picture for those engaged in a war to free Belgium.

*

Although Trotsky's Paris writings for *Golos* and its successors did not always appear in the exact form that he may have wished, one cannot say that the censor was particularly 'brutal' when he doctored Trotsky's work. Out of a plethora of articles submitted for approval between November 1914 and December 1916 only three were rejected outright.[38] One can read the partially censored articles without feeling that Trotsky's revolutionary socialism was being too heavily repressed or, even worse, being turned into reactionary social-patriotism. From a comparison of partially censored contributions against their fuller versions one discovers that Trotsky managed to say most of what he wanted to say, if not always in the language he wanted to employ. Trotsky himself was even able to reprint one of his partially censored articles in its censored form as an illustration of the theory of permanent revolution as he conceived of it during World War One when the book *Results and Prospects* was issued in Moscow in 1919.[39] As the following several chapters will show, his contributions to the radical Russian émigré press in Paris during World War One are a rich source for discovering his views on a whole range of issues as the 'war to end all wars' was being fought.

4
Lenin and the Bolsheviks

In 'The Eighteenth Brumaire of Louis Bonaparte' Karl Marx wrote that the 'tradition of the dead generations weighs like a nightmare on the minds of the living'.[1] Marx's view is particularly pertinent to Trotsky's political biography. His pre-1917 relations with Lenin and the Bolsheviks were to haunt him after he joined them in 1917. This was especially true during the disputes which surrounded the struggle to be Lenin's successor. The protagonists' overriding consideration was to claim a special closeness to Lenin. The nature of an individual's history with Lenin became of supreme importance. Each had an interest to construct a picture of harmony between themselves and Lenin, and to accentuate disharmony between others and Lenin.

Bolsheviks who opposed Trotsky had a rich store of material from which to draw: starting with the spilt between Lenin and Trotsky at the Second Congress of the RSDLP of 1903, and ending with disagreements between the two during Bolshevik rule. Stalin and his supporters did not waste this opportunity and attacked Trotsky for his anti-Leninism and non-Bolshevism. In turn, Trotsky responded by defending his Leninist pedigree.

The use of Leninism as a criterion of correctness also left its mark on subsequent writings by historians of this period. In Trotsky's case this has resulted in some historians writing accounts of a strong line of demarcation between Lenin and Trotsky.[2] Others interpret relations between the two as those of a gradual convergence. Disputes are explained away or softened by references to circumstances which were made irrelevant by the 1917 Revolution.[3] The suspicion remains, however, that whatever the interpretation, an honest evaluation of documents has not been the overriding consideration in reaching conclusions. This is for several reasons. First, as long as the USSR existed, Russian historians were limited either in access to documents or to what they could publish openly.[4] Second, Trotsky is a figure who arouses political passions and many Western interpreters have written their accounts more from a political point of view than from any other.[5] Third, translations of many of Trotsky's writings have been long available and this has permitted several non-Russian reading researchers to produce biographies of Trotsky, but without the ability to incorporate obscure, untranslated and often crucial documents into their versions.[6]

Of course these remarks do not apply to all historians who have addressed this topic in the recent period. Brian Pearce, for example, has written an excellent piece on one aspect of this chapter's topic.[7] However, we differ from Pearce's contribution in two respects. To begin with, our focus is wider than the issue of 'revolutionary defeatism in Lenin and Trotsky'. Indeed, the current work will present the first full account of relations between Trotsky, Lenin and the Bolsheviks from the outbreak of war to the February Revolution. Furthermore, although Pearce noted Trotsky's difficulties post-1924 in presenting his pre-October relations with Lenin, he gave no account of how this sensitive topic was approached in the very first years of Bolshevik rule. In contrast, we will illustrate how the actual content of the polemics which raged between Trotsky and Lenin and the Bolsheviks during World War One became obscured first by the Bolsheviks in collaboration and then in dispute, and how, in turn, these distorted positions entered the accounts of historians writing on the 1914–17 period. This chapter, therefore, is both a history and a historiographical analysis of its topic.

During the war the main forums for communication between Russian Social-Democrats continued to be the publication and distribution of newspapers, journals and pamphlets. This form of intercourse was obviously complicated by conditions of war. However, apart from circulation and financial problems, Russian socialists enjoyed a relatively free environment for the pursual of debates. The Bolsheviks published *Sotsial'Demokrat*, *Kommunist* and *Sbornik Sotsial'Demokrata* in neutral Switzerland; *Novyi Mir* was produced in America; and even in Paris, where Trotsky wrote for *Golos*, *Nashe Slovo* and *Nachalo*, the censor was not particularly concerned by the appearance of articles contributing to polemics raging between various fractions of Russian Social-Democracy, especially as they were of interest to a minority audience and written in a foreign language.[8]

Russian Social-Democrats were already split along fractional lines at the outbreak of World War One. In the months prior to August 1914 Trotsky had continued his campaign for unity, most notably in the journal *Bor'ba*.[9] Events of such magnitude as war can interrupt a settled pattern of debate and throw people and groups into alliances which, up until that point, they would not have seriously considered. Thus, an opportunity arose for a realliance of Russian Social-Democratic fractions around a common programme on the war.

Trotsky outlined his political response to the war in a series of four articles of January and February 1915, published in *Golos* and *Nashe Slovo*. Here he continued his analysis of the war as a revolt of the productive forces against the narrow confines of state boundaries, which he had first argued in the Preface to *War and the International*. According to Trotsky, one had to clearly understand the causes and nature of the world conflict in order to construct a viable political programme. It was of no use merely to demand peace. One had to offer real solutions which could act as a rallying call for revolutionary action for a just peace:

> It is very naive to say that we should not complicate our struggle for peace with slogans of a broader character. We would not want a peace in which Belgium, Northern France ... etc were annexed by the victorious country, becoming the source of a future conflict. We do not intend to drop questions of Poland, Alsace-Lorraine and Serbia from the order of the day – we want to resolve them. We do not believe these can be solved by militarism, and we express this disbelief in our demands for the war's end. To call for peace while sweeping its programme aside would be to take a backwards step, down a blind alley ... such a political stance is powerless to win over to its side the enthusiasm, heroism, and willingness for self-sacrifice currently exploited by militarism.[10]

For Trotsky, the war was being fought across two geographical centres, each at different stages of historical development. In South-Eastern Europe – Russia, Austria and the Balkans – the main issue was the creation of nationally independent, stable states as a prerequisite for capitalism. This area was thus beset by problems of the first stage of bourgeois development. In Western Europe – Britain, France and Germany – the nation-state had been created over the previous three centuries. These countries were grappling with the major problem of the final stage of imperialist development: the need to abolish artificial state boundaries. The productive forces demanded the extension of the economic base. In terms of the policies of the Great Powers of the day this meant one of two things: either victory and domination by Britain or by Germany. Trotsky realised that Britain was allied to France, but he asserted that the antagonism between Britain and Germany was 'the basic moving force of the present war'.[11] He argued that Britain and France had been united by the 'German danger', but he also claimed that perceptions of this danger were rooted in different concerns. France's main worry, due to its 'halting population growth and extreme down-turn in the tempo of economic development',[12] was to preserve its existing position on the world market and as a world power. Britain's interest was to ensure that no continental power, France or Germany, became so powerful in Europe so as to be able to launch an attack on British expansion, which was to be achieved on the basis of its colonial acquisitions. According to Trotsky, Germany pursued the most aggressive foreign policy at that time as this corresponded to the condition of its industry, the most quickly developing in Europe. In this way the expansionary plans of Britain and Germany lay at the heart of the world conflict:

> capitalism saturated in the framework of the national state and the rebellion of the productive forces against this framework, aspiring to a further and greater widening of the economic base to include colonies in the economic activity of the mother country, is the essence of the imperialist policy of the great powers. The collision of national imperialists brought about the present war.[13]

For Trotsky, the combination of tasks of different historical origin gave the war its peculiar character and gave rise to some of its illusions. The struggles of the advanced countries, for example, could be seen as part of the ostensibly liberating struggle for national independence taking place in the backward countries. However, Trotsky argued that the dominating factor was the concerns of the Great Powers. He recognised the importance of the national pretensions of, for example, Serbia and Belgium as playing an important part in the conflict, but he also perceived them as secondary issues. Thus, Serbia and Belgium had become involved in the war only because they were geographically situated on the map of the expansionary plans of the Great Powers. Moreover, the peoples struggling for national independence could not follow the route taken by the advanced nations when they faced tasks of a similar nature. The nation state was already an anachronism. For example, Trotsky claimed that each Balkan nation had too narrow a base for economic development. Even an enlarged Serbia would mean that other nationalities would fall into dependence upon Germany, Russia or even Serbia itself, and this could only give rise to a prospect of further 'liberation' conflicts. For Trotsky, the only answer to the peculiar combination of tasks of a pre-capitalist nature in an environment dominated by the needs of the final imperialist stage of capitalism was the enlarged state form of a Federative Balkan Republic.

According to Trotsky, the establishment of a Federative Balkan Republic would have several significant advantages. First, it would answer the need of a wide territorial base for economic development. Second, it would be a democratic state structure in which various nationalities would be able to express their individuality without threatening the cultural requirements of others. Trotsky combined these two points thus: 'It neutralises nationalism in the economic sense, freeing economic development from dependence upon the distribution of separate ethnic groups on the map of Europe.'[14] Finally, the Federative Balkan Republic would be better equipped to defend the interests of the Balkan peoples from possible aggression from Russia or Germany.

Trotsky also argued for the establishment of a transnational state structure, specifically a Republican United States of Europe, for Western Europe. In this area the interests of further economic development demanded an integrated economy organised under a single European state. Obviously, Trotsky did not see national problems as particularly pressing in West Europe as in South-Eastern Europe; his case for a United States of Europe remained at the level of economic considerations. For Trotsky, this urgent task could be realised in one of two ways. First, German imperialists had planned the forceful unification of Europe under their domination. Trotsky acknowledged that this represented a genuine attempt to resolve an issue that had to be resolved; it was a 'progressive historical need refracted, however, through the Junker-militaristic, reactionary-caste state apparatus of Germany'.[15] However, this attempt was bound to fail. One could not bring about the cohabitation and cooperation of peoples through militarism. Furthermore, what chance had plans for a Europe under the tutelage of the Central Empire when this Empire itself was disintegrating? 'The wonderful professor-Junker-stock-market utopia is the plan to turn the whole of Europe into a new Austria-Hungary when the old Austria-Hungary is being torn to shreds.'[16] Alternatively, the European proletariat could arise and create an all-European dictatorship of the proletariat in the form of a Republican United States of Europe. For Trotsky, not only was this the only way to achieve the desired goal, but the preconditions for it had been prepared by the very process which demanded the formation of a United States of Europe:

> Destroying the framework of the national state as too narrow for the development of productive forces, the war also destroys them as a base for social revolution ... Currently, social revolution stands before us if not as a world problem in the direct and immediate sense of the word, then in any case as a European problem. In present circumstances all proletarian movements in their very first steps will inevitably aspire to expand the framework of their national limitness and in the parallel movements of the proletariat of other countries seek to find a guarantee of their own success.[17]

Thus, Trotsky's analysis and prognosis envisaged a struggle for peace under the slogans of the creation of two federative republican state structures; the first in the Balkans and the second across Europe. In his concluding remarks in the final article he did add, however, that the responsibility for the further economic development of backward regions would rest upon the United States of Europe.[18]

While Trotsky was expounding his views Lenin and the Bolsheviks were publishing their reaction to the war in their newspaper *Sotsial'Demokrat*, issuing their first manifesto of the war in number 33 of 1 November 1914.

This manifesto shared several assumptions of Trotsky's writings of the time. First, the war was characterised as a struggle of the advanced imperialist nations for markets in which the dynastic interests of the backward nations were also involved. Second, and probably most important from Trotsky's point of view, the manifesto called for the formation of a Republican United States of Europe as the 'immediate political slogan of European Social-Democracy.'[19] Like Trotsky, the manifesto distinguished between 'proletarian' and 'bourgeois' versions of a United States of Europe, declaring that:

> the formation of a Republican United States of Europe, distinct from its bourgeois version which is prepared to 'promise' whatever is demanded if only to entice the proletariat into chauvinism. Social-Democracy will explain the falsehood and the foolishness of

this slogan without the revolutionary overthrow of the German, Austrian and Russian monarchies.[20]

However, the manifesto also departed from Trotsky's analysis. First, it expanded the basic aims of the war from pure imperialist antagonisms to a desire to 'distract the working masses from the internal political crises of Russia, Germany, Britain and other countries.'[21] Second, although *Sotsial'Demokrat* viewed the battle as the British and French bourgeoisie fighting against their German counterparts, no distinction was made between British and French interests. For *Sotsial'Demokrat* both countries wished to 'seize German colonies and end competition from a nation distinguished by a more rapid economic development'.[22] Third, and here begins what were to be the most significant differences, the manifesto made no mention of a struggle for peace with a defined peace programme. Instead, *Sotsial'Demokrat* called for 'turning the imperialist war into a civil war',[23] and referred to a resolution of the 1912 Basel Conference as authority for the correctness of this stance. Fourth, the manifesto considered the defeat of one of the two warring camps from the perspective of whose defeat would be the most useful for socialism. The conclusion reached was that

> for us, Russian Social Democrats, there can be no doubt that from the point of view of the working class and the labouring masses of all nationalities in Russia the lesser evil would be the defeat of the Tsarist monarchy, the most reactionary and barbaric government, oppressing the most national groups and the greatest human mass in Europe and Asia.[24]

Finally, *Sotsial'Demokrat* did not call for the establishment of a Republican United States in the Balkans as well as in Europe. For *Sotsial'Demokrat*, the main cleavage was between advanced and backward countries. Socialists in backward countries were told to struggle for the defeat of their governments in order to introduce democratic changes: 'democratic republics (with equal rights, including the right to national self-determination), the confiscation of landowners' land and the eight-hour working day.'[25] It would be up to socialists in the advanced countries to bring about the defeat of their country so as to stage a socialist revolution:

> in the advanced countries the war makes a socialist revolution the

first priority. This becomes more urgent the more the war's burdens are placed upon the proletariat's shoulders, and the more active the proletariat's role will be in rebuilding Europe when the horrors of modern 'patriotic' barbarism, which utilises capitalism's undoubted technical achievements, are over.[26]

The Bolsheviks were to return to their programmatic response to the war at the Conference of the Foreign Section of the RSDLP, held in Bern between 14–19 February 1915. The conference resolutions widened the differences between the Bolsheviks and Trotsky, most notably, a 'United States of Europe' was omitted. The only idea advanced under 'Slogans of Revolutionary Social-Democracy' was that of 'turning the imperialist war into a civil war', and five points of action were listed as the first steps towards this goal.[27] Moreover, *Nashe Slovo* was not favourably reviewed in 'Relations to other Parties and Groups':

> elements grouping around *Nashe Slovo* vacillate between platonic empathy to internationalism and aspirations of unity at any cost with *Nasha Zarya* and the Organisational Committee.[28]

At this stage, i.e. between November 1914 and the end of February 1915, both Trotsky and Lenin and the Bolsheviks developed their programmes knowing the stances adopted by the other. In early November 1914 Eintracht, a section of the Swiss Social Democratic Party, organised a meeting in one of Zurich's large halls. Trotsky attended and delivered a speech, although when he subsequently made reference to this meeting in two of his published writings he did not expound upon its contents.[29] However, Lenin was also present and his notes made at the conference were published in volume 14 of *Leninskii sbornik* (1930). These notes enable us to reconstruct some of the themes addressed by Trotsky. First, he declared his solidarity with Eintracht's resolution, which called for a struggle to end the war with the aim of implementing a 'peace programme' – i.e., no forced annexations, no war indemnities, the right of nations to self-determination and a United States of Europe free of standing armies, secret diplomacy and feudal castes.[30] He then considered the relationship between his policy of a struggle for peace and the resolution of the 1912 Basel Conference. For Trotsky, there was no contradiction between the two:

in order to start the German proletariat's fight againt its bourgeoisie one must first of all end the war raging between the German
and French proletariat. The first slogan for a civil war is an end to
the imperialist war.[31]

Lenin highlighted this section of his notes with a square bracket
down the left-hand side and labelled Trotsky's argument 'sophistic.'[32]
Further in his notes he commented, 'Let the speaker declare his
opposition to the Basel Conference.'[33] Later, when writing of
S. Vainshtein's view that little separated the positions of Lenin and
Trotsky, Lenin registered his contempt by writing of 'rebellious anar-
chism' (Trotsky) and 'scientific socialism' (Lenin).[34]

However, Trotsky also made somewhat of a favourable impression
on Lenin. Thus, for example, when he referred to his disagreements
with Kautsky Lenin wrote of a 'firmer tone and more profound considerations'.[35] Moreover, when M. Ratner declared his intention to argue
against Trotsky Lenin found his tone to be 'demagogic and very
distasteful'.[36]

Indeed, at the beginning of 1915 the idea of cooperation between
Trotsky and *Nashe Slovo* on the one side and Lenin and
Sotsial'Demokrat on the other was broached. The cause was the decision to call a conference of socialist parties of the Entente countries,
to be held in London in February 1915 and organised by the Belgian
social-patriot Vandervelde.[37]

The initiator of the correspondence was the editorial board of *Nashe
Slovo*, who approached the Bolshevik Central Committee and the
Menshevik Organisational Committee, among others, in an attempt
to forge an anti-social patriotic bloc. The full text of this approach was
not published in the newspaper, and the editors of volume 17 of
Leninskii sbornik (1931) claim that the Institute of Marxism-Leninism
did not possess a copy of *Nashe Slovo's* letter.[38] We are thus forced to
rely upon references made to the letter to learn of its contents. From
Lenin's reply, written in Bern on 9th February 1915, we discover its
date and basic intentions:

In your letter of 6th February you propose a plan of action against
'official social patriotism' regarding the London Conference of
socialists of the 'allied countries' of the Entente.[39]

Lenin responded favourably, declaring that he accepted the offer of
joint action 'with pleasure'.[40] He then stressed the necessity of utilis-

ing all opportunities of conducting this struggle and outlined a draft declaration on the London Conference, to be signed by *Sotsial'Demokrat* and *Nashe Slovo*. This declared the war an imperialist war, the product of an age in which the bourgeois nation-state was an anachronism. Lenin listed an eight-point programme of action, intended to fulfil the Basel resolution: 1) the break-up of national blocs in all countries; 2) a call to workers of all countries to use political and economic means to struggle against their bourgeois governments; 3) a harsh condemnation of all voting for war credits; 4) socialists should resign from Belgian and French governments, and it should be recognised that joining governments and voting for war credits is as big a betrayal of socialism as that perpetrated by German and Austrian Social-Democracy at the outbreak of war; 5) the formation of an international committee to propagate the idea of revolutionary mass action against one's own government; 6) all attempts at the establishment of fraternal relations between the soldiers of warring countries should be supported; 7) women socialists of warring countries should strengthen their efforts to propagandise the aforementioned points; and 8) Russian Social-Democracy should be supported in its struggle against tsarism. The letter from *Nashe Slovo* must also have mentioned the possibility of teaming up with the Bund and the Organisational Committee, as Lenin felt it necessary to warn that they stood for 'official social-patriotism.' However, he also asked to be kept informed of how these organisations responded to *Nashe Slovo*'s suggestions.

Thus, the overall tone of Lenin's reply was positive, and he even went so far as to make concrete suggestions for furthering cooperation. However, this positive tone was at odds with the pessimism he expressed on the likelihood of the success of the *Nashe Slovo* project in a letter to A. Shlyapnikov of 11 February 1915:

> We answered *Nashe Slovo* that we are happy with its suggestion and we sent our draft declaration. Agreement is unlikely, for Akels'rod, apparently, is in Paris and Aksel'rod is a social chauvinist, wanting to reconcile Germanofiles and Francofiles on the soil of social-chauvinism. We will see which is dearer to *Nashe Slovo* – anti-chauvinism or Aksel'rod's friendship.[41]

In the meantime, *Nashe Slovo* published three separate declarations on the London Conference. The first was signed by Martov on behalf of the Organisational Committee and Lapinski representing the Polish

Socialist Party.[42] This statement criticised the calling of the London Conference for several reasons. First, socialists should not be invited because of their nationality, a criterion underpinned by imperialist assumptions: 'We refuse to recognise the principle of grouping the proletariat along the lines of the temporary coincidence of the interests of their class enemies.'[43] Second, by limiting invitations the organisers were accepting and strengthening the splits in the Second International which had occurred at the outbreak of the war. Third, only an internationalist stance, considering the views of socialists of all countries, could restore the International. For Martov and Lapinski, if they were to expose the imperialist roots of the war and to struggle for peace, socialists had to avoid aligning themselves with any of the warring nations. Only in this way, the authors were convinced, could socialists guarantee themselves an influence over the terms of a future peace. They requested that delegates at the London Conference refrain from passing any resolutions which could play into the hands of the class enemy. In a footnote to the declaration, which appeared after the Conference had ended, Martov and Lapinski announced that they would have voted against the resolutions eventually adopted by the meeting.

The second declaration was *Nashe Slovo*'s own, in the form of a mandate passed by the editorial board on 13 February 1915. This seven-point programme was censored in the newspaper: half of point two and all of point six were lost.[44] However, Lenin and other socialists had access to the full text, which was published in *Berner Tagwacht* of 20 February 1915, and later translated into Russian from the German in volume XVII of *Leninskii sbornik*.[45] *Nashe Slovo* also declared the London Conference a betrayal of the principles of socialist internationalism, and called for socialists to attend the Conference so as to demand a gathering of socialists of all countries. Then, using the contents of Lenin's letter to its editorial board, a programme of action was listed not in order to turn the imperialist war into a civil war but as part of a struggle to end the war.[46]

Third, in *Nashe Slovo* of 4 March 1915, the declaration of the Bolshevik Central Committee was published. This text was also censored, points 2–4 and the concluding sentences were blank. The declaration began by pointing out that the London Conference was supposed to be for socialists from Belgium, Britain, France and Russia, but Russian Social-Democrats had not received invites. The hope was then expressed that Russian Social-Democracy's hostility to the Conference had been made clear to delegates gathering in London, otherwise 'we would have good reason to accuse you of hiding the truth.'[47] The Central Committee made demands similar to those outlined in its letter to *Nashe Slovo* which had then been used by *Nashe Slovo* itself: the immediate withdrawal of socialists from governments; a condemnation of voting for war credits; and, finally, the recognition that Austrian and German Social-Democracy had committed terrible crimes against socialism and the International, and that Belgian and French socialists had hardly acted any better.

Nashe Slovo followed the publication of these declarations with an article enlightening readers on the steps it had taken to coordinate the actions of Russian socialists on the London Conference.[48] An editorial outlined its intentions in approaching the Bolshevik Central Committee and the Menshevik Organisational Committee:

> Not long before the Conference the editorial board of our newspaper sent to representatives of our party in the International Socialist Bureau, Aksel'rod and Lenin, letters which proposed that in the interests of a struggle with 'official social patriotism' steps should be taken to ensure that no accidental invitations could be sent to a social-patriot, not sharing the views of the RSDLP, to speak on behalf of Russian Social-Democracy, and that any Conference invitations should be issued through official representatives of our party in the Internationalist Socialist Bureau. Our offer, obviously, also proposed a coordination of action of internationalist elements of Russian Social-Democratic delegates.[49]

Readers were then informed that both Aksel'rod and Lenin had agreed to coordinate activities, and that the basic points of Comrade Lenin's draft declaration had been incorporated into *Nashe Slovo*'s mandate. The editorial concluded with a confident statement of the success of the *Nashe Slovo* initiative to date:

> In this way we see that maintaining an internationalist socialist position, *unifying Social-Democratic internationalists of all fractions* – a stable base for joint revolutionary action is created. It is our profoud belief that the coordination of action of all revolutionary internationalist elements of Russian Social-Democracy is not only possible and desirable but is also absolutely essential.[50]

This optimistic mood was also reflected in 'Where is the majority?'[51] This editorial took issue with Plekhanov's assertion that a majority of

Russian workers and socialists supported his patriotic stance on the war. *Nashe Slovo* reported that Plekhanov cited two pieces of support-ing evidence. First, Martov had declared that his own followers did not agree with him. Second, Lenin had published a worker's letter which stated that the Russian proletariat did not wish to hear talk of Russia's defeat. These two points were then dismissed as insufficient grounds for drawing such a conclusion. First, it was pointed out that Martov was speaking of the editorial board of *Nasha Zarya*, a group which did not represent a majority of Russian workers and which had no organisational base. Second, it was argued that just because workers did support Russia's defeat they wanted instead a victorious Entente. It was claimed that Russian socialists could disagree over the appeal of a call for Russia's defeat and yet be united in opposition to social patriotism, a unity which was in fact forming. The editorial listed the party groups (including the Bolshevik Central Committee, the Menshevik Organisational Committee and the Bund) which were hostile to Plekhanov, while a footnote highlighted the fact that differ-ent tendencies had united around *Nashe Slovo*'s initiative on the London Conference. Two further processes of unification around points of view opposed to Plekhanov's were mentioned: first in Petersburg and second among Social-Democratic deputies in the State Duma. The editorial concluded that the only way in which Russian Social-Democracy could prevent one single voice from claiming to represent the movement as a whole was for fractional groups to unite around a stand against social patriotism.

It was this article, combined with *Nashe Slovo*'s evaluation of the negotiations surrounding the London Conference, that Lenin found objectionable. In his reply to *Nashe Slovo* Lenin had stated that he considered the Organisational Committee social-patriotic. Now *Nashe Slovo* was claiming that he was agreeing to join a coalition which included arch social-patriot Aksel'rod. Moreover, he was probably annoyed that *Nashe Slovo*, claiming to have incorporated the funda-mental points of his draft declaration into its programme, appeared to be undermining his party's copyright over 'internationalism'. Indeed, to be fair to *Nashe Slovo*, its mandate and Lenin's draft project were very similar in content and in their use of language. However, afraid of being steamrollered into an alliance with which he did not want to be associated, Lenin went onto the offensive.

On 23 March 1915 Lenin despatched a letter to *Nashe Slovo*.[52] He began by expressing support for the idea of the unification of all Social Democratic internationalists. However, he also pointed out that there had to be sufficient ideological agreement to make unification possible. In order to discover whether this existed Lenin asked for clarification of *Nashe Slovo*'s position on several points. First, did it agree that the struggle against Plekhanov and Aleksinskii had to be waged not via declarations, but through real work in which, in order to qualify as an organisation, one needed experience of years of contact with the masses and not simply issue a newspaper. Second, Lenin questioned why *Nashe Slovo* had included the Bund in its list of internationalists. After all, he argued, their newspaper the *Informatsionnyi Listok* 'is clearly based on German chauvinism.'[53] Third, internationalism excluded from its ranks any advoacte of an 'amnesty', i.e. that socialists should regroup after the war without accusations of guilt against one another:

> Any concessions, any agreements with Kautsky and the Organisational Committee are absolutely impermissible. The most decisive struggle against the theory of 'amnesty' is the *conditio sine qua non* of internationalism ... And here we ask – is there agreement between us on this crucial question?[54]

Why, Lenin continued, did *Nashe Slovo* think that the Organisational Committee was internationalist? Was it not obvious from its most prominent representative Aksel'rod, for example, that it was replete with chauvinists? Lenin did not rule out further cooperation with *Nashe Slovo*, but he emphasised that, 'We will be very glad to receive a full and clear answer to all of these questions. Only then will it be possible to think of the future.'[55]

These sentiments were expressed in a slightly harsher tone in 'On the London Conference'.[56] Here Lenin emphasised that he had labelled the Bund and the Organisational Committee social-patriots in his letter to *Nashe Slovo* of 9 February 1915: 'Why does *Nashe Slovo* hide the truth, remaining silent about this in its editorial of issue 32?'[57] Furthermore, in an attempt to take control of the negotiations and to preserve his party's distinctive stance, Lenin stressed differences between his draft project and *Nashe Slovo's* declaration:

> Why keep quiet on the fact that in our draft project we also spoke of the betrayal of German Social-Democrats? *Nashe Slovo*'s declaration omitted this crucial, 'basic' point. Neither we nor Comrade Maksimovich accepted this declaration nor are we able to. As a result, united action with the Organisational Committee did not

happen. Why then does *Nashe Slovo* fool itself and others, believing
that grounds exist for united action?[58]

In this (public) article Lenin made it absolutely clear that if there was
to be joint action, then it would be a case of *Nashe Slovo* coming to
share *Sotsial'Demokrat*'s position, not vice versa: 'It remains only to
hope that from vacillations between "platonic empathy with internationalism" and reconciliation with social-chauvinism *Nashe Slovo*
moves to a more determined position.'[59]

In reply to Lenin's letter, *Nashe Slovo* defended its inclusion of the
Organisational Committee and the Bund in the ranks of internationalists.[60] For *Nashe Slovo*, the groups to which it had appealed were
united in their opposition to the war and it was this fact that, in its
opinion, enabled joint action. Moreover, *Nashe Slovo* argued that it
was possible to exaggerate differences and in this way fall into the trap
of condemning internationalists as social-patriots. So, for example, it
would be correct to say that the Organisational Committee was wrong
in its view of the newspaper *Nasha Zarya*; but, at the same time, it
would be incorrect to conclude from this that the Organisational
Committee supported social-chauvinism. According to *Nashe Slovo*,
Sotsial'Demokrat had also made this mistake in evaluating the Duma
fraction as social-chauvinist: '[the Duma fraction] did not balk at
excluding Man'kov from its ranks because of his militaristic speech.'[61]
Furthermore, *Nashe Slovo* continued, it was possible for undoubted
internationalists to waver on crucial matters: 'witness (including
Sotsial'Demokrat) the uncertain position in relation to the slogan of
struggle for peace, under the banner of which internationalist activity
currently takes place.'[62] Finally, on the issue of an amnesty, *Nashe
Slovo* stated that it was against the reformation of the International
based on the principle of mutual acceptance of nationalist positions
taken up during the war. However, at the same time, *Nashe Slovo*
argued that it did not want to exclude cooperation with any group at
too early a stage:

> ... it would have been a mistake, in the beginning of the war when
> both Liebknecht and Rühle were at one with the majority of
> German Social-Democracy, to have demanded an abyss between
> them and us and to have constructed our tactics on this basis ...
> the revolutionary minority which we, the internationalists, now
> constitute should resolve issues of preserving or sacrificing party
> unity from point of view of expediency, i.e., depending upon what

type of organisational form will guarantee us the most influence over the course of the class movement in each separate case.[63]

Nashe Slovo concluded by hoping that it had removed any doubts which the Central Committee had had on the viability of further cooperation. However, we have no record of the Central Committee responding. Indeed, it is not even possible to say with certainty when *Nashe Slovo* replied to Lenin's letter of 23 March 1915. The editors of volume XVII of *Leninskii sbornik* date *Nashe Slovo*'s letter 'after 25 March'.[64] What is clear is that Trotsky blamed Lenin for the breakdown of the negotiations and for harming the internationalist cause. The following is from his letter to Radek of 8 June 1915:

> The meeting which *Nashe Slovo* proposed (Ts.K, O.K. and NS) could have played an important role now. The internationalists would have been the decisive force and the vacillating O.K. would have been forced to firm-up ... Lenin destroyed this meeting. Why? Out of pure fractional considerations, not allowing collective authority to replace his own personal authority, seeing in himself, in the last analysis, the axis of world history. This is a terribly egocentric person ... and this terrible egocentricism brings us no less difficulties than the Mensheviks' vacillations.[65]

The next development of note was an offer from the Central Committee to Trotsky of cooperation on its new journal *Kommunist*, the first (double) issue of which appeared in August 1915. No copy of this offer has ever been published. We are forced to guess the time of its composition and reconstruct its contents from Trotsky's response, printed in *Nashe Slovo*.[66] The Central Committee's offer was probably made sometime towards the end of May 1915. This date is the most likely as the Central Committee included a copy of its introduction for the new journal, dated 20 May 1915 when it was published later that year.[67] Assuming that Trotsky would not leave this letter without a reply for long, such a dating would also fall nicely into the timescale of Trotsky's printed reply of early June 1915.

In his 'Open Letter to *Kommunist*' Trotsky declined the offer of participation. First, he highlighted serious programmatic differences between himself and the Bolsheviks: the Central Committee's rejection of the slogan struggle for peace; the Bolshevik's preference for Russia's defeat as the 'lesser evil' which, for Trotsky, shared the same methodological grounds as social-patriotism; and, finally, Trotsky did not agree with the way in which the Bolsheviks delineated social patriotism in organisational terms. Second, Trotsky claimed that these differences in themselves would not be an obstacle to cooperation if the Bolsheviks were establishing an open discussion journal. However, for Trotsky, *Kommunist* was 'sad evidence that you subordinate your struggle against social patriotism to considerations and aims for which I under any circumstance could not accept responsibility'.[68] Most annoying for Trotsky was the fact that in its introduction to *Kommunist* the editorial board had included a list of people and groups which it considered to share its opposition to social-patriotism. This list included the five imprisoned Duma deputies but excluded Trotsky and *Nashe Slovo*. According to Trotsky, this list represented 'a distortion of the truth for fractional reasons'.[69] After all, he pointed out, the views of the five condemned Social-Democratic deputies were the same as the Social-Democrats remaining in the Duma. If there was any lack of revolutionary clarity in the first statements issued by Social Democratic deputies then, for Trotsky, this was the responsibility of all deputies – both in and out of prison. Moreover, recent speeches by Social-Democratic Duma representatives gave a 'rebuff to all attempts to lead the masses into social-patriotic depravity'.[70] The fact that the Bolsheviks could ignore the Social-Democrats in the Duma while welcoming Monat and the Independent British Socialists into their ranks merely testified to the fact that their conclusions were drawn 'neither for political clarity nor in the interests of the International [but] for fractional gain which I cannot support'.[71] Trotsky concluded by stating that in actual fact *Nashe Slovo* was closer to the Bolsheviks than any of the groups named in *Kommunist*. Only one of two conclusions could be drawn: 'you keep silent about [*Nashe Slovo*] because of murky considerations; if not it looks as though you have no allies in the International.'[72]

Trotsky's unequivocal reply, based upon the differences which clearly separated him from the Bolsheviks, raises the question: why did the Central Committee appeal to Trotsky? There are several possible reasons.

First, there had long existed the suspicion in the Bolshevik camp that Trotsky's calls for unity were a form of 'non-fractional fractionalism', i.e., a device to strengthen Trotsky's own influence in Russian Social-Democracy. This could be demonstrated if Trotsky were to turn down an offer of cooperation. Second, some Bolsheviks may have looked upon Trotsky as occupying the most internationalist stance of all in the *Nashe Slovo* editorial board. They had no doubt followed his dispute with Larin concerning Trotsky's relation to the Organisational Committee,[73] and they may have desired to push Trotsky, through participation in the production of *Kommunist*, further into the Bolshevik camp. Third, if Trotsky was perceived as being closer to the Bolsheviks than to anyone else and as being the main figure behind *Nashe Slovo*, then coopting Trotsky could have been seen as a way of increasing Bolshevik influence over a daily newspaper – something the Bolsheviks were not producing but clearly wanted to produce.[74] Thus, there might have been tensions among Bolsheviks – between those supportive and dismissive of Trotsky. Trotsky's response to a letter sent directly to him could provide evidence for one side or the other, in this way ending what might have been (or threatened to be) a long running dispute. Certainly this was the claim made in *Kommunist* itself. In a footnote to 'Russian Social-Democracy and Russian Social-Chauvinism'[75] Zinoviev described the events surrounding the offer to Trotsky as a successful and amusing 'experiment':

> Regarding the letter Trotsky involuntarily gave *Kommunist's* editorial board several minutes of real mirth. Some of the editors had predicted Trotsky's pompous vacuously-phrased answer word for word. (Trotsky, like Turgenev's well-known hero, is even silent in vacuous phrases) … The 'demonstration's' outcome was obvious. After Trotsky's open letter it became clear to all that for him it was more important to be allied to the liquidationist Organisational Committee than to Russian internationalists.[76]

Whatever the reason, or combination of reasons, for the Central Committee's approach Trotsky was certainly annoyed. The 'Open Letter' was soon followed by a further attack on *Sotsial'Demokrat* in the third instalment of an editorial series, 'Our Position', published between May and July 1915.[77] In earlier contributions Trotsky had criticised *Sotsial'Demokrat* for its opposition to the slogan struggle for peace:

> Parliamentary declarations from socialists of various countries, international women's conferences etc. testify to the huge role of the slogan 'struggle for peace' in mobilising the left and what a massive political error was commited, and to a significant degree continues to be commited, by *Sotsial'Demokrat* attempting to dismiss this slogan as that of the pacifist and Papist camps.[78]

Now Trotsky turned his attention to the issues of splits and unity among Russian Social Democrats. In particular, he answered *Sotsial'Demokrat*'s accusation that *Nashe Slovo* was not drawing the necessary conclusions from a struggle against social-patriotism, i.e. a split with the Organisational Committee. For Trotsky, internationalists should remain within organisational structures, even if they were in the minority, in order to win them over to internationalism: 'Splitting is not our slogan but the winning of organisations.'[79] He pointed to Liebknecht, Monat and the Independent Labour Party as instances of remaining within old groupings to win them over to internationalism. However, as well as rejecting the 'artificial splitting' proposed by *Sotsial'Demokrat*, Trotsky stated that splits were permissible in certain circumstances. For instance, splits could arise from the struggle for internationalism itself. However, in such cases 'the proletariat should be made aware that splitting was unavoidable and responsibility for it rests on those who are using discipline in the service of the class enemy'.[80]

In the fourth, final, instalment of 'Our Position' Trotsky applied his general arguments on unity and splits to the specific case of Russian Social-Democracy.[81] He began by distinguishing Russian Social-Democracy from its Western European equivalent. For instance, Russian socialists had split into organisational fractions long before the war during disagreements over specifically Russian issues (most notably the nature of any forthcoming Russian revolution), whereas German socialists coexisted within one broad organisation. According to Trotsky, stances adopted on the war had led to a regrouping in Russian socialism which, as elsewhere, had cut across old allegiances. However, so strong was the tradition of ideological and organisational fracture that, among Russian socialists, three groups had survived into the war: *Sotsial'Demokrat*, the August Bloc, and *Nashe Slovo*.[82]

For Trotsky, several dire consequences for Russian internationalism had followed. First, the proletariat had been thrown into confusion by the outbreak of the war and organisational disunity compounded this confusion. Second, although internationalists were objectively closer in their outlook to one another than to anyone else, competing organisational interests mitigated against a general coming together, i.e. negotiations for unity tended to be founder on the rocks of organisational myopia. For Trotsky, the urgent task was to unite all internationalists (he mentioned the Organisational Committee, the Central Committee and *Nashe Slovo*) so that henceforth there would be two identifiable groups in Russian socialism: Social Democrats and social-patriots. He illustrated how this could be achieved through a scenario of the possible unification of three proletarian organisations in Petrograd: the Petrograd Committee, the Unification Group, and the Initiative Group. Supporters of merger were urged to remain within their current organisation and argue their case. Trotsky hoped that the Initiative and Unification groups would become more decisive in their campaign against social patriotism and the Petrograd Committee would free itself of fractional arrogance. In this way the three groups would converge politically, providing the prerequisite for their reformation into one organisational structure. By not calling for the formation of a fourth 'progressive' fraction Trotsky claimed that he was refuting the accusations of 'organisational platform' and 'non-fractional fractionalism' made by *Sotsial'Demokrat* and the August Bloc. Despite a lack of success to date Trotsky saw the future as belonging to his position:

> We have taken the initiative to call, appealing to the 'leaders', for the joint elaboration of a common effective platform of the internationalist majority of Russian Social-Democracy. So far our efforts have produced no practical results, but we do not intend to despair. The logic of our attempts penetrates a lot deeper than the official leaders. On our side is the far mightier logic of the situation itself. We shall repeat our attempt and no doubt more than once. Tomorrow we shall meet face to face at an international gathering of internationalists. We hope that it will ... bring us together and ease our closer unifictaion in the framework of Russian Social-Democracy. Working for this we do not doubt the vitality of this position – far both from ideological-political formlessness and from organisational-fractional absolutism.[83]

However, Trotsky's arguments cut no ice with the Bolsheviks. For Zinoviev, for example, Trotsky's plans for unity were doomed to failure because his political platform was the most,

> vacuous and unprincipled ever to have existed in Russian Social-Democracy. Taking a piece from the liquidationists and a piece from the Pravdists, 'to worm oneself' between the Central Committee and the Organisational Committee – in this consists the simple philosophy of 'Trotskyism'. It is obvious that no-one can respect this.[84]

Zinoviev argued that eclecticism was no path to socialism. Russian Social-Democracy had passed the test of the outbreak of war because the Bolshevik Central Committee had pursued a long-term policy of splitting from revisionists. Protecting ideological purity had enabled the Central Committee to occupy a principled position against social-chauvinism. Trotsky's policy of reconciliation of all tendencies could result only in the burying of Russian socialism, just as socialism had been buried alongside the triumph of opportunism in Western Europe:

> Opportunists reduced Social-Democracy to the level of a national liberal workers' party. Now the question is should we assimilate the social chauvinists, can one somehow cohabitate with social chauvinists, or is our sense of socialist self-preservation still so alive in us that we can muster enough strength to split with bourgeois corrupters of socialism and maintain our independence? The issue is should there or should there not be socialism.[85]

Zinoviev cited several facts which illustrated Trotsky's support of opportunism and social-chauvinism. First, Trotsky located the collapse of the Second International solely to the peculiarity of the previous epoch.[86] For Zinoviev, this was a one-sided and confused formulation. After all, Trotsky had said nothing of the nature of opportunism as such. Why should Trotsky omit any reference of the ideological side of the matter? Because, Zinoviev answered, his call for the formation of a single party from various tendencies was a cover for reconciliation with social-chauvinism. Second, despite permitting splits when political expediency demanded, after a year of war Trotsky had still not split from Russian social-chauvinists. Third, Trotsky insisted that there were no differences which separated the five sentenced Social Democratic deputies from the rest of the Duma fraction. How could this be, asked Zinoviev, when Chkheidze and others rejected everything that the five stood for? Did Trotsky not know that Chkheidze supported the social-chauvinist publication *Nasha Zarya*? Was Trotsky unaware of Chkheidze's participation in meetings at which the question of how best to supply the army was discussed? Was Trotsky blind to the fact that Man'kov had been expelled because his open avowal of social-chauvinism was harmful to a cause which needed to hide its true intentions so as not to alienate workers? Had Trotsky not read Plekhanov's patriotic justification of Chkheidze's refusal to vote for war credits: that one could not give money to a government unfit to ensure the defence of the homeland? Did Trotsky really not know why tsarism itself had singled-out the five for 'special' treatment? According to Zinoviev, Trotsky knew all of this but he lied because he was 'chained to the Organisational Committee and to social-chauvinism like a convict to a wheelbarrow'.[87] The attack on Trotsky concluded with a prediction of his full conversion to social-chauvinism:

> At the present moment, under the influence of an optical illusion, it is possible that Trotsky's newspaper appears to be an organ of a particular, independent direction. In order to create a newspaper of *Nashe Slovo*'s type in Paris one need have no connections with the Russian workers' movement. When the matter comes to a serious struggle before the masses in Russia then it will once again become clear that we have only two serious independent platforms: our party and the party which forms *Nasha Zarya*, behind which Trotskyism will always be forced to keep up with.[88]

Lenin also went on to the offensive against Trotsky, most notably in two articles of late July 1915. 'On the defeat of one's own government in the Imperialist War' declared defeatism to be the axiom of a revolutionary class during a reactionary war.[89] Trotsky was labelled a 'hopeless servant of the social-chauvinists' for his claim that defeatism shared the same methodological grounds as social-patriotism.[90] Lenin argued that the Bern Resolution had made the issue absolutely clear, even for people like Trotsky who could not think: 'the proletariat should desire the defeat of their own government in *all* imperialist countries.'[91] For Lenin, Trotsky's views were expressed in the same 'puffed-up phrases by which [he] always justifies opportunism'.[92] This analysis of Trotsky as social chauvinist was pursued in 'On the state of affairs in Russian Social-Democracy'.[93] Here Lenin listed three groups which coexisted in *Nashe Slovo*: first, two editors who were close to *Sotsial'Demokrat*; second, Martov and the *okisty*; and, finally, Trotsky who 'as always does not agree with the social chauvinists but is in all practicalities at one with them (thanks, by the way, to the 'lucky mediator' – it seems as though this is how to call it in diplomatic language? – Chkheidze's fraction).'[94]

Trotsky did not respond directly to either of Lenin's articles. However, in early September 1915 he published what was his fullest case against defeatism to date.[95] He acknowledged that Russian Social Democrats had agreed even before the hostilities that Russian engagement in a war would fatally weaken its state order. However, he also pointed out that, for several very good reasons, none of the Russian socialists had called for war as a means to further the cause of revolution. First, war becomes a substitute path to revolution only when there is no class able to act as a revolutionary force, a condition not met in Russia. Second, war is too uncertain a factor to place at the centre of one's strategy; it could give the necessary push to revolution but this was not guaranteed. Third, the consequences of war and defeat are a disrupted and often ruined economy, hardly the best starting-point for a new revolutionary order. Fourth, the defeat of one country presupposes the victory and strengthening of another, and 'we do not know of any European social and state organism which the European proletariat would wish to see strengthened. At the same time, we in no way assign Russia the role of an elected state whose interests should be subordinated to the interests of the development of other European peoples.'[96] Finally, military defeat, as well as stirring a population to action, can also paralyse a nation and 'perhaps in first instance the revolutionary movement of the proletariat'.[97]

So, relations between Trotsky and the Bolsheviks were far from the state of harmony which Trotsky hoped would be achieved at a meeting of internationalists to take place in Zimmerwald, starting on 5 September 1915. In his first reports from Zimmerwald which, because of restrictions imposed by the censor, appeared in *Nashe Slovo* of early October 1915 Trotsky devoted several articles to an evaluation of the activities of Lenin and the Bolsheviks.

'Our Groupings' reported how the Bolsheviks, together with the Polish Opposition, held a pre-conference meeting to decide on a joint programme.[98] The article began with the claim that Lenin was isolated. According to Trotsky, Lenin had argued that the slogan struggle for peace was devoid of revolutionary content. However, he 'did not attract any support.'[99] The reader was then informed that the 'Leninist tendency' put forward two documents in draft form: a tactical resolution and an appeal to the masses. The tactical resolution contanied a denunciation of the war as an imperialist war, a condemnation of Kautsky and of the notion of 'civil peace', the demand for a struggle for peace and for a break with legalism. Trotsky welcomed this resolution, viewing it as a 'whole series of "retreats" by *Sotsial'Demokrat*', and arguing that to the extent that this represented a move towards *Nashe Slovo's* position there was now an absence of 'all that demarcates *Sotsial'Demokrat* from *Golos* and *Nashe Slovo*'.[100] He also emphasised, in block letters, that if *Sotsial'Demokrat* was to continue to adopt a more internationalist stance it would be forced to abandon its fractionalist position:

> We can only a hundred times note with satisfaction that IN SO FAR AS THE GROUP SOTSIALDEMOKRAT ENTERS ONTO THE INTER-NATIONAL ARENA IT WILL BE FORCED TO A GREATER OR LESSER EXTENT TO ABANDON THE SECTIONALIST LANGUAGE WITH WHICH IT HAS ATTEMPTED TO ARTIFICIALLY SPLIT RUSSIAN INTERNATIONALISTS.[101]

After expressing regret that the tactical resolution was defeated when it was put to the vote, Trotsky issued a cautionary note: the slogan of struggle for peace had not been written into the resolution in a sufficiently decisive and principled manner.[102]

Three days later Trotsky painted a far more pessimistic picture of Lenin's machinations. Events occurring on the eve of the conference illustrated just how far a mood of hostility had set in between the two. 'The Russian Section of the Internationalists' recounted how Lenin had tried to prevent *Nashe Slovo* from having its own representative at the conference.[103] According to Trotsky's report, Lenin had argued that since half of the editorial board of *Nashe Slovo* belonged to the Organisational Committee there was no need for a separate place to be set aside for *Nashe Slovo*. Lenin also claimed that this had already been agreed with the Organisational Committee. The Organisational Committee disputed this, while Trotsky attacked Lenin's assertion of the links between *Nashe Slovo* and the Organisational Committee – had not *Sotsial'Demokrat* itself written that the Organisational Committee had decided to boycott *Nashe Slovo*? Lenin dropped his proposal amid all of this wrangling, but there was obviously no love lost between Lenin and Trotsky, the latter claiming that the proposal would have been rejected if it had been put to the vote.

In this and in other articles written from the Zimmerwald Conference Trotsky proudly defended the achievements of *Nashe Slovo*'s 'non-fractional' stance. For example, he emphasised that it was now entering its second year, playing a crucial role as an organ used by revolutionary internationalists struggling in the Balkans, Russia, Italy and especially in Germany where the fact that *Nashe Slovo* (unlike other socialist publications from neutral countries) was produced in Entente-aligned France had special significance.[104]

'Basic Theses' reported the background to the adoption of the Zimmerwald Manifesto.[105] Lenin put forward a resolution demanding a programme of struggle to launch a civil war against imperialist governments. Trotsky criticised this plan as ignoring the need first of all to unite the proletariat against a war which was exhausting vital human and technical resources: 'In order for the German proletariat to turn their cannons 42 against the class enemy they should first of all not target them on their class brothers.'[106] He acknowledged that Lenin considered Trotsky's espousal of a struggle for peace as a half-retreat to pacifism but, for Trotsky, it was exactly this that made Lenin's position 'sectionalist'. Furthermore, Trotsky argued that the Leninists were inconsistent in their evaluation of pacifism, sometimes correctly identifying it as a desire to ensure that war would not occur again while retaining capitalism and, at others, calling pacifism part of the 'revolutionary-class struggle for peace as a central task of the moment.'[107] However, Lenin's proposal was rejected. A Commission of the Conference asked Grimm and '*Nashe Slovo*'s representative' to elaborate a programme acceptable to all. This was done and passed unanimously. The Leninists attempted to add an amendment, criticising Kautsky's position and approving Liebknecht's. This was also rejected as too personal for a document bearing a general appeal. Trotsky made it clear that he was not satisfied with the Manifesto. For him, it did not outline a full programme of peace and its relation to a revolutionary struggle. The Manifesto had a pacifist tone which, given the critical and not creative mood which existed among parties dominated by social patriotic leaderships, he accepted as an inevitable compromise. Nevertheless, Trotsky viewed the Manifesto as a step forward when many socialist parties remained in a state of crisis after their recent capitulations.

Lenin also produced his version of what had happened at Zimmerwald, seizing this opportunity to continue his struggle against Trotsky. *Sotsial'Demokrat* carried the Zimmerwald resolution in full on its front page, bearing Lenin's signature of approval on behalf of the Russian delegation.[108] However, Lenin and his comrades stressed that the first 'internationalist' conference of the war had not issued a truly internationalist manifesto. The evaluation of Zimmerwald was similar to Trotsky's: a necessary compromise which would eventually be replaced with a real revolutionary Marxist appraisal of current events.[109] However, Trotsky and the Bolsheviks differed over the meaning of a real Marxist approach. In a back-page report of the 'also-internationalists' at Zimmerwald Trotsky was criticised for his opposition to Radek's theses of a struggle against opportunism and the centre, and for mass revolutionary activity.[110] The report claimed that

French and German delegates were the first to object to Radek's views. Trotsky then supported them, declaring that he did not know what Radek meant by 'mass revolutionary activity'. *Sotsial'Demokrat* retorted that Trotsky's 'revolutionary activity' never went beyond the idea of votes for war credits. Although it was admitted that Trotsky had recommended Lenin's resolutions be submitted to the commission which would elaborate a common statement, the *Nashe Slovo* correspondent was described as having 'struggled with all his might against a revolutionary Marxist appraisal'.[111]

The same issue of *Sotsial'Demokrat* contained one further assault on Trotsky's views. In 'The War and the Revolutionary Crisis in Russia' Zinoviev criticised Trotsky's evaluation of the coming revolution in Russia.[112] In the series of articles 'Military Catastrophe and Political Perspectives' Trotsky had argued that recent changes in Russian society meant that the proletariat was the only class willing and able to carry out a revolution.[113] The peasantry had become yet more stratified and conservative, the proletariat could hope to attract only proletarian and semi-proletarian elements from peasant ranks. For Trotsky, the revolution would not only be proletarian in form but also in content, i.e., it would be a socialist revolution. According to Zinoviev, Trotsky's schema ignored the importance of Russia's bourgeois-democratic movements as well as underestimating the peasantary's potential to play a revolutionary role. Furthermore, he argued that Trotsky was wrong to call for a socialist revolution in Russia. Zinoviev repeated the view outlined in *Sotsial'Demokrat*'s war manifesto of November 1914: in backward countries, including Russia, there should be a democratic revolution, socialist revolution was possible only in the advanced countries of Western Europe.

Trotsky responded to only one of the above articles, focusing upon the criticisms of his actions at Zimmerwald.[114] *Sotsial'Demokrat*'s version of events was refuted as a 'distortion'. After all, Trotsky had stated that he considered the Manifesto to be deficient from a revolutionary Marxist point of view. More over, elaborating the Manifesto in conjunction with Grimm hardly amounted to a full-blown struggle against Marxism. Trotsky also responded to an 'extremist' critique of Zimmerwald advanced by the Dutch Tribunists.[115] He belittled the Dutch ultra-radicals, noting the ease with which one could preserve purity when one led five hundred people in a neutral country which would not become a centre of revolutionary activity. The point was, however, that if one remained in the confines of one's own fraction one lost a sense of perspective of what could possibly be achieved at any particular moment. Trotsky added that from Paris he could have written of Zimmerwald as a capitulation to social-chauvinism. He used this thought as a background against which he ridiculed Zinoviev:

> In mood it have the same tone in which Zinoviev writes his articles (Zinoviev, as is well-known, always writes one and the same article) and would not have been distinguished from Zinoviev's article – well, apart from better literary style![116]

By the end of November 1915 both Lenin and Trotsky were levelling criticisms at the other, but over different issues. Lenin chose to concentrate on the differing perceptions of what type of revolution would occur in Russia. Trotsky had once again stated his case for the establishment of a socialist workers' government in a polemical article directed against Aksel'rod and the Organisational Committee.[117] Lenin seized the opportunity to express his view on the debate and went onto the offensive against Trotsky.[118] His main criticism was that Trotsky was blind to the crucial role of the peasantry in a revolution which would lead to a 'revolutionary democratic dictatorship of the proletariat and the peasantry'.[119] For Lenin, Trotsky's arguments would advantage only Russian liberalism which 'by "denying" the role of the peasantry do not urge the peasantry to revolution!'

Trotsky, however, continued to focus on how the Zimmerwald Manifesto was produced, polemicising with Martov.[120] The dispute centred around Martov's evaluation of Trotsky's reportage of the Zimmerwald Conference. For Martov, Trotsky had incorrectly identified three groups: the extremists (Lenin) who called for a civil war; the right (Ledebur) who demanded peace but without any clear plan of how to achieve it and who refused to condemn social nationalism; and the centre (*Nashe Slovo*) who put forward the slogan struggle for peace which would act as a rallying call for the revolutionary mobilisation of the proletariat. Trotsky defended his classification of the various political tendencies at the conference and included a damning characterisation of Lenin and the Bolsheviks:

> misunderstanding the significance of the slogan struggle for peace as a slogan of mass proletarian struggle, subordinating political action to organisational splitting, hostility to those not sharing the basic principles of their political programme and to those not bowing down before each point of their sectionalist programme. If

this group was the most crystallised, this would correspond fully to its exclusionist tendencies.[121]

As well as presenting the Bolsheviks as a closely knit sectionalist group Trotsky also pinpointed friction within the Bolshevik camp. In particular, he (once again) claimed that Lenin was out of step with his supporters, pointing out Lenin had initially refused to sign the Zimmerwald Manifesto unless it was amended. Lenin then backtracked and signed. For Trotsky, the message was obvious: 'even [Lenin's] closest allies were not prepared to be so sectionalist'.[122]

Trotsky's insistence of the sectional nature of Lenin's politics was not only based upon his experiences at Zimmerwald. At some point in 1915 Trotsky resigned from his membership of Paris's Internationalist Club because he thought it run by Lenin's extremist sectionalists. In 1921 Tanya Lyudvinskaya, the secretary of the Paris section of the Bolshevik fraction during World War One, sent a copy of Trotsky's letter of resignation to Istpart. In her covering letter she informed the Party historians that the Club was established by the Paris section of the RSDLP(b) with the intention of 'uniting all groups occupying an internationalist position on the war.'[123] She dates Trotsky's letter at May or June 1915, but it was clearly written after Zimmerwald. Louis Sinclair's dating of December 1915 is probably the more accurate.[124]

In the letter Trotsky claimed that the Paris Club could not fulfil its aim of uniting internationalists since it clearly was a sectionalist organisation. After all, he pointed out, the Club's practice of passing resolutions would inevitably alienate some comrades. The resolutions which were passed, 'receiving a completely accidental majority', supported the Zimmerwald extremists. This left Trotsky with no option but to resign:

> Since I disagreed with the Leninist delegation's conduct at Zimmerwald, since I supported the Leninist delegation at the conference only in so far as its basic line corresponded with revolutionary internationalism and with all my energy struggled against it when it attempted – true, unsuccessfully – to leave its sectionalist, fractionalist, extremist stamp on the conference, threatening even not to sign the conference manifesto – then naturally, not uniting with the Leninists in Zimmerwald, I am even less able to unite with them through the auspices of the Paris Club.[125]

For Trotsky, that the majority of the Club's members supported

Lenin's Zimmerwald resolutions without considering other groups' 'yet again illustrates the fractional character of the Club's decisions'.[126] Trotsky stressed that the reasons for his resignation were principled, and not sour grapes.

In November and December 1915 Lenin and Trotsky made conflicting claims about whose programme was gaining most support among the Petrograd workers. They were given this opportunity by the tsarist government which, in the summer of 1915, decided to allow the workers to elect representatives to the War-Industries Committees. The elections were held in September 1915.[127] Zinoviev reported that the Bolsheviks received ninety votes against the social-chauvinist's eighty. This was no thanks to *Nashe Slovo* and Trotsky who, in the election campaign had whitewashed the social-chauvinists, labelling their publication *Utro* 'internationalist'. For Zinoviev, Trotsky paid the consequences. With no clear policy of his own, Trotsky

> again turned out to be a dead end. There is simply no place for him in the Russian workers' movement. Either you support Chkheidze, which means backing Plekhanov and Guchkov, or you are for the RSDLP, which means opposing Chkheidze. The objective situation places the question thus.[128]

In his rejoinder to Zinoviev Trotsky did not claim the ninety internationalists for himself, stating that exact figures on the ideological-fractional breakdown of the internationalist majority were not available. However, it was clear that the Mensheviks and the internationalist minority of the Narodniks had been counted in the ninety. Trotsky admitted that the Bolsheviks were a significant group among the worker deputies, but even they had not supported specific slogans advanced by *Sotsial'Demokrat*. On the contrary,

> There was a repetition only on a much larger scale, and not at the start but in the fifteenth month of the war, of what occurred at the trial of the five S-D deputies: the defeatist slogan, i.e., nationalism turned inside out, was rejected not by 'chauvinists' and 'government lackeys', as *Sotsial'Demokrat* labels all its opponents, but by the *whole revolutionary-internationalist vanguard of the Russian proletariat*. We hope therefore that *Sotsial'Demokrat* will not force us to comment again on its sorry ideological and political confusion.[129]

Whatever misgivings Trotsky had about the compromise which lay at the centre of the Zimmerwald Manifesto, he clearly viewed it as more successful for him than for the Leninists. In a series of articles between 29 January and 13 April 1916 Trotsky attempted to fill what he saw as the main lacuna left by Zimmerwald, the absence of a detailed peace programme. In the opening instalment Trotsky repeated his view that the Leninists had been forced to give ground at Zimmerwald:

> Opponents of the struggle for peace (Leninists) capitulated without a struggle: they could not but see that the movement arises everywhere under the slogan struggle for peace.[130]

Lenin's alternative of turning the war into a civil war was then dismissed as 'putting the question abstractly-extremely and not revolutionary politically'.[131]

A central component of Trotsky's peace programme was the need to establish a United States of Europe. In their first Manifesto of the war the Central Committee had also supported this idea. Lenin had then divided the United States of Europe into a political and an economic aspect. He accepted the term politically but he also said that it must be evaluated more fully from an economic point of view. He then came out against the slogan both politically and economically. Trotsky discussed the developments in Lenin's position in the fourth and fifth contributions of 'A Peace Programme'.

First, he examined the arguments expounded in a footnote to Zinoviev's and Lenin's brochure *Socialism and the War*, published in the Summer of 1915. Here Zinoviev and Lenin stated:

> In No. 44 of our party's central organ, *Sotsial'Demokrat*, there was an editorial article in which the economic flaws of the slogan 'United States of Europe' were illustrated. Either this is a demand which is unrealisable under capitalism, proposing the establishment of a regulated world economy under a share-out of colonies, spheres of influence and so on. Or this slogan is reactionary, signifying a temporary alliance of the great powers of Europe for a more successful exploitation of the colonies and for robbing the more quickly developing Japan and America.[132]

Trotsky dismissed these arguments as an 'administrative dispatch' written in a 'telegraph style'.[133] He used the example of industrial trusts to illustrate how the two Bolsheviks had concentrated on only one (reactionary) side of the issue. He pointed out that trusts were also a means to more exploitation, but to end one's analysis here could be done 'only by a Chelyabinsk Narodnik'.[134] Marxists also viewed trusts as progressive phenomenon in that they would be utilised as part of a future socialist organisation of production. Trotsky hoped that, 'the authors of the aforementioned brochure draw from this analogy the necessary conclusions in applying them to the United States of Europe.'[135]

Trotsky devoted a whole article to a consideration of Lenin's arguments expounded against a United States of Europe.[136] Lenin rejected the United States of Europe for two reasons: 'first because it combines with socialism, and second, because it can lead to an incorrect acceptance of the impossibility of the victory of socialism in one country and of the relation of this country to the rest.'[137] Trotsky criticised Lenin's objections on four grounds: logical, logistical, methodological and empirical.[138]

Trotsky likened Lenin's view that the United States of Europe would be combined with socialism and therefore any talk of it in the present could only give rise to the aforementioned illusions to the reason why the Dutch Tribunists rejected the slogan the rights of nations to self-determination, i.e. that this problem would be resolved under socialism and any mention of it beforehand could only create the impression that it could be resolved under capitalism.[139] He also pointed out that Lenin thought the nationality problem a task for the present epoch, leaving him in the contradictory position of assigning the national democratic demarcation of states to imperialism while denying that imperialism could bring about the democratic unification of states, i.e., a United States. For Trotsky, 'such a picture is absurd whether one takes it politically, economically or synthetically.'[140]

Trotsky's second objection to Lenin's critique of a United States of Europe was that Lenin had ignored an important logistical consideration, i.e., he had leaped over the bridge which linked the present (capitalism) to the future (socialism). In assigning the United States of Europe to the future Lenin, claimed Trotsky, had omitted social revolution. And, for Trotsky, 'the European Republican Federation is the state instrument of social revolution and outside this it turns into a democratic abstraction'.[141] In other words, the formation of a United States of Europe was the means by which the coming revolution would realise itself, so to ignore the slogan of a United States of Europe meant that one was out of step with reality and left with an empty and meaningless analysis.

Trotsky linked Lenin's logistical error to his methodological short-comings. Thus, for instance, he characterised Lenin as a thinker in whom 'revolutionary democratism and socialist dogma live side by side without ever having been amalgamated into a living Marxist whole'.[142] Regarding Lenin's thoughts on the issue of the rights of nations to self-determination, Trotsky discerned the victory of the revolutionary democrat over the socialist doctrinaire, the latter 'did not have time to express his doubts regarding the realisation of self-determination on a capitalist basis'.[143]

Trotsky's final assault on Lenin went right to the heart of their differing perceptions of the nature of the epoch and of the coming revolution. Lenin had stated that the time when socialism was only a European problem was over. For Lenin, uneven political and economic development meant that a socialist revolution would occur first in one or in several states. There would then follow a whole epoch of struggle in which the remaining capitalist states would be conquered until the establishment of a United States of the World. Lenin did not predict where or when this process would begin, but he emphasised that one could not separate out Europe as a special entity in itself.[144] In response, Trotsky outlined a diametrically opposed scenario. While he accepted Lenin's assertion of a law of uneven development under capitalism which 'it is useful and necessary to repeat', he also insisted that 'in comparison with Africa or Asia, all of these countries are a capitalist "Europe" ripe for socialist revolution'.[145] Ultimately, Trotsky viewed Lenin's worry of the imper-missibility of a successful revolution taking place in one country under Trotsky's outlook as sharing the same theoretical ground as social-patriotism:

> To view the perspective of social revolution through the prism of the nation state is to fall victim to the same national limitness which is the essence of social patriotism ... One should not forget that in social patriotism there is that vulgar reformism and national revolutionary messanism which thinks that its state ... is the one to lead humanity into socialism. If the victory of socialism was possible in the limits of one more prepared nation this messanism, connected with the idea of national defence, would have its relative historical justification. But in actual fact it does not have this. Struggling for the preservation of the national base of the social

revolution by such methods which undermine the international ties of the proletariat means to undermine the revolution which has to start on a national basis, but which cannot be limited to it under the present economic and military political interdependency of the European states, never before revealed with such force as precisely in this war. This interdependency, which will immediately and directly condition the coordination of action of the European proletariat in revolution, is expressed in the slogan of a United States of Europe.[146]

In the midst of all this wrangling one further attempt was made to bring Trotsky and Lenin together. The mediator was Henrietta Roland Holst who wanted Lenin and Trotsky to contribute to the journal *Vorbote*, two issues of which were published in January and April of 1916. Trotsky replied to Holst's offer after he had received the journal's first number.[147] He refused to be in any way connected with it. Trotsky's main objection was that Holst wanted the journal to be a coalition journal, whereas in reality it was firmly in the hands of the Leninists. As such the journal was notable mainly for its paucity of content, for 'Russian extremism is the product of an amorphous and uncultured social environment where the first historical movement of the proletariat naturally demands a simplification and vulgarisation of theory and politics.'[148] Furthermore, Trotsky excluded the possibility of bringing the Leninists over to the side of cooperation. After all, he pointed out, had they not criticised Holst's contribution for its opposition to the Dutch extremists? According to Trotsky, he 'knew this public too well to be surprised by anything'.[149] For Trotsky, the journal's base was far too narrow for it to be able to attract wide support and to be successful:

> I do not think that this journal can attract serious support amongst the German and French workers' movements. I know too well with what contempt the leaflet of the Zimmerwald Left was dealt with here so have not to have any doubts on this score. In the final analysis you should not forget that the Leninists do not have – and in my view cannot have – any supporters either in Germany or in France or in Britain. The Russian and Dutch extremists together cannot found the International.[150]

Trotsky was to refer to his disagreements with Lenin and the Central Committee one more time in *Nashe Slovo* before it was closed by the

French police on 15 September 1916. This concerned Lenin's assertion in *Sotsial'Demokrat* that nothing separated Chkheidze from the social patriotic newspaper *Prizyv*:

> Trotsky can rant against our fractionalism, hiding behind the rantings (the old recipe of Turgenev's ... hero!) of his supposed non-fractional 'appearance' that some so and so from Chkheidze's fraction 'agrees' with Trotsky and swears his leftism and internationalism and so on. But fact remains fact. There is no hint of serious political differences not only between the O.K. and Chkheidze's fraction but also between both these institutions and ... *Prizyv*.[151]

In the first instalment of 'Our Duma Fraction' Trotsky criticised Chkheidze for not making it clear that imperialists and social-patriots were guilty of propagating a 'defencist' ideology.[152] However, at the same time he praised the deputy for disrobing social patriotism, and he cited the following extract from Chkheidze's speech: 'what to them [the social patriots] is holy is lying and deceitful.'[153] In view of this Trotsky claimed that it was simply nonsense to equate the two. One month later Trotsky was far more critical of the Social-Democratic fraction, claiming that the deputies were 'passive internationalists'.[154] This more damning appraisal was further developed in September 1916. Here Trotsky labelled Chkheidze's call for the setting up of mutual aid organisations as a response to high prices as 'deplorable'.[155] However, Lenin was not overly impressed with Trotsky's critique of Chkheidze:

> *Nashe Slovo* and Trotsky ... have more and more been forced by the pressure of events to struggle against the O[rganisational] C[ommittee] and Chkheidze ... but to this day they have not yet uttered the decisive words. Unity or split with Chkheidze's fraction. They dare not contemplate this![156]

After Trotsky was deported from France to Spain at the end of October 1916, his circumstances were not conducive to the steady production of polemical articles. He was to regain contact with a readily available forum for the expression of his views only after he landed in New York on 13 January 1917. There he quickly became involved with the publication of the Russian émigré journal *Novyi Mir*, edited by Bukharin, Kollantai and Volodarsky. His attention was soon to be absorbed by the news of the outbreak of the February Revolution in Russia and he wrote no articles in which he directly polemicised with Lenin and the Central Committee.

However, this does not mean that hostility between the two had in any way receded. Thus, for example, in a letter of 17 February 1917 to Kollantai we learn of Lenin's continuing contempt for Trotsky. Kollantai must have informed Lenin that Trotsky had attempted to forge an alliance against Bukharin:

> It was just as wonderful to learn from you of N. I. Bukharin's and Pavlov's victory in *Novyi Mir* ... as it was sad news of Trotsky's bloc with the right for a struggle against N. I. Bukharin ... – left phrases and a bloc with the right against the whole left!! Trotsky should be exposed (by you) although with a short letter in S-D![157]

So, despite attempts at the establishment of cooperation relations between Trotsky and Lenin and the Bolsheviks from August 1914 to February 1917 remained fraught with suspicion and hostility. This mood seems to have continued right up to the time of Trotsky joining the Bolshevik Party. After all, during the negotiations between the Bolsheviks and the Inter-Districters Trotsky stipulated that, 'I cannot call myself a Bolshevik.'[158]

The subsequent problem for Trotsky was how to represent these war time relations when he came to compose his Collected Works around the beginning of the 1920s, i.e. when he was a member of the Bolshevik government.

The first post-revolutionary reference made by Trotsky to his World War One disputes with Lenin was in the Introduction, first written in 1919 and then revised in 1922, to the first volume of *War and Revolution*.[159] Here Trotsky did two things. First, he acknowledged that *Nashe Slovo* and *Sotsial'Demokrat* had adopted different stances during the war. However, he limited these disagreements to three: *Nashe Slovo* rejected defeatism; *Sotsial'Demokrat* rejected the slogan of struggle for peace and supported the notion of civil war; and, finally, *Nashe Slovo* declared that the coming revolution would be a socialist revolution whereas *Sotsial'Demokrat* insisted that it would be a 'democratic' dictatorship of the proletariat and peasantry.[160] Thus, he did not mention the disputes concerning the United States of Europe and those centring around accusations of fractionalism. Second, Trotsky claimed that *Nashe Slovo* and *Sotsial'Demokrat* were poles apart at the outset of the war and then gradually moved closer together. Credit for this convergence was given to *Sotsial'Demokrat*, whose criticism

> was ... undoubtedly correct and helped the left-wing of the editorial board to oust Martov, in this way giving the newspaper, after the Zimmerwald Conference, a more defined and irreconcilable character.[161]

Of course, the pattern of relations between Trotsky and the Bolshevik Central Committee had not followed the curve drawn by Trotsky in the above scenario. In fact, there had been initial agreement on the need to establish a United States of Europe, then negotiations of joint action during the London Conference, and after this the onset of a stable course of opposition and occasional acrimonious outbursts. However, in *War and Revolution* Trotsky constructed a picture of increasing harmonisation in two ways.

First, as Bukharin pointed out in the mid-1920s, he simply left out most of the articles in which he had polemicised with Lenin and the Bolsheviks.[162]

Second, Trotsky falsified other articles to make them conform to his convergence thesis. For example, in the second volume of *War and Revolution* there is an article 'Conclusions', ending a section devoted to the Zimmerwald Conference and claiming to be from *Nashe Slovo* of 3 and 6 October 1915.[163] The impression is given that 'Conclusions' is a coherent article spread over two issues. It begins by talking of a pre-conference Bolshevik meeting and throughout the piece one reads 'meeting' as signifying that reference is still being made to this gathering of Bolsheviks. The evaluation of the meeting is very favourable and it is claimed that the differences between *Nashe Slovo* and *Sotsial'Demokrat* had been eliminated. However, 'Conclusions' was in fact made-up from two separate and unconnected reports, one (discussed above) in which Trotsky noted that *Sotsial'Demokrat* was moving closer to *Nashe Slovo* but significant differences remained, and another in which Trotsky presented a glowing account of the success of Zimmerwald in general.[164] Trotsky also changed the whole thrust of his original analysis of some convergence between *Nashe Slovo* and *Sotsial'Demokrat* by omitting crucial sentences when he merged the two articles to form 'Conclusions.' The first paragraph of 'Conclusions' ends with the claim that Lenin had 'showed that the slogan of struggle for peace was deprived of revolutionary content'.[165] The subsequent sentence in the original that Lenin had not attracted any support was simply cut; as was the text in block capitals in which Trotsky had emphasised that *Sotsial'Demokrat* would have to abandon its fractionalism if it were to adopt an even more internationalist position, together with the footnote which stated that the Bolsheviks had not formulated the slogan struggle for peace in a sufficiently decisive way. Thus, from the 1924 text one would think that Trotsky had recognised Lenin's persuasiveness in October 1915!

When Trotsky falsified his writings of World War One his sensitivity extended beyond Lenin. Thus, for instance, in 'Dutch Extremists' he dropped the paragraph where he had ridiculed Zinoviev for his vacuousness and poor prose style.[166]

At this stage Trotsky's endeavours to present past disputes in a more favourable light received some backing from his Bolshevik colleagues. When Zinoviev gathered his war time writings for publication in the fifth volume of his Collected Works he cut his more taunting references to Trotsky. For example, the claim that the Bolsheviks had written to Trotsky offering cooperation on *Kommunist* as part of an 'experiment' did not appear in the reprint of 'Russian Social-Democracy and Russian Social-Chauvinism'.[167] Zinoviev did retain the part of this article which was very critical of Trotsky, but he added an explanatory footnote which stated that:

> During the war L. D. Trotsky attempted to occupy an intermediary position and 'reconcile' the Central Committee and the social chauvinists, advancing his usual view on the necessity of patience. The war's events prodded him leftwards. None the less the characterisation of his position during the war remains true and factual.[168]

This equilibrium was upset by Trotsky's publication of his essay 'Lessons of October', used as an introduction to the third volume of his Collected Works.[169] This essay became a contentious issue as it was interpreted as part of a Trotsky campaign to become the new leader of the party and state.[170] Trotsky had not referred to World War One in this essay, but this did not prevent this period from being brought into the remit of the debate. Many leading party figures wrote rejoinders to Trotsky's 'Lessons of October'. In their contributions to the debate Kamenev and Bukharin gave expositions of the disputes which raged between Trotsky and the Central Committee during the war.[171] These accounts highlighted the issues of civil war or struggle for peace, defeatism, unity with Chkheidze, the Zimmerwald Left and the role of the peasantry in the Russian Revolution. This approach was to become the standard version of Stalinist historiography.

Trotsky returned to the positions taken by Russian socialists during World War One in *My Life*, *History of the Russian Revolution* and in *The Stalin School of Falsification*, all of which stressed the gradual convergence of Lenin's and Trotsky's views. In his autobiography, for example, Trotsky claimed that the 'essentially secondary disagreements which still separated myself from Lenin in Zimmerwald disappeared into nothing in the coming months'.[172] Both *My Life* and the *History* state that, by April 1917, only Lenin and Trotsky shared the same evaluation of the future development of the Russian Revolution – the former expounding his view in his famous April Theses and the latter in his articles of March 1917 in *Novyi Mir*.[173]

In this way the ground was laid for the approaches subsequently adopted by historians of this period. Deutscher followed Trotsky's interpretation and his willingness to do so must be set against a generally accepted view of the falsity of Stalinist historiography. Indeed, given the nature of Stalinist oppression one can well understand Deutscher's inclination to believe Trotsky, just as one can well understand Soviet historians repeating the views taken by Trotsky's protagonists following the publication of 'Lessons of October'. The most full-blown process of deStalinization to have occurred in the former Soviet Union, under Gorbachev, however, witnessed a further twist of the tale. In their desire to abandon the falsities of Stalinist historiography, some Russian historians uncritically accepted Trotsky's version of events. For example, Pantsov argued that the analyses produced by Trotsky and Lenin in March/April 1917 are 'obviously identical'.[174] However, an examination of the documents written during World War One reveals a story of almost continuous opposition between Trotsky and Lenin and the Bolsheviks.

The next chapter will examine whether Trotsky was able to establish and maintain better relations with the Menshevik section of the RSDLP.

5
Martov and the Mensheviks

At the outbreak of World War One the leading Mensheviks were on various sides of the new military frontiers, and lacked a central organ through which they could inform each other of their respective responses to the war. They could, however, communicate by mail, not all of which was confiscated by the military censorship.[1] In 1924 the Russian Revolutionary Archive in Berlin published Aksel'rod's and Martov's letters. This correspondence enables us to trace Martov's efforts to orientate himself in the new environment of war.

He first of all worried about the fate of comrades spread across Europe, mentioning Uritskii, Semkovskii and Trotsky,[2] and was not himself happy at being trapped in Paris. First of all he was devoid of any means of support and, furthermore, he felt there was nothing for him to do. Above all, he wanted to go to Zurich and discuss matters with Aksel'rod. *Vorwärts*, the German Social-Democratic Party's newspaper, continued to reach Paris, but reading of its support of the vote for the war credits only convinced him that German comrades had 'brought shame upon the banner of Marxism and in a scandalous manner ended their hegemony in international socialism'.[3] For Martov, only the Mensheviks possessed the personnel versed in Marxism to save the honour of revolutionary socialism. In letters to Aksel'rod he soon raised the issue of how and with whose participation a journal could be established. The possibility of working with Plekhanov and Lenin was broached and dismissed, Martov declaring: 'I would prefer if we, the Mensheviks, spoke for ourselves.'[4] He insisted that only a combative publication could answer the needs of the moment: 'we have to try to exert a moral influence on Russians abroad, to prevent them from losing all hope in social-democracy, given its fall from grace. We need to come-out against illusions and opportunism of both a German and Slavonic origin.'[5] Indeed, Martov had the chance to fulfil this aim when he was asked to take overall control of the recently formed Russian internationalist newspaper *Golos* but, as he himself admitted, he let this opportunity slip through his hands:

> *Golos*, it seems, is everywhere considered as mine. This is not alto-gether comfortable, since a fair amount of stupidity appears in it. In actual fact I lost the opportunity of taking it under my wing. It was founded by unemployed printers and they asked me to head it. I was convinced that with the censorship it would be impossible to say anything and I declined. Then the printers called for a first meeting and matters progressed little by little. Now we have to consider the 'rights acquired' by the *vperedist* Ivan Bezrabotnii, one 'party-bolshevik' and a mediocre liquidationsist. One cannot dismiss the possibility that, for example, Lenin will be invited to cooperate and so on.[6]

Martov also considered *Golos* to be 'amateurish', and this low opinion of *Golos*'s 'professionalism' no doubt played its role in his refusal to become editor in chief. At the same time, however, it did not prevent him from submitting several articles.

In contributions of September, October and November 1914 Martov consistently pursued an anti-war line. He derided attempts to present the war as a 'war to end all wars', or as a 'just war', as ideological justi-fications of the bourgeoisie's aggressive intentions. Wars, he made clear, would occur as long as capitalism existed. In one piece he highlighted a declaration of some Russian industrialists, from *Promyshlennosti i Torgovli*, that a clash of Russian and German economic interests had brought forth the conflict, as evidence of imperialism's guilt for the war. Martov was particularly appalled by 'comrades' who argued that the war was, for some, a 'war of defence' which could be condoned on socialist principles, or that it was neces-sary to declare a 'civil peace' for the duration of the hostilities. It was in this connection that he polemicised with Plekhanov, rejecting the 'Father of Russian Marxism's' case that an economic determinist analysis led to support for Russia's war effort, and wrote an obituary notice on *Vorwärts*, which had renounced class struggle while the war lasted. Contrary to the German newspaper, Martov insisted that class struggle on an international basis in order to wrest power from the bourgeoisie was the only way to resolve the problems which had led to war. The first slogan of this struggle, he thought, should be 'peace'. Finally, he publicised the activities of the Mensheviks in the Duma and one Serbian socialist who had voted against the war credits, welcomed the first signs of anti-war sentiment voiced by Liebknecht in Germany, the Italian party's resolutions to keep Italy neutral, and the attempts of the Dutch and Swiss parties to restore ties between socialists situated on both sides of the war zones, to stress that not all Marxists had capitulated before the 'social-chauvinist' fury.[7]

These writings earned Martov Lenin's guarded praise, the latter declaring that 'Martov, if one judges by the Parisian *Golos*, is holding-up very well..rebuffing German and French chauvinism ... but he dare not declare open war against all international opportunism and its "mighty" defender, the "centre" of German Social Democracy'.[8] Although Martov did not mention all the arguments taken by Trotsky in the first months of the war, the United States of Europe being a notable absence, Trotsky himself could not but have been impressed by Martov's 'internationalism'. Indeed, Deutscher claims that Trotsky 'rejoiced' at the prospect of a bloc with Martov and Lenin around a common response to the war.[9] Be that as it may, only one month passed after Trotsky's arrival in Paris in mid-November 1914 before his relations with Martov became strained.

The cause of the breakdown in relations was Martov's response to several chauvinist announcements made by his Menshevik colleagues. To begin with the Menshevik-liquidationist broadsheet *Nasha Zarya* published contributions which backed Russia in the war. One of its correspondents, G. Cherevanin, for example, held German militarism to account for causing the war and urged Germany's 'defeat'.[10] Then *Sotsial'Demokrat* carried the reply sent to Vandervelde by a Menshevik-liquidationist group in St Petersburg. In August 1914 the Belgian socialist minister had appealed to Russian comrades not to hinder their country's war efforts which were of vital importance, he said, to the Entente's cause.[11] The St Petersburg Menshevik-liquidationists assured Vandervelde that they viewed him and Belgian's workers as conduct-ing a 'just cause of self-defence against aggressive Prussian Junkers which threaten democratic freedom and the proletariat's liberating mission'.[12] They hoped that German Social-Democracy, the 'mighty vanguard of the international proletariat', would participate in the fight against Prussian militarism, and regretted that 'Russian condi-tions' deprived them of the chance to join a war ministry. Despite this, and despite the fact that they had to guarantee that Tsarism did not become the centre of European reaction, the Menshevik-liquidationists said that, in their work, they would comply with Vandervelde's request. In return, they asked the Belgian minister to oppose the war if it ever became transformed into a war of aggression by the Entente. In an editorial supplement *Sotsial'Demokrat* commented that the Menshevik-liquidationsits, as a tendency, had declared itself to be social-chauvinist: 'Martov's voice against chauvinism', it claimed, 'now stands alone among the liquidationists.'[13] Finally, there appeared in *Golos* itself a summary of Aksel'rod's stance on the war, compiled from an interview he had given to *Bremer Bürger-Zeitung*, a German left-radical publication, and a conversation with *Golos's* (Menshevik) correspondent R. Grigor'ev.[14] Aksel'rod expressed his amazement that some socialists had rejected the defensive/aggressive war distinction, condemning the conflict as 'imperialist'. He accepted that none of the warring sides represented 'progress' which, he maintained, was vested in the international proletariat struggling for peace. Furthermore, he did not doubt that each imperialist country had had an interest in attack. But, he said, this did not mean that in the events that had led to war it was impossible to distinguish 'relative guilt'. From this perspective, Germany had acted first and therefore was the aggressor. Aksel'rod urged relativism in two more senses. First, he explained various national Social-Democratic parties' support of mobilisation orders as reflecting a level of social development in which each separate proletariat was still infected with fears for 'its' homeland. Hence, he argued, one could not condemn the German proletariat any more than one could blame the Belgian workers for taking up arms in their country's defence. After pointing out that 'explanation does not mean condoning', he highlighted the tactics which each section of the International should have adopted after war had been declared, taking into account relative guilt for causing the war and the workers' nationalism. German socialists should have admitted that the war was 'adventurism' on behalf of its ruling classes and abstained during the vote on war credits. The French party, on the other hand, had a duty to vote for the war budget but should have added that while supporting France in its hour of need, the French Socialist Party did not want its country used as a bulwark to Russian absolutism. Finally, judging the most desirable outcome to the war, Aksel'rod argued that one had to distinguish one type of defeat from another. The complete destruction of one country would be disastrous since it would obstruct economic progress and lead to future conflicts. A mild defeat for Russia would not, contrary to Plekhanov, mean total enslavement by Germany, but the establishment of a democratic order.

Martov was certainly placed in an awkward situation by these developments. On the one hand he did not want to admit that, three months into the hostilities, he was isolated among a fraction to which he had belonged since 1903. To do so would, he felt, play into the hands of the Bolsheviks, a fraction with whom he disagreed on the war and other issues. Why then break from a group on an issue which would most likely disappear along with the war itself when there were other points to take into account? On the other hand, Martov could not deny that there existed real differences between himself and the St Petersburg liquidationists and his old friend Aksel'rod. A whole range of questions now confronted Martov, most notably, could unity in Menshevik ranks be maintained despite opposing views on the war or would the fraction split into hostile camps?; if a split was to occur who would be left in control of the fraction – himself or the Petersburg group?; finally how would this affect his standing in *Golos*? After all, the Mensheviks had still not organised their own publication and Martov did not want to be left without any means of propagating his views. In the end he decided to pursue a dual strategy: on the one hand, to play down the extent of disagreement among the Mensheviks, in this way trying to counter Lenin's efforts to force him to split from his friends, and, on the other, to stress the internationalist element in Menshevik thinking, in this way attempting to placate his colleagues on *Golos*.

In a letter to *Golos*, 'On My Supposed Isolation', Martov claimed that *Sotsial'Demokrat* was in cynical fashion trying to make fractional gain out of the current tragedy.[15] The Bolshevik publication knew, he said, that it was lying when it wrote of Martov's isolation. After all, had not Aksel'rod and two (unnamed) Menshevik collaborators on *Golos* spoken out against chauvinism? As far as the 'Petersburg statement' was concerned Martov also thought it contradictory and confused but, he wondered, what else could one expect from people both isolated from émigré leaders and confronted with the pro-war announcements of such authorities as Plekhanov, Guesde and Vandervelde? Moreover, Martov argued that one had to focus upon all aspects of the Petersburg document. If one did this, one found not only reasons for criticism but also grounds for praise. For Martov, the Petersburg liquidationists had given at least three indications of their non-chauvinism: (1) they had not connected 'Prussian militarism' to a demand for Germany's defeat but to the activities of the German proletariat; (2) social-chauvinists would not call German Social-Democracy 'mighty'; and (3) they were anti-Tsarist, not a chauvinist trait. Martov corrected *Sotsial'Demokrat* for stating that the Petersburg group was a Menshevik tendency; the reply to Vandervelde had not been sanctioned by the Duma fraction or by the Organisational Committee. Finally, although he admitted that he had no exact information about the situation in Russia, Martov was convinced that comrades there did share his views.

Martov's rejoinder probably satisfied his immediate demands as leader of the Mensheviks. Indeed, he could even claim some success. He continued to be closely involved in *Golos*, and P. B. Aksel'rod's name was not removed from its list of participants.[16] However, he did not escape from this incident unscathed. An editorial comment on Martov's letter to *Sotsial'Demokrat* denied that his defence had saved the Petersburg liquidationists from the charge of social-chauvinism. The call 'not to oppose the war' was the logical outcome of the views expounded by the social-chauvinists Plekhanov, Guesde and Vandervelde and not by internationalists of the *Golos* mould. Yes, the liquidationists had warned of tsarism becoming a centre of reaction but, asked *Golos*, would not calling a halt to revolutionary activity when the state was armed to the teeth only make this more likely? *Golos* agreed with Martov that 'fractional obsessions' should not cloud one's view of contemporary standpoints, but was not Martov himself guilty of this when he evaluated his own group's statements? In conclusion, *Golos* stated that the times demanded that people apply the clearest critical acumen and, in this particular case, this meant issuing a rejection of the liquidationist's chauvinism.

Martov's attempt to find a compromise solution to his difficulties not only earned him a public rebuff from *Golos*, it also soured his personal relations with Trotsky. During December 1914 Martov fulfilled his desire to travel to Switzerland to converse with Mensheviks. He returned to Paris at the beginning of January 1915 armed with propositions that Aksel'rod and other Mensheviks in Zurich should join *Golos*'s editorial board, and that Trotsky should contribute to a planned Menshevik publication. From a letter to Aksel'rod we learn that Martov encountered Trotsky's hostility on two issues. Trotsky felt Martov was not splitting from *Nasha Zarya* out of 'fractional considerations' and that his Zurich colleagues wanted to turn *Golos* into an exclusively Menshevik broadsheet. Then, on a more personal matter, he was convinced that Martov had conspired to arrange a less than desirable reviewer for his pamphlet *War and the International*:

I have not reached agreement with any of the proposed contributors to our *sbornik* because upon my return I encountered opposition from Trotsky on another point – the supposed pretensions of the people in Zurich to make *Golos* a 'fractional organ'. He concluded this from Zurich's proposed agreement with the editorial board and the inclusion of the former into the latter. During the first conversation with him on this matter he made me lose all patience and I said a few harsh things to him. I therefore decided to delay talk of the *sbornik* until our relations have softened a little. This happens from time to time. He reproached me for not breaking with *Nasha Zarya* out of fractional bias, even though it now stands on a Plekhanovite position. But this is only the half of it. Even worse, he thinks I engaged in some kind of intrigue, that I encouraged Zolov to write an article about his book in Grimm's newspaper. I thought that I had rendered him a service but it turns out that he was offended that Grimm himself did not write the review ... and with a sincerity that almost touched me, convinced me that I had hit upon Zolov so that a committed liquidationist and not some Leninist would write about his brochure and, in this way, out of fractional considerations, any initiative on Grimm's behalf would be forestalled. I can see you shaking your shoulders, reading this rubbish. To be fair to Trotsky it has got to be said that I myself put this idea into his head, for in a fit of temper I said to him: if Zolov had not written the review, Grimm would not have written it but, in all likelihood, Grisha Zinov'ev who would have sworn at you for the slogan of peace and so on. This was an argument about whether Zolov had done Trotsky a good turn and Trotsky decided that I had let my machiavellianism slip out. In a word, once again I will have to walk around him as one walks around a table with a china ornament on it.[17]

Trotsky's differences with Martov were not limited to personal relations, they also spilled over into *Golos*'s editorial board meetings. The fact that Trotsky and Martov did not see eye to eye at these gatherings has long been recognised.[18] Less well known, however, are the articles over which the two clashed. Some examples of these disputed texts can be gathered from Martov's correspondence. Further in the letter quoted above, for instance, we find the following account of the threats and compromises which accompanied the penning of *Golos*'s editorial on the Copenhagen Conference, attended by Dutch and Scandinavian socialists on 16–17 January 1915:

In number 100 of *Golos* you can read an address, sent in the name of 'editors and co-workers' to Copenhagen. The censored spots revealed Russia's annexionist policy and explained the slogan of peace. This text which was first of all worked out by a *vpredist* and myself was, under the pretext of a 'supplement', radically changed from top to bottom with Trotsky's support against other members of the commission ... I had to come face to face with a completely simple and simple-minded understanding of the crisis which we are living through and break a lance over every word. Finally I had to threaten not to add my signature after they had wasted all my efforts. Instead of an explanation of the proletariat's confusion by the psychology of the previous period, they inserted hackneyed phrases about the reformism in which the workers were raised. My 'ultimatum' led to a toning down of this section.[19]

Even when the two agreed, joint action proved to be impossible. When news of the intention to hold a conference of Entente socialists in London became known, for example, Martov drew up a three-point programme which he intended to take to this gathering.[20] In a letter to Aksel'rod, Martov recounted how he had asked Larin to obtain official invitations so that three representatives of the Menshevik Organisational Committee could attend: himself, Aksel'rod and Trotsky. He then went on to say that despite approving Martov's programme, Trotsky refused to go to London as part of an Organisational Committee delegation. The extent to which 'fractional considerations' played a crucial role in this instance is clear from Martov's commentary:

In the finish he [Trotsky] said that, in an emergency, he could represent *Bor'ba* as part of the OC delegation, as was the case in Brussels, with the right to conduct a separate line ... I replied that on a joint mandate I could not accept these concessions for Trotsky and that therefore I would ensure that a mandate was issued to us without Trotsky. I think that no other outcome was possible, although his presence might have been useful; but, on second thoughts, even this is in doubt if he, for example, took it into his head, if only to emphasise his independence and 'reconciliationess', to reach agreement with Lenin.[21]

The next opportunity for Trotsky to cooperate with Martov came during negotiations to start a new newspaper after *Golos* was closed by the French authorities on 18 January 1915. Martov was still trying to include the Zurich Mensheviks on the projected editorial board and Trotsky, worried that he would find himself in a minority among the Mensheviks and bound to them by the formal rules of editorial unity, at first refused to join *Golos*'s replacement, *Nashe Slovo*. As is clear from Martov's letter to Aksel'rod, this did not prevent Trotsky from attempting to limit the Mensheviks' influence on *Nashe Slovo* from the 'outside':

> Instead of *Golos Nashe Slovo* has begun to appear. I agreed to join its editorial board. I was invited along with Trotsky. He refused on the grounds that he was too busy, but, really, he does not want to commit himself. I am convinced of this, seeing how he influences the non-Menshevik part of the editorial board ... terrorising them with the prospect of being swallowed-up by our threesome ... If we are not careful, he, with 'the best intentions', will split the editorial board and the newspaper will loose any 'unification' significance.[22]

The ground for Trotsky's eventual cooption onto *Nashe Slovo*'s editorial board was most probably laid by Martov's renunciation of *Nasha Zarya*'s chauvinist line, published in the very first issue of *Nashe Slovo*.[23] After all, Trotsky would be unlikely to join a publication that associated itself with chauvinism, even if it did so negatively by not printing a critique of *Nasha Zarya*. The appearance of Martov's 'announcement' can probably be explained by the following factors. First, Martov had resisted making a public statement against *Nasha Zarya* while he lacked backing from Menshevik colleagues. To do this alone would be to admit that Lenin was right. However, by late January 1915 Martov had received a letter from fellow Menshevik Dan in which the latter also opposed *Nasha Zarya*. Martov published Dan's letter alongside his statement in *Nashe Slovo*, and he did so to stress Menshevik unity. Second, Martov's colleagues on *Nashe Slovo* were most likely pushing him to make an anti-*Nasha Zarya* announcement. This would hopefully stop Lenin from accusing *Nashe Slovo* of harbouring closet chauvinists, and ease relations with Trotsky who, as Martov himself recognised, had friends on *Nashe Slovo*'s editorial board. Forced into action by various pressures, Martov admitted that he was torn with anguish when he made his anti-*Nasha Zarya* statement. On the one hand, he wanted to make his opposition to something he did not believe in clear; on the other, he did not want to damage the standing of the Menshevik fraction. Not least, would his public remarks not be used by Trotsky?

> I made this 'splitting' with a great 'anguish' in my soul, for I foresee that, as a result, we, who have been most united in spirit up to this point will split and, from another, I am aware that every sign of disintegration is exploited and will be exploited to an even greater degree by the specialists in disrobing 'fractionalism' who, in actual fact, slyly use even a great world tragedy and catastrophe to tiny fractional advantages. Antid Oto [Trotsky] is a case in point. With him (he is here) I have to (preserving, as far as possible, good personal relations) be constantly on guard.[24]

If Martov hoped that he could prevent antagonism between sections of *Nashe Slovo* and parts of the Menshevik fraction from appearing in *Nashe Slovo*, in part by keeping on good terms with Trotsky, he was to be sorely disappointed. Although he could claim the occasional victory, in the coming months it was Trotsky's views which more and more came to dominate.

On 13 February 1915 Trotsky distanced himself from the Organisational Committee by issuing a statement in which he denied that he bore any more responsibility for the policies of the Organisational Committee than for any other section of the party.[25] Then, at the beginning of March, Trotsky published a two-part critical evaluation of *Nasha Zarya*'s commentary upon the Copenhagen Conference, which appeared in the first issue of the Organisational Committee's newly established *Izvestiya*. In the first part of this critique Trotsky focused upon *Nasha Zarya*'s claim that, since the proletariat had proved itself unable to prevent the war, socialists had to support the side whose victory would bring most benefit to economic and political progress, i.e., the Entente. For Trotsky, this view misunderstood the conditions in which the workers would engage in revolutionary activity. He reconstructed the logic of the *Nasha Zarya* group thus: the Second International overestimated the strength of the working class as a factor in international relations. Therefore the masses would have to throw their weight behind one of the great power blocs as a supplementary force. Contrary to this, Trotsky argued that the proletariat had *underestimated* its strength in the pre-war epoch. This, he thought, was quite natural for what was a period of 'mighty world reaction' for, 'revolutionary self-sufficiency ... awakens and is strengthened during epochs of instability which put the oppressed class in a situation from which the only escape is revolution'.[26] And, according to Trotsky, the war was creating conditions ripe for violent class struggle. This explained why the revolutionary internationalists, unlike *Nasha Zarya*, urged the proletariat to free itself of nationalism and to pursure its own, social-revolutionary policy. In the second instalment Trotsky took issue with *Nasha Zarya*'s perception of the Entente as most embodying progress. He made it clear that the war was not a clash of political forms, democratic (Entente) versus feudal (Central Powers), but a battle for colonies between capitalist nations. In thinking otherwise *Nasha Zarya* had simply accepted imperialist propaganda:

> One of the most important ideological means for putting the whole democratic state organisation at the service of imperialist aims is the idea, the myth, the legend that the war is conducted 'for democracy against militarism'. Taking this legend on board the Petersburg liquidationists, like *Nasha Zarya*'s editorial board, can only hinder critical thought, easing the work of social forces deadly hostile to socialism and democracy.[27]

During April 1915 Martov was able to claim limited success in his battles on *Nashe Slovo*. On the negative side, Trotsky gained a majority to delay the publication of Martov's reply to Radek's censure of the Menshevik I. Izvol'skaya for belonging to a fraction which did not conduct a decisive struggle with social-patriotism in its own ranks.[28] After this dispute Martov, in a letter to Semkovskii, wrote that it was once again 'impossible to approach Trotsky'.[29] On a more positive note, he did ensure that, in a declaration on fractions within Russian Social-Democracy, *Nashe Slovo* stated that it did not consider itself a separate group and that, while it recognised that old alignments were still in force, it would maintain good relations will all those who held an internationalist position, irrespective of fractional alignment.[30] This victory, however, proved to be short-lived. The following months not only saw *Nashe Slovo* in dispute with Aksel'rod but, through polemics with the Organisational Committee's *Izvestiya*, with the whole Menshevik fraction.

In an interview with *Nashe Slovo*, Aksel'rod outlined his latest thoughts on the war. He began by stating that the war had shown that nationalism and internationalism were two mutually exclusive principles. According to Akels'rod, the Second International had proven inadequate to the task of preventing the outbreak of hostilities because nationalism dominated it. For him, it followed that only an internationalisation of the tactics of the workers' movement would stop this from reoccurring. Looking forward to this, Aksel'rod thought that current divisions on the war would not determine who would stand where: 'I cannot imagine Plekhanov in the opposing conservative camp after the war ... I agree with criticism of *Nasha Zarya*'s current line in relation to the war, but I consider the attempt to harden these differences into fractions as, to put it mildly, premature.'[31] It was from this perspective that Aksel'rod rejected Lenin's 'fanatical splitting', insisting instead that social-chauvinists should also be invited to any gathering intended to unify Russian social-democrats. Only then, reasoned Aksel'rod, would it become clear if social-chauvinists and internationalists had already formed two hostile camps. On the war, Aksel'rod said that he disagreed with Lenin's call for Russia's defeat, the best outcome would be 'neither victory nor defeat' for all sides.[32]

It was left to Trotsky to spell out *Nashe Slovo*'s differences with Aksel'rod. Trotsky noted his agreement with Aksel'rod in so far as the latter counterposed nationalism and internationalism, and rejected splitting without just cause. But, for Trotsky, Aksel'rod was so concerned about Lenin's manoeuvres, that he refused to raise the issue of the irreconciliability of internationalism and social-chauvinism as this would kill-off the old groupings in Russian Social-Democracy. In turn, Trotsky pointed out, this left Aksel'rod in the contradictory position of opposing the only means by which his call for the internationalisation of the workers' movement could be realised, i.e. a clear split of internationalists from social-chauvinists. Furthermore, in light of Aksel'rod's acceptance that nationalism and internationalism were hostile principles, Trotsky puzzled over Aksel'rod's desire to maintain contact with Plekhanov. Whether the 'Father of Russian Marxism' returned to the fold or not was, Trotsky stated, irrelevant. Plekhanov's current position was chauvinistic and confusing the workers and it was the clear obligation of revolutionary internationalists to oppose him. Finally, Trotsky objected to Aksel'rod's view that social-chauvinists should be invited to a unification conference along with internationalists. According to Trotsky, this would only complicate the process of fractional realignment and hinder the struggle against social-chauvinism: 'so that the irreconcilable ideological-political demarcation from the social-patriots in all groups ... is not accompanied by the preservation, and even the complication of party chaos, it is necessary that an ideological and actual unification of internationalists of all fractions takes place parallel with this process.'[33]

At the same time as the above dispute with Aksel'rod appeared, *Nashe Slovo* began to issue a series of editorial articles, 'Our Position', penned by Trotsky, which examined how the issues raised by the war affected the old groups in Russian socialism. Their central message that the outbreak of the war had opened a new era which demanded a realignment of social-democrats into new blocs, internationalist versus social-patriots, was a direct challenge to Martov's and Aksel'rod's attempts to preserve the Menshevik's ideological and organisational integrity.

The first instalment began by conceding some ground to Martov and Aksel'rod; it was admitted that not all of the issues of the pre-war era had since disappeared. However, Trotsky argued that such remnants had been radically transformed. Most notably, reformism and revolution now stood as clearly opposed tactical and programmatic principles: the former had turned into social-imperialism, 'expecting a new set of social reforms from military victories', while the latter, which in the pre-war reformist era had been compelled to develop its possibilist features, had come to signify a struggle for power by the proletariat. It was with these changes in mind that *Nashe Slovo* considered a regrouping of forces into 'revolutionary internationalists' versus 'social-chauvinists' as progressive, since this 'corresponds with new tasks of world importance ... the attempt to preserve the old ideological-organisational groups, ignoring their relation to the central facts of our epoch, war and imperialism, is profoundly reactionary and doomed to failure.'[34]

In the second article of this series Trotsky rejected Aksel'rod's contention that one's relation to the war would not determine one's post-war politics. It was in this connection that Aksel'rod hoped that he would one day once again join hands with Plekhanov. For Trotsky, the contrary was true. An individual's war programme 'not only determines the direction of political activity at the present moment (pro- or anti-war), but also to a significant degree pre-determines those groups which will finally take shape after the war'.[35] He justified this by claiming that association with militarism during the hostilities would fatally infect an individual with a social-chauvinist, nationalistic outlook. In the remainder of this contribution Trotsky outlined three approaches to the war which, given the inevitable disintegration of the centre, could be reduced to two: social-chauvinist and revolutionary-internationalist.

In the third instalment of 'Our Position' Trotsky outlined how *Nashe Slovo*'s policy on unity and splits was unique. The previous chapter noted how Trotsky responded to *Sotsial'Demokrat*'s critique that *Nashe Slovo* was not decisive enough in splitting from social-chauvinists. In this section he also tackled the Organisational Committee's accusation that *Nashe Slovo was* pursuing a splitting policy, both in Russian Social-Democracy and in the International. Although it was unlikely that either side would be satisfied with his reply, Trotsky presented his newspaper's case. It was against artificial splits, hence the dispute with *Sotsial'Demokrat*, but, at the same time, unlike the Organisational Committee, it was not prepared to avoid an open struggle against social-patriotism out of a fear that this would lead to a split. It was this sin that Trotsky thought Aksel'rod and Semkovskii guilty of when they argued for unity among the old group-ings in Russian socialism in the first issue of the Menshevik Organisational Committee's *Izvestiya*.[36] Trotsky highlighted two harmful consequences of their view. First, it helped the social-patriots confuse the proletariat. One example of this was their refusal to admit that *Nasha Zarya*'s stance on the war rejected a revolutionary struggle against Tsarism.[37] Second, it hindered the internationalist section of the Organisational Committee from conquering it from within. If internationalists were to follow Aksel'rod and Semkovskii's advice, Trotsky concluded, they would be committing political suicide:

> We cannot ... shut our eyes to the fact that in the old socialist parties the majority is for social-patriotism: from this it follows that the key to unity and organisational discipline is also in their hands. If the internationalists, the persecuted minority, voluntarily limited the field of their activity to unity and discipline at any price, they would make their struggle dependent upon the organi-sational liberalism of the Social-Patriots.[38]

The above warning of the dangers inherent in the Menshevik's stance on unity gave Semkovskii just enough time to pen a rejoinder for the second number of the Organisational Committee's *Izvestiya*. In 'Demagogy and Discrimination' Semkovskii protested against Trotsky's 'polemical-discriminatory style [which] obviously aims at forming a third "nonfractional" fraction'.[39] This response probably made little impression on Trotsky. After all, it only confirmed his presentation of the accusations of fractionalism levelled at him and *Nashe Slovo* by the Organisational Committee. However, Semkovskii's note did cause some upset in Menshevik ranks. In a letter to Aksel'rod, for example, Martov argued that Semkovskii was overestimating Trotsky's potential to harm the Menshevik fraction. Moreover, Martov disagreed with the logical conclusion of his colleague's case: his resignation from *Nashe Slovo* and the closing of Menshevik ranks. He thought it more important to retain links with the audience among which Trotsky was conducting his 'disorganising tactics', and pointed out that the untimely appearance of Semkovskii's note had rendered Martov's plans for *Nashe Slovo* to publish a compromise resolution on the Organisational Committee impossible.[40] In their turn Aksel'rod and Semkovskii thought Martov was making too many concessions by remaining within *Nashe Slovo*, and at one point Aksel'rod even threatened to quit the Organisational Committee's Secretariat because of his disagreements with Martov.[41]

Although Martov was proved right and *Nashe Slovo* did not publish a conciliatory statement on the Organisational Committee, he did manage to achieve a 'civil peace' on the editorial board. It was agreed that the continuation of Trotsky's series 'Our Position' would, for the time being, be suspended. This 'civil peace' was soon broken, however, when Gri'gorev sent a letter to *Nashe Slovo* protesting at the Paris publication's 'persecution' of the Organisational Committee for its supposed lethargy in exposing social-patriotism. Why level such charges only at the Organisational Committee, Gri'gorev asked, when the Bolshevik Central Committee and the group *Bor'ba*, to which Trotsky belonged, also housed social-patriots? In an obvious reference to the language employed by Trotsky's pre-war journal, *Bor'ba*, Gri'gorev concluded that *Nashe Slovo*'s selectivity on this matter aroused the suspicion that it was engaging in 'nonfractional fractionalism of recent times.'[42]

Nashe Slovo published two replies to Gri'gorev, one from the editorial board and one from Trotsky. The former pointed out that it was aware of social-patriotism in, for example, the Bolshevik fraction. However, it had focused its attention on social-patriotism in the Organisational Committee as it was precisely among the Mensheviks that social-patriotism had the most influence and was doing the most harm: 'Does Gri'gorev think that the statements of individual Bolsheviks have the same effect as *Nasha Zarya*, one of the most influential sections of the August Bloc? Certainly not.'[43] In response to the accusation of 'nonfractional fractionalism' the editors stated that *Nashe Slovo*'s stance was independent of all fractions and it was precisely this that enabled it to respond critically to the crisis besetting the International and Russian Social-Democracy. In his reply to Gri'gorev Trotsky repeated his view that the Foreign Section of the Organisational Committee had deliberately tried to mislead by claiming that the Petersburg liquidationists had not repudiated a revolutionary struggle against tsarism. He admitted that a former contributor to *Bor'ba*, An, was currently spreading social-patriotic propaganda. But, he pointed out, fellow members of *Bor'ba* both in and out of Russia were criticising An. Therefore Gri'gorev was quite wrong to consider An within *Bor'ba* as a case analogous to the Petersburg liquidationists within the Organisational Committee:

> We cannot comprehend in what sense An's individual sin, which in *Bor'ba* immediately met with a decisive rebuff, can be considered in the same league as the Petersburg group, which over the head of its organisation communicated with the Belgian patriotic minister Vandervelde ... and, unfortunately, did not receive in the sphere of its activities the rebuff that it fully deserved.[44]

The question of *Nashe Slovo*'s relation to the Organisational Committee was not exhausted by the above exchanges. Martov attempted to dampen the flames of the polemic between *Nashe Slovo* and *Izvestiya*. He tried to clear up any misunderstanding that the two publications were engaging in fractional warfare. He pointed out that *Nashe Slovo* provided a forum for internationalists of all fractions who occupied an anti-war position. Thus *Nashe Slovo*'s aim was not to replace old fractions, but to provide an outlet for all those who opposed nationalism. Hence, while *Nashe Slovo* would criticise individual documents as and when it saw fit, it would not conduct a consistent campaign against groups as if it itself formed a fraction. For Martov, the recent polemic between *Nashe Slovo* and *Izvestiya* was an example of a localised dispute. The fact that the two publications agreed on most issues surrounding the war meant that current disagreements could soon be forgotten and friendly relations reestablished.[45]

However, Martov did not meet with the support of his fellow editors. In an editorial reply his colleagues pointed out how his statement diverged from the real aims of *Nashe Slovo*. Contrary to Martov, *Nashe Slovo* did have its own 'general-political inter-party position'. Moreover, *Nashe Slovo* thought its programme would form a focus around which a new unification of Russian Social-Democrats would occur, *replacing* the pre-war divisions. This belief, they made plain, issued from a conviction that the war had opened a new era in which the old fractions were no longer relevant. Furthermore, *Nashe Slovo* saw its programme as *hastening* this process. Had Martov forgotten the editorial of issue 85 which had made these points clear and which he had helped to elaborate?[46] It was *Nashe Slovo's* intention to continue its work and 'if the historically formed fractions attempt to avoid this, this is not our fault but their sorrow'.[47]

One might have thought that Martov would resign from *Nashe Slovo* after the latter had spelled out its intention to replace the old fractions, including Martov's Mensheviks. However, in a letter to Semkovskii he expressed his satisfaction that his differences with some of *Nashe Slovo's* co-editors had been made public, declaring that 'our hands are now free'.[48] Perhaps he then took his colleagues' advice and reread *Nashe Slovo's* editorial of issue 85, for he soon penned a letter in which he cited from this same text, drawing support for his interpretation of the Paris publication's aims.[49] For Martov, the crucial section of issue 85 was that which read, 'Accepting that the fractional ... groups which formed in the previous epoch are at the present moment the only forum in which internationalists can come together, *Nashe Slovo* thinks its task of unifying internationalists excludes loyalty to any one fraction, as it rejects the artificial unification of its supporters into a special fraction, opposing the old groups.'[50] From this paragraph Martov could justify both the existence of his fraction and his cooperation on *Nashe Slovo*. He warned against those who wished to use the crisis in socialism brought about by the war to the advantage of old fractions, including former 'non-fractional fractionalists'. Only the flexible formula which he had highlighted could, he argued, enable the joint activity of all internationalists.

If Martov intended the above letter to be the first shots in an open battle for control of *Nashe Slovo*, it soon became apparent that he had lost. Much to Martov's chagrin,[51] Trotsky's editorials, 'Our Position', began to reappear, not only as a continuation of a series but also as an editorial response to Martov. Here Trotsky did not deny that pre-war divisions among Russian Social-Democrats had retained their significance. On the contrary, he admitted that long-standing ideological and organisational affiliations could not but be carried over into the new epoch opened by the war. However, he pinpointed two harmful consequences of internationalists failing to overcome fractional allegiances during the war. One the one hand, disagreements with social-patriots in one's own ranks could be avoided in the interests of unity and, on the other, the activities of internationalists of other fractions could be ignored as one's own fraction claimed exclusive rights to 'internationalism'. Trotsky obviously had Martov in mind when he spoke of the former danger and *Sotsial'Demokrat* in view when he mentioned the latter. He reiterated *Nashe Slovo*'s aim of overcoming old fractions by uniting internationalists from all organisations, and threw the following warning at Martov:

> In so far as *Nashe Slovo* undertakes new interpretations of socialism, rejecting the old groups, it is accused of 'splitting' and is suspected of fractional intrigue. To refute these suspicions we can recommend nothing other than what we have done so far, i.e., to further the irreconcilable struggle against social-nationalism and socialist eclecticism.[52]

Following his defeat Martov resolved to join Aksel'rod in Switzerland, which he did in August 1915. His biographer, Israel Getzler, does not connect these two events, merely asserting that 'by August 1915 [Martov] had been practically squeezed out [of *Nashe Slovo*]'.[53] A different picture emerges from Alfred Rosmer's reminiscences of Paris during World War One: 'Pretty vehement controversies brought him [Martov] into conflict with Trotsky, after which he decided to settle in Switzerland.'[54] Certainly relations deteriorated so far that the two tried to score points against each other in constant exchanges of insults,[55] and in a letter to Aksel'rod of late July, Martov admitted that the disputes were badly affecting his health:

> Eternal money worries have sapped my strength for work. I am not able to exploit fully the best source of making money – *Vorwärts*; but, by the way, perhaps the constant squabbles in *Nashe Slovo* have proved more fatal, ruining my nerves and, now and then, making an invalid out of me.[56]

Martov's retreat to Switzerland did not mean that disputes between Trotsky and the Mensheviks ceased. On the contrary, as early as mid-September 1915 *Nashe Slovo* published a three-part article by the Menshevik Martynov, which criticised Trotsky's 'peace programme'. For Martynov, the appearance of Trotsky's 'Our Political Slogan' in *Nashe Slovo* in late February 1915 marked a turning-point in the Paris newspaper's understanding of whether the war had increased the likelihood of socialism. 'Our Political Slogan' stated that the war signified a new era of historical development which contained two options: either continued capitalism, with the inevitability of new wars, or socialism via proletarian revolution. The objective prerequisites for socialism were already to hand, it remained only for socialist agitators to enlighten the proletariat. It was for this agitational purpose that Trotsky argued that calling for the *status quo ante* ('Peace without annexations') was reactionary, for only a revolutionary socialist peace programme (a United States of Europe, resolving the economic diffi- culties and nationalism which had led to war), could convince the proletariat that conquering state power and declaring peace was viable.[57] Before this, Martynov pointed out, *Nashe Slovo* had claimed that nationalities problems would continue after the war. At best the bankruptcy of militarism and of the bourgeois classes would be revealed to the proletariat who would learn an important lesson: 'Europe can only pull itself out of this vicious circle by overcoming imperialism, i.e., by liquidating capitalism.'[58] For Martynov, conflict- ing perceptions of 'the new epoch opened by the war' underpinned two radically different expectations of what could be achieved through the war: one, modest, which predicted a positive lesson for the workers, instilling in them a knowledge necessary if they were to respond to socialist agitation; the other, high, which foresaw the proletariat seizing state power and resolving economic and cultural problems through its peace programme. In contributions to *Nashe Slovo* Martynov showed why he did not envisage any concrete and positive political structures being brought about by the war's end.

It was not that he disagreed with Trotsky's case for a United States of Europe, an idea which he had admired since Kautsky first formu- lated it in 1908. Nor did he deny that capitalism had 'objectively' ripened for a transition to socialism, amply illustrated by the way capitalism had adapted to military conditions. His concern with Trotsky's analysis was that it reduced a 'historical epoch' to a 'histori- cal moment'. Citing Martov as supporting evidence, Martynov stated that the subjective requirements for a realisation of socialism – a complete break with nationalism, capitalist ideology and traditions, i.e., the internationalisation of the workers' movement – could only be attained over the course of several stages of the *post-war* era. Trotsky, on the other hand, thought 'beginning with a struggle for ending the war the revolutionary mobilisation of the mass will conclude with the proletariat seizing power'.[59] By telescoping a whole period into a single moment, Martynov argued that Trotsky had ignored the complexities involved in guaranteeing the subjective aspect of his programme, which left him with unrealisable expectations. For example, the establishment of a United States of Europe demanded a certain level of consciousness and organisation from the proletariat, and 'as the collapse of the Second International has shown we still need to create them'.[60] Furthermore, Martynov highlighted two ways in which Trotsky had misunderstood the significance of the slogans 'Neither victory nor defeat' and 'No forced annexations'. Trotsky rejected these as a hollow return to the pre-1914 situation which had caused the war, and as based upon a belief in the 'weakness of militarism multiplied by our weakness'.[61] But, countered Martynov, if the proletariat managed to halt the war before the victory of one side or before a general exhaustion had set in, not only would the workers have saved thousands of lives, they would also have prevented a greedy peace, increasing the strength of reaction on one side and desires for revenge on the other. And, he added, how could these huge victories be taken as a sign of weakness? Next, Martynov attacked Trotsky's conception of the *status quo ante*:

> Of course a peace without annexations would be a return to the past in the sense of state boundaries, but the correlation of class forces would have radically altered *inside* each state to the advantage of the proletariat. When each proletariat is convinced that the gold promised by its imperialists is a chimera, this is a huge conquest for socialism for the proletariat realises that imperialism is its hostile enemy.[62]

This returned Martynov to the nub of his dispute with Trotsky. The former thought that the best one could hope for from the war was a positive change in the workers' consciousness. This would be but the first stage of a long process of preparing them for socialism. Hence, the negative slogans of 'Peace without annexations' and 'Neither victory nor defeat' were most appropriate for the current stage of the proletariat's development. The latter viewed the advanced workers, at least, as ready to lead the proletariat to construct a United States of Europe. For Martynov, however, Trotsky had miscalculated the nature of the epoch and of the workers, condemning Trotsky and his over-ambitious and unrealistic programme to political isolation.

Trotsky was brought face to face with his Menshevik adversaries at the Zimmerwald Conference. In a report from Zimmerwald Trotsky wrote that Aksel'rod, speaking on behalf of the Organisational Committee, had delineated two approaches adopted by Russian

Social-Democrats to the war: one, supported by a minority, called for Russia's defeat; the other, backed by the overwhelming majority, including *Nasha Zarya* and the speaker, demanded the convoking of a Constituent Assembly which would take Russia out of the war. Trotsky then dismissed the slogan of a Constituent Assembly as 'hiding irreconcilable differences on the war and the absolutely contradictory tactics recommended by each'.[63]

In a subsequent letter to *Nashe Slovo* Aksel'rod did not dispute Trotsky's concluding comments on the political consequences of his remarks since, he pointed out, the Paris correspondent had not accurately presented what he had actually said in Zimmerwald.[64] He admitted that he had highlighted two basic approaches to the war, but these had been: (1) internationalists struggling for peace to end the war and restore the International; and (2) nationalists such as the German centre. Furthermore, contrary to Trotsky's report, he had deliberately avoided mentioning defeatism so as not to touch upon disagreements at what was a unification conference. Devoid of any exact figures, Aksel'rod claimed that he did not say, and could not have said, that a majority in Russia backed the call for a Constituent Assembly. He had noted that the Foreign Section of the Organisational Committee had sent a proclamation to Russia which demanded the convocation of a Constituent Assembly, and it was in this context that he had expressed a hope that this would meet with majority approval. Finally, Aksel'rod confirmed that he had placed *Nasha Zarya* in the internationalist camp.

'A reply to P. B. Aksel'rod' accepted the Menshevik's factual corrections to initial reportage adding, however, that these qualifications only confirmed Trotsky's original analysis of the dire consequences of Aksel'rod's views. Here Trotsky had in mind his opponent's reiteration that *Nasha Zarya* was internationalist. How could this be, asked Trotsky, when the Menshevik publication differed from the latter? *Nasha Zarya* approved the French Socialist Party's pro-war stance whereas internationalists condemned it as deadly hostile to socialism; *Nasha Zarya* in its reply to Vandervelde had agreed not to hinder the Entente's 'just war', rejecting the internationalist's revolutionary struggle against tsarism. Hence, concluded Trotsky,

> I wrote that 'It is clear that the demand for a Constituent Assembly can presently play only one role: hiding irreconcilable differences on the war and the absolutely contradictory tactics recommended by each.' Aksel'rod's objections confirm in essentials my warnings.

I can be comforted by the fact that my sins on secondary matters indirectly acted to bring out clarity on the main issue.[65]

Martov's relation to *Nasha Zaraya*'s successor, *Nashe Delo*, was at the centre of Trotsky's next confrontation with a Menshevik. This dispute grew out of Lozovskii's request, in the form of an open letter in *Nashe Slovo*, to Volonter and Veshnev to repudiate Aleksinskii's assertion, made in *Sovremennyi Mir*, that they had opposed *Nashe Slovo*'s 'Germanophilism' during editorial board meetings.[66] Veshnev obliged, although he protested against the polemical tone of Lozovskii's letter.[67] After receiving no reply from Volonter, Lozovskii addressed another open letter to him, in which he suggested that Volonter's differences with *Nashe Slovo* over organisational issues had now spilled over into ideological-political matters:

> The fact that we now have ideological-political differences should be clear from the fact that you, without any qualification, wrote in the fighting organs of the Russian social-patriots together with Maslov, Levitskii and other homeland patriots who are deeply hostile to *Nashe Slovo*'s internationalism. Is it possible for a ... co-worker of *Nashe Slovo* to remain silent when ... *Sovremennyi Mir* hauls the newspaper over the coals? ... Is it possible to write in *Nashe Delo*, laying a bridge between internationalism and social-patriotism when, as you know, *Nashe Slovo* considers the gulf between these two variants of socialism to be unbridgable and all types of joint literary activity inadmissible?[68]

Volonter may have been unmoved by Lozovskii's open letters, but they certainly aroused Martov's indignation. In a letter to *Nashe Slovo* he said that he was surprised by Lozovskii's reference to *Nashe Delo*.[69] After all, anyone reading Lozovskii's letters would think that *Nashe Slovo* had banned its contributors from appearing in *Nashe Delo* when Martov knew that this was not so. He once again reminded *Nashe Slovo* of its editorial of issue 85 which stated that the Paris newspaper was against the break-up of old fractions at any cost, and that comrades could remain within old organisations on the condition that they propagate internationalist principles. This, he claimed, was the case with Volonter's contributions to numbers 3 and 4 of *Nashe Delo* which had been opened-up to opponents of 'self-defence'. Martov also pointed out that he had warned his co-editors on *Nashe Slovo* of his intention to write an anti-social-patriotic article for *Nashe Delo*, which, because of censorship, had not appeared, and had not been censured at the time. Was it not the case, Martov asked, that *Nashe Slovo* itself had published contributions from known social-patriots (Deich, Leder, Borisov and Aleksinskii)? And was it not also true that *Nashe Slovo*'s writers had worked alongside social-patriots in socialist (*Sovremennyi Mir*, *Sovremennik*, *Novyi Mir*) *and* (with an obvious stab at Trotsky) non-socialist newspapers (*Vestnik Evropy*, *Kievskaya Mysl*)?

On the following day there appeared an editorial comment on Martov's letter, penned by Trotsky. This conceded Martov's point that no formal resolution banning him, or anyone else, from submitting articles to *Nashe Delo* had ever been passed. At the same time, however, Martov was reminded that five of the seven editors had expressed their opposition to his plans because, as in fact turned out to be the case, they thought that the censor would rush to the defence of the 'fighting organ of Russian social-nationalism.' In these circumstances Martov's (muted) contribution to *Nashe Delo* could only serve as a smokescreen, both for *Nashe Delo* itself and for all 'intermediary, swaying or unprincipled elements'. Moreover, a distinction could be drawn between cooperation for bourgeois and social-patriot publications. Martov had confused matters by placing *Vestnik Evropy* and *Kievskaya Mysl* on the same level as *Nashe Delo*. The former belonged to a tradition which had long ago differentiated itself from Marxism. It was clear that when soocialists worked for the bourgeois press they had not entered into an alliance with the bourgeoisie. But, since social-nationalism was an outgrowth of Social-Democracy which had still to separate itself clearly from Marxism, the joint activity of internationalists with social-patriots in social-patriotic publications could only have several detrimental consequences: 'confuse, retarding the necessary and salutary process of splitting and blunting the advanced workers' revolutionary vigilance.' Then, *Nashe Slovo* objected to how Martov had used its objection to splits at any price to justify joint political work with social-patriots. The Paris newspaper's stance, it pointed out, meant that internationalists and social-patriots could coexist in one organisation for a certain while and under certain conditions, most notably if internationalists could conduct an open struggle with social-patriots to force the masses to choose between the two. And, in this battle for influence, *Nashe Slovo* insisted, internationalists could only pursue their own line in their own publications: 'one can do battle with the enemy on shared territory, but one cannot do battle with it in a shared publication.' Finally, *Nashe Slovo* stated that the occasional social-patriotic article on its pages and Martov's work for *Nashe Delo* were incomparable. Most instances of the former had occurred in the first months of the war when rival tendencies were in the process of forming and, on top of this, when such cases had been repeated in the recent period, they had been accompanied by editorials to illustrate the impossibility of cooperation with social-patriots. *Nashe Slovo* reminded Martov that he had recently signed the Zimmerwald Manifesto, whose signatories were obliged to conduct an irreconcilable struggle with social-patriotism. For this, 'international-ists have to close *their* ranks, create *their* organs and *their* support base for revolutionary activity'.[70]

Martov kept this dispute alive by replying.[71] He thanked *Nashe Slovo* for accepting that Lozovskii had had no grounds for condemning Volonter. On his own account he stated that he had ignored the coeditors' objections to his planned cooperation on *Nashe Delo*, since he suspected that they disliked it, the successor to *Nasha Zarya*, out of fractional considerations. These suspicions were confirmed by *Nashe Slovo*'s characterisation of *Nashe Delo* as the 'fighting organ of Russian social-nationalism' when it was a forum for discussion. After reemphasising that he was criticising social-patriotism in *Nashe Delo*, he reminded his Parisian colleagues that there was no Zimmerwald resolution obliging comrades to do battle against defencist ideology. Indeed, Lenin's resolution condemning *Nasha Zarya* had been rejected. In hounding Martov and other Mensheviks for putting the case for internationalism in *Nashe Delo*, he warned *Nashe Slovo* that it was not uniting internationalists, but setting them against one another.

The idea that *Nashe Slovo* was working against its stated aim of uniting internationalists raised the temper of the debate. In its (Trotsky's) comment on Martov's defence, *Nashe Slovo* not only repeated that *Nashe Delo* was a social-patriotic publication which internationalists had to criticise to the fullest extent, it also accused Martov of trying to convert the Mensheviks to social-patriotism. Of course, *Nashe Slovo* pointed out, Martov found it easier to write for *Nashe Delo* once he had discounted the views of his five colleagues. However, that the latter had not acted out of fractional concerns was evident because Martov had also had to ignore the disquiet of his 'own' revolutionary-Menshevik internationalists. A recent resolution of London-based revolutionary-Mensheviks argued for a 'merciless struggle with social-patriots (Plekhanov, *Nashe Delo*, etc.)'. After defending its statement that Zimmerwald had obliged its signatories to conduct an irreconcilable struggle with social-patriots, *Nashe Slovo* told Martov that his 'internal-fractional policies' could not keep the Paris newspaper and the revolutionary-Mensheviks apart. In effect a battle for the Menshevik fraction itself was declared:

> We do not doubt that ... amongst the worker-Mensheviks there are hundreds of revolutionary cadres for whom ties with revolutionary internationalists of all fractions are more dear than purely-fractional, politically-reactionary ties with *Nashe Delo*'s social-patriotic staff ... Menshevik-revolutionaries cannot be kept from us, just as we cannot be kept from them: we fight for one and the same aim. It is for them, and for all internationalists, to judge the drawn-out conflict between Martov and our editorial board.[72]

In the midst of this conflict Trotsky and Martov also clashed over their respective accounts of the Zimmerwald conference. This dispute started when Martov protested against Trotsky's 'subjective' reportage of what had actually taken place in the Swiss village between 5–8 September 1915. A reader guided by Trotsky's journalism would conclude that three groups had battled for influence: the left, the centre and the right. These distinctions would, he said, be familiar to anyone who knew the history of Russian Social-Democracy. However, although the Russian delegates at Zimmerwald had made important contributions, Martov emphasised that this gathering of internationalists had not repeated a set Russian pattern. In actual fact, the conference had divided into two groups: one made-up of eight delegates, led by Lenin, who wanted the conference to be the beginning of a Third International; and another, the majority, who thought that they were planning a struggle for peace to restore the Second International. The only other debate, whether German Social-Democracy should be condemned, also witnessed a minority/majority split; the former headed by Ledebour who said 'no' and the latter who answered 'yes'. According to Martov, Trotsky had created a third fraction by splitting the majority, most notably by portraying the Organisational Committee as a right-wing group, opposed by a centre majority headed by *Nashe Slovo*. On the issue of a struggle for peace, for example, Trotsky said that *Nashe Slovo* considered it a revolutionary-class tactic whereas Aksel'rod and Co. thought of it in non-class struggle terms. In reality, as was evident from the Organisational Committee's suggested amendment to the Zimmerwald Manifesto, not discussed at the conference because time ran out, the Mensheviks viewed a struggle for peace as a first step in the new era of sharpening class contradictions, which conference participants should apply all their efforts to turn into a second step. Hence the Mensheviks had been at one with the majority on this matter, and this explained why *Nashe Slovo*'s 'splitting gestures ... led nowhere: a third tendency *did not emerge*.'[73] Finally, Martov argued that Aksel'rod and Trotsky had agreed on the issue of German Social-Democracy, although they approached the matter from different starting-points. But, he regretted, Trotsky's subjectivism had turned Aksel'rod's passing remark that German comrades were more worthy of condemnation than their French and Belgian counterparts into a whole tendency which the conference had supposedly rejected.

In his defence, published over two issues of *Nashe Slovo*, Trotsky turned Martov's accusation on its head: if he had suffered from too much subjectivism, Martov had written under 'the burden of objectivity'. This became clear, if one compared Martov's perceptions of what had happened at Zimmerwald with what had actually occurred. Trotsky began by correcting Martov's definition of the extremist group. They were unique not because they demanded the establishment of a Third International, but because they wanted to turn the war into a civil war. He then outlined the points which separated the revolutionary from the pacifist internationalists, most importantly for the former a struggle for peace was a revolutionary demand, opposing the proletariat to the whole of bourgeois society and to social-patriotism, while the latter rejected revolutionary methods of struggle out of hand. In presenting matters thus Trotsky argued that he had not simply viewed international socialism through the prism of a well-established divisions among Russian socialists. Indeed, he asked whether 'our homeland groups' were not 'a refraction of international socialist tendencies'.[74] After all, the three groups which he had noted were evident in all European countries. In Germany, for example, the equivalent of the Russian passive internationalists (Martov and the Organisational Committee) was the fraction in the Reichstag, of the extremists (Lenin and the Central Committee) the group Lichtstrahlen, and of the revolutionary internationalists (*Nashe Slovo*) Liebknecht and his comrades. Hence it was not accidental that three draft declarations were submitted at Zimmerwald, each of which represented an individual tendency; just as it was no accident that it was Trotsky who had been asked to draw-up the final version as it was his group, which included Rakovsky, Grimm and Henrietta Roland Holst, which had guaranteed that anything at all was achieved at Zimmerwald. Furthermore, Trotsky claimed that he and his supporters had quarrelled with the passive internationalists, Ledebour, Moragi, Aksel'rod and others, on all the major points of discussion. Why then had Martov lumped the two groups together? This question returned Trotsky to Martov's 'objectivity', which reflected, he said, the Menshevik fraction itself, composed equally of opponents and supporters of *Nashe Delo*. Martov did not wish to upset this balance, and it was this which explained his insistence that two forces, internationalists and extremists, had clashed at Zimmerwald:

> Martov's position ... which enables him to see the watershed between Marxism and extremism, at the same time forces him not to note the watershed between revolutionary Marxism and passive internationalism. But, with Martov's permission, this watershed does not disappear when somebody, wishing to preserve a spiritual equilibrium, ignores it. For however mighty Martov's objectivity, the objectivity of political development is mightier.[75]

The dispute about what had happened at Zimmerwald carried over into the New Year when, in January 1916, *Nashe Slovo* published Martov's reply to Trotsky's reply.[76] Martov questioned each of Trotsky's factual corrections. He asked *Nashe Slovo* to name the points over which Trotsky had clashed with Aksel'rod, for he did not know of any. He then threw the notion that Zimmerwald had been a victory for Trotsky into doubt. After all, the final manifesto made no mention of the struggle for peace growing over into a conquest of state power by the proletariat, just as there was no reference to a general battle with social-patriotism in the section condemning French and German Social-Democracy. Finally, Martov asserted that Trotsky had falsely put comrades into a group of 'revolutionary internationalists'. Grimm, for example, had recognised that there were two groups at Zimmerwald: one of eight headed by Lenin and another of the rest. In conclusion, Martov asked why, if he was so absorbed by fractional intrigue, had one of the extremists, Radek, supported his proposed amendment to the manifesto?

In what was to be the final word on this affair in *Nashe Slovo*, Trotsky declined the opportunity to, in turn, show the falsity of each of Martov's assertions. 'To take the mosaic apart stone by stone would', he declared, 'be to waste the readers' and the newspaper's time.' Instead, he would continue to critically analyse the positions of the three groups, extremists, revolutionary and passive internationalists, 'rooted in the life and actions of the socialist parties in the current epoch',[77] as they emerged on individual issues as time went by.

Trotsky's first opportunity to fulfil his promise came soon after the conclusion of his 'Zimmerwald debate'. In the second instalment of his 'Peace Programme', for example, Trotsky contested Martynov's belief that the only sensible slogan under which the proletariat should struggle to end the war was 'Peace without Annexations'. He agreed with Martynov's view that a huge effort from the proletariat would be required to prevent territorial conquests from the current world conflict. However, it was for this very reason, he stated, that the proletariat should not limit itself to Martynov's 'minimal programme':

> a decisive struggle of the proletariat directed against imperialist pretensions, whatever slogan it is conducted under, will weaken the ruling classes and strengthen the proletariat. But from this it does not follow that in its struggle the proletariat should aim to restore the old map of Europe, not advancing its *own programme of state and national relations*, firmly rooted in the basic tendencies of economic development, the revolutionary character of the epoch and the socialist interests of the proletariat.[78]

In later parts of this series Trotsky made it clear that a proletarian peace programme had to include the demand for the establishment of a United States of Europe.[79] When he examined opposition to this, as we have seen, Trotsky focused mainly upon Lenin's objections. He did, though, make the following comment upon Martynov's 'passive-possibilist' critique:

> Comrade Martynov takes us from an 'abstract', i.e., from a social-revolutionary, posing of the question to 'concrete' and 'realisable' tasks under the banner of a peace without annexations. But a peace without annexations would demand from the proletariat such revolutionary power that it would not be able to limit itself to the conservative-negative programme of *status quo ante*.[80]

In his last dispute with the Mensheviks while working as a journalist in Paris, it became clear that Trotsky and *Nashe Slovo*, on one side, and Martov and the Organisational Committee's *Izvestiya*, on the other, had irreversibly parted company. This polemic surrounded the election of worker representatives to the War-Industries Committees, bodies created to help conduct Russia's war effort, which took place in

September 1915. In his first reports of these elections Trotsky recounted how candidates standing on behalf of the Organisational Committee and the August Bloc, despite holding viewpoints ranging from 'Plekhanovite to electic-internationalist', were, as a group, defencists. Hence, he concluded, the Organisational Committee and the August Bloc had joined the social-patriotic camp.[81]

The third issue of *Izvestiya* contained two challenges to Trotsky's account of the August Bloc. A. Martynov identified four competing 'August Bloc' groups within the War-Industries Committees: (1) an insignificant number of Plekhanovite nationalists; (2) opportunists, seeking to team-up with the bourgeois opposition; (3) the majority, aspiring to oppose the bourgeoisie with an organised proletariat to overthrow tsarism and to ensure that Russia's war aims remained 'defensive'; and (4) internationalists who had stood for election on a 'struggle for peace' ticket.[82] Then, Semkovskii pointed out that Mensheviks had argued for internationalism in the elections to the War-Industries Committees 'without any reference to patriotism'.[83]

Trotsky subjected these articles to ruthless criticism in the long-running series 'Social-Patriotism in Russia'.[84] He stated that for *Izvestiya*'s claims to have any validity, anti-defencist statements should have been issued from meetings of the War-Industries Committees. Actually, as was clear from the latest pronouncements of the Petrograd and Moscow groups, *'the politics of the workers' groups in the War-Industries Committees is social-patriotic'*.[85] According to Trotsky, the leader of the August Bloc in Russia was not the fictitious Menshevik-internationalist Dan, but the social-patriot Gvozdev. If the various viewpoints outlined by *Izvestiya* were examined, he argued, they were all social-patriotic. About the Plekhanovite social-nationalists there could be no argument. The reformists, seeking progress within capitalism, had quite naturally allied with the bourgeoisie; opportunism 'is forced to follow the bourgeoisie into nationalism and imperialism', i.e., like Gvozdev, be social-patriotic. The politics of the third tendency, to use the War-Industries Committees to struggle with the bourgeoisie was, Trotsky stated, ruled out by the nature of the War-Industries Committees. In other words, revolutionaries in the War-Industries Committees would be corrupted by the social-patriots and forced to serve the latter. As regards the final tendency, the internationalists, Trotsky argued that their tactic did not make sense. After all, he asked, how could one struggle for peace in a body that did not resolve questions of war and peace? The only means by which the War-Industries Committees could have served agitational purposes was if the internationalists had attended once, simply to declare their opposition to defensive organisations. This, he said, would have answered the revolutionary policy of cutting all ties with the social-patriots. However, Dan demanded that internationalists remain within the committees for national defence and this, for Trotsky, meant 'rejecting the revolutionary mobilisation of the masses against the war'. The Organisational Committee's stance was so pernicious, according to Trotsky, since worker opposition to the War-Industries Committees depended upon internationalists remaining true to their principles: 'if bourgeois nationalism had met from all leading Social-Democratic groups and centres, a solid phalanx of internationalists ... it would have stumbled across an insurmountable class barrier and its experiment would have ended in failure.'[86] In not recognising that its 'internationalists' had played a crucial support role to the outright social-patriots of the Gvozdev mould, Trotsky accused the Organisational Committee of penning a 'literary mockery of political facts'.

In a reply to Trotsky, Martov claimed that *Nashe Slovo* had engaged in its own form of subterfuge in its coverage of the War-Industries Committees.[87] In particular it had, he said, remained silent on the activities of the Petrograd Unification Group. At first sight this appeared puzzling. After all, articles on the Unification Group, which *Nashe Slovo* considered its own, often used to appear in it. Why then had this group not been mentioned in relation to the War-Industries Committees? Because, Martov answered, the Unification Group had split over the issue of the worker elections, some demanded a boycott but most were for participation. And, he added, the leader of the latter fraction, as he had learnt from *Sotsial'Demokrat*, was none other then Gvozdev.[88] See now who was harbouring social-patriots! Not only had *Nashe Slovo* remained silent on the Unification Group it had, Martov stated, out of the same fractional considerations, falsely labelled the Organisational Committee social-patriotic. In order to refute this he cited from, among other documents, a proclamation issued by the Initiative Group of Social-Democratic Mensheviks. This justified participation in the War-Industries Committees on the grounds that they provided a platform from which workers' demands could be advanced. Moreover, the Initiative Group declared that it had fulfilled its election promise of entering the War-Industries Committees 'not for defencism ... but to struggle for peace, freedom and socialism.' This corresponded, Martov said, to a distinction which *Nashe Slovo* had not discerned. Comrades in Petersburg had been elected to *save*

Russia, i.e. repulse the enemy *and* liberate the country from tsarism. In Moscow, on the other hand, the workers had elected candidates on a purely defencist platform. According to Martov, 'defending Russia' was social-patriotic, but not 'saving Russia'. Given this evidence, only those who consciously wished to lie could say the Organisational Committee was social-patriotic.

In his reply to Martov, Trotsky asserted that the Menshevik leader had not followed his own advice of sticking to 'the facts'. *Nashe Slovo* had never frequently printed articles on the Unification Group. This would have been impossible, according to Trotsky, since news of its activities reached Paris only very occasionally. It was equally untrue to say that the Unification Group was absent from *Nashe Slovo*'s analysis of the elections to the War-Industries Committees. On no less than two occasions its correspondent Boretskii had, for example, criticised the Unification Group for not being sufficiently firm against social-patriotism.[89] Similarly, Martov had misled the reader by declaring that *Nashe Slovo* had ignored the information concerning Gvozdev's allegiance contained in *Sotsial'Demokrat*. In actual fact, Trotsky pointed out, a full editorial had faithfully announced that Gvozdev was a *former* member of the Unification Group.[90] He then told Martov that he had read the Initiative Group's proclamation and had correctly identified it as social-patriotic, since it recommended participation in the War-Industries Committees on a defencist basis. This programme had, he said, most recently found expression in the defencist resolutions of the War-Industries Congress. Trotsky's main words of advice to Martov were:

> before levelling new accusations at us on the basis of ... indirect evidence it would be better to make enquiries at our offices by letter: this would spare Martov from further ... negligence and more importantly spare *Nashe Slovo* from polemics which bring no good.[91]

Ten days later *Nashe Slovo* reprinted Martov's statement from *Izvestiya*, in which he declared that he was following Ber's example and resigning from *Nashe Slovo*'s editorial board. Martov explained that he had not done this while there was a 'slim chance that the majority of the editorial board would reach an agreement, protecting the minority from at least the worst excesses of fractional intrigue'.[92] However, his colleagues' refusal had removed any 'moral and political responsibility' that could be laid at Martov's door for *Nashe Slovo*.

Trotsky responded to Martov's resignation on behalf of the whole editorial board. He began by questioning Martov's assertion that Ber had left *Nashe Slovo* at an earlier date for much the same reasons as Martov. Although Ber had had disputes with the majority of his editorial colleagues, these differences had been accurately represented in *Nashe Slovo*. It was for this reason that Ber had not once levelled the accusation of fractional intrigue at his co-editors. Indeed, when Martov had sought his 'guarantee' he had been opposed by, among others, Ber and several leading Menshevik internationalists. For Trotsky, Martov's formal resignation would have no influence on *Nashe Slovo* since over the previous year the two had clearly parted company. Thus, for example, when *Nashe Slovo* had criticised the Organisational Committee for harbouring social-patriots, Martov spoke of the Paris newspaper's 'fractionalism'. Similarly, Martov had opposed *Nashe Slovo* on a whole series of other points, including: (1) a critique of Aksel'rod's social-patriotism; (2) the characterisation of *Nashe Delo* as the ideological base of social-patriotism; (3) the call to Menshevik internationalists to join like-minded colleagues of other fractions in an open struggle against social-patriots serving on the War-Industries Committees; and (4) the distinction between passive internationalism and social-revolutionary internationalism. Trotsky expressed no regret that Martov had formally broken all ties with *Nashe Slovo*. Rather he declared that the battle for influence over the Menshevik internationalists would continue:

> If Comrade Martov at the height of a struggle with social-patriotism considers it necessary to remove from himself the very 'hint' of *moral* (!) responsibility for the only Russian internationalist daily newspaper in which he enjoyed unlimited rights of criticism, then on our behalf we declare that *not for one minute will we remove from ourselves the obligation of moral and political responsibility which falls on us, as a non-fractional newspaper, for the ideological struggle and political work of the revolutionary Mensheviks*.[93]

The question of the loyalties of the Menshevik internationalists lay at the centre of Trotsky's next article on the War-Industries Committees. 'Without Substance' reported that opposition to the Organisational Committee's defence of participation in the War-Industries Committees was growing within Menshevik ranks in Russia. Trotsky's evidence was taken from the fourth issue of the Organisational Committee's own *Izvestiya*, in which there had appeared a letter from Mensheviks in Petersburg.[94] This had made several points, most notably, from Trotsky's point of view, that Menshevik workers were not defencists and that the Petersburg Mensheviks would resign if the Organisational Committee did not adopt an anti-defencist line. The Petersburg Mensheviks were convinced that as soon as the Menshevik's leaders declared opposition to defencism, social-patriotism would collapse. While he welcomed the demands made of the Organisational Committee, Trotsky puzzled over *Izvestiya*'s editorial comment on the Petersburg communication which, it claimed, confirmed its earlier view that leading circles of the August Bloc had been forced to take-up a defencist position because of pressure from below. For Trotsky, 'irony becomes disbelief when faced with this unheard-of confusion'.[95]

Documents issued by Menshevik groups in Russia and published in *Izvestiya* also provided the material for Trotsky's next comment on 'internationalism' in the War-Industries Committees.[96] This time, however, the Paris correspondent could find no points of agreement between himself and the Russian Mensheviks.[97] According to Trotsky the two declarations which had appeared in the fifth number of *Izvestiya*, the first signed by the Petersburg Initiative Group and the Moscow Social-Democratic Group and the second only by the former, were examples of the way in which workers were brought to serve the imperialist state. Ostensibly both documents proclaimed their allegiance to Zimmerwald. They then said, however, that a Russian revolution was possible only if the proletariat allied with the bourgeoisie. Therefore internationalists, while refusing responsibility for the war, should join the War-Industries Committees as part of a campaign to link-up with the bourgeois opposition. For Trotsky, this train of reasoning was faulty. It misunderstood bourgeois opposition which was not revolutionary, but a means to 'discipline the workers and subordinate them to the imperialist band-master'.[98] A bloc with the bourgeoisie could only lead the workers to imperialism. This was the means by which the proletariat was tied to the imperialist state. Workers who were not willing to serve the bourgeoisie under the openly social-nationalist Plekhanovite banner, would most likely do so under the leadership of 'Zimmerwaldists': 'Just as the liberal opposition is needed by the imperialist bloc for taming ... the bourgeois nation, so war-industrial "internationalism" is necessary for bringing the workers to heel.'[99] Second, the Moscow and Petersburg Mensheviks had not understood what Zimmerwald stood for, for this conference made the Russian revolution dependent not upon the bourgeoisie, but upon the international proletariat. The tactic which followed from this, argued Trotsky, was an independent class policy of open hostility to the bourgeoisie. Hence, Trotsky concluded, one had to break with bourgeois organs of defence and abandon the War-Industries Committees.

In his final piece on the War-Industries Committees dispute, marking the end of his last clash with the Mensheviks while working for *Nashe Slovo*, Trotsky first summarised his differences with the Organisational Committee. Trotsky thought that 'internationalists' participating in the War-Industries Committees were committing themselves, and the workers who followed them, to social-patriotism. Only opposition to the War-Industries Committees could, he argued, 'become an important moment in the development of international-ist tactics'. The Organisational Committee, on the other hand, as was clear from Martov's article in *Nashe Slovo* of early April 1916 (discussed above), did not consider participants in the War-Industries Committees *a priori* defencists. Trotsky then highlighted that not all of the Organisational Committee had been consistent on the elections to the War-Industries Committees. In a document issued in Berne in February 1916, for example, Martov had written that, 'More than 100,000 workers in Petersburg voted against participation in the War-Industries Committees, refusing responsibility for the war.' Subsequently, in *Nashe Slovo*, this self same Martov had claimed that in Petersburg candidates had stood for Russia's saviour, and not its defence, as part of a justification *for* participation in the War-Industries Committees! One more example of Menshevik duplicity was mentioned. Here Trotsky focused upon the brochure *Kriegs und Friedensprobleme der Arbeiterklasse*, recently issued by the Mensheviks to enlighten foreign comrades of their approach to the current prob-lems facing Social-Democracy. It was the brochure's structure that most offended Trotsky. It began with a reprint of the draft manifesto submitted by the Organisational Committee and the Polish Socialist Party to the Kienthal Conference of 24–30 April 1916 which, for Trotsky, gave a 'confused' exposition of Zimmerwald's response to the war.[100] However, this draft manifesto had attached to it the declara-tions of the Petersburg and Moscow Mensheviks which called for cooperation with the bourgeoisie. If, he said, the Mensheviks had wanted to inform comrades of the real nature of their programmatic response to current issues, the appeals of the Petersburg and Moscow groups should have been placed at the front and not the back of the brochure. The fact that they had not done so, he concluded, suited the

Organisational Committee's task of hiding its social-patriotic interior with an internationalist exterior:

> We assert that *not one* foreign internationalist, reading the first document, would guess that its authors recommend defencism with the intention of joining-up with the imperialist bourgeoisie ... from the point of view of *political truth* there is no name for such a way of informing foreign comrades ... this method inevitably follows on from the official-semi-official politics of the August Bloc which has two faces: one false, international-Zimmerwaldist, and the other natural – Gvozdevist.[101]

*

There is a certain amount of irony in Trotsky's disputes with the Mensheviks. His call for the unification of internationalists of all fractions, for example, was opposed on two fronts: from the Bolsheviks for not being decisive enough and from the Mensheviks for being too hasty and too radical; although both Bolsheviks and Mensheviks agreed that Trotsky was engaging in 'non-fractional fractionalism'! A perception shared by Bolsheviks and Mensheviks also underpinned their disagreement with Trotsky on another matter, that of the United States of Europe. Both fractions argued that Trotsky, in calling for the establishment of this transnational state structure as a way of ending the war, was compressing a historical epoch into a historical moment. Leaving these ironies to one side, however, Trotsky's main bone of contention with the Menshevik's Organisational Committee was that its internationalism was passive, i.e. it did not recognise the need for an open and complete break of all ties with social-patriots. For Trotsky, passive internationalism was particularly harmful since it herded workers, who under a different leadership would have engaged in revolutionary activity, into the social-patriotic pen. The next chapter will examine Trotsky's relations with the outright, and not masked, social-patriots who were also in Paris during World War One.

6
Russian Social-Patriotism in Paris

If Trotsky's polemics with the Bolsheviks, on the one hand, and his disputes with the Mensheviks, on the other, show that he did not have a monopoly on a Russian Social-Democratic response to the war, Russian social-patriots in Paris prevented Trotsky from being the sole voice of Russian émigré opinion in the French capital. In a collection issued in Paris in 1915 several Russian social-patriots outlined a core set of beliefs: Germany, by attacking Serbia and breaking Belgium neutrality, was responsible for the war; a German victory would be harmful for democracy; a German victory would retard Russia's economic development and would not be good news for Russia's workers; and, finally, Germany must be defeated.[1] Prominent members included journalists working for the newspaper *Novosti*, Yakovlev (*Novoe Vremya*), Belorussov (*Russkia Vedomosti*) and the editorial board of *Prizyv*, a weekly newspaper which began publication in the autumn of 1915.[2]

Trotsky's first skirmish with the social-patriotic circle in Paris followed Aleksinskii's citation of a section of Trotsky's pamphlet *War and the International* in the final instalment of his 'War and Socialism',[3] which criticised German Social-Democracy's pro-war stance. In making this point he referred to Trotsky's just-published work:

> In his interesting [Lausanne] essay Comrade Trotsky cites a member of the German Social-Democratic Party's Central Committee who, in conversation with Trotsky, explained the disappointing behaviour of the party's leading circles at the beginning of the war by a highly simple consideration: if we had opposed the war the government would have confiscated our party funds! But a

Social-Democratic Workers' Party draws and should draw its tactics from class [*klassovikh*] interests and not from ... those of the kitty [*kassovikh*].

I have often had to comment on these reason with which several comrades 'explain' and condone German Social-Democracy.[4]

Thus, Aleksinskii cited Trotsky as the source of a German comrade's views, and then stated that he had been forced to reject similar attempts to whitewash German Social-Democracy by other (unnamed) socialists. His report of the contents of Trotsky's pamphlet seems just and accurate. After all, in *War and the International* Trotsky wrote,

Perhaps never before had the spirit of organisational inertia dominated so freely in German Social-Democracy as in the past few years which directly preceded the great catastrophe; and there can be no doubt that the question of preserving the organisation – the kitty, the workers' houses, the printing presses – played a very large role in determining the position of the fraction in the Reichstag in relation to the war. The first argument which I heard from one of the leading German comrades (Mol'kenbur) reads: 'if we had acted otherwise we would have doomed our organisation to death.'[5]

However, in a 'Necessary Correction' Trotsky insisted that, contrary to Aleksinskii, he had not explained German Social-Democracy's backing of the German government out of a concern for its funds and that he had not used this explanation to justify the German Social-Democratic Party. Trotsky pointed out that in the very same pamphlet he had told the German socialist: 'You have fatally undermined the authority of German Social-Democracy and you have killed the International.' As Trotsky emphasised, 'this does not look like a "justification"'.[6] Finally, in an obvious dig at Aleksinskii's approval of French and Belgium socialists' calls for a war of self-defence, Trotsky said that he had also truthfully characterised shameless semi-patriots who used their attacks on German Social-Democracy as an excuse to concoct a 'patriotic mixture of France ... and Petrograd under the internationalist flag'.[7]

The Swiss town of Lausanne also featured in the series of events which led to Trotsky's first critical response to the views of the most famous Russian social-patriot residing in the French capital, Plekhanov. *Golos* readers had been able to become acquainted with Plekhanov's view of the war from a report of one of his speeches.[8]

Plekhanov blamed Germany for bringing Europe to war. He pointed out that on the eve of hostilities even German Social-Democratic leaders had accepted this. However, these self same German socialists had then failed to oppose German militarism, instead justifying German actions under the slogan 'each nation has a right to existence'. For Plekhanov this was 'laughable'. How could German socialists seek refuge in this while denying Belgium that very right? He also dismissed the argument that German Social-Democrats had to support their government as it was defending itself from tsarism: 'everyone knows that the German crown was one of the strongest bulwarks of Tsarism'.[9] For Plekhanov, the out and out opportunism of German Social-Democracy derived from its disregard for principles and from its concern about popularity:

> German Social-Democracy did not have sufficient strength to struggle with chauvinism and preferred to sacrifice principles than to sacrifice its influence over the masses, if only provisionally.[10]

One illustration of the German party's theoretical carelessness was the German radicals' claim that they voted for war credits for the sake of party unity. Plekhanov said that he was against splits, but not when principles were at stake. Recent German events pointed to the sorry state of affairs that inattention to theory could lead: *Arbeiterzeitung* had abandoned class politics for the politics of race. The extent of Plekhanov's disgust for German Social-Democracy was evident from his demand that radical changes would have to be undertaken in the German SDP before relations with it could be restored.

Plekhanov's condemnation of German socialists was matched by his fervent support of socialists who had voted for and even joined the war time governments in the Entente countries. According to Plekhanov, Russian, French and Belgium socialists were duty-bound to fight their countries as they were acting in self-defence. Socialist conferences had stipulated that socialists could join bourgeois ministries in exceptional circumstances and, asked Plekhanov, were not current events 'exceptional'? Furthermore, he defended socialist attempts to win over neutral countries to the Entente. Proletarian diplomacy should maximise the fight against those guilty of infringing justice: 'If one is content to avoid the war, this is not an internationalist policy but narrow-nationalism.'[11]

Golos then reprinted one of Plekhanov's letters from the British socialist broadsheet *Justice*.[12] In this Plekhanov located the war's origins in Germany's desire for economic supremacy. He argued that a German victory would undermine Russia's base for economic development and, 'since economic development underpins social and political progress, Russia, if defeated, would forfeit all, or almost all, possibility of finishing Tsarism.'[13] Plekhanov warned socialists not to be fooled by the trickery of the German general staff. If the Entente lost, progress in Western Europe would take a backward step.

Trotsky responded to Plekhanov's case after the 'father of Russian Marxism' had developed his views in the pamphlet *O voine* (1914).[14] For Trotsky, Plekhanov's writings were the saddest testimony of the recent collapse of socialism. Although he agreed with Plekhanov's condemnation of German Social-Democracy, he argued that Plekhanov had added nothing to what had already been said in the Russian socialist press. Moreover, Plekhanov's claim that German Social-Democracy fell because it wanted to preserve its popularity was dismissed as a non-explanation. Unfortunately, this was not surprising, for Plekhanov and German Social-Democracy shared the same presuppositions: 'For both the criterion is not the social-revolutionary tasks of the international proletariat but the interests of national capitalism viewed from a national workers' policy.'[15]

Trotsky's then criticised Plekhanov's distinction between Germany's 'offensive' and Russia's 'defensive' war. According to Plekhanov, Austria-Hungary had broken the European peace by attacking Serbia, whereas Russia had to support Serbia so as to retain influence in the Balkans. Trotsky attempted to discredit this view of a less rapacious tsarist diplomacy by pointing to Russia's appalling record of interference in the Balkans. Romanian, Bulgarian and Serbian Social-Democrats distinguished between Hapsburg and tsarist policy only by labelling the latter's approach more 'dishonourable and dangerous'.[16] Second, one could easily construct a list of Russia's cynical and self-interested acts in the Balkans, including: in 1876 Bosnia and Herzegovina had been conceded to Austria in return for Austrian neutrality in the event of a Russo-Turkish war; Russian endeavours to turn Bulgaria into its satrap had led to the formation of an anti-Russian party in Bulgaria; in 1908–09 Russia pushed Serbia into a war with Austria and then betrayed the Balkan nation and so on. Trotsky trusted that the memory of the Balkan peoples was better than Plekhanov's. Finally, Trotsky claimed that Russia joined the war not out of a concern for Serbia's independence but to use the Serbian cause to gain Galicia. Had Plekhanov not considered a scenario in which *'Tsarist diplomacy would abandon Serbia to the Hapsburgs as it abandoned Bosnia 38 years ago in exchange for Galicia,* without which tsarism will not cease fighting'?[17]

In his conclusion Trotsky returned to Plekhanov's argument that Austria had pushed Russia into war. He accepted Plekhanov's reference to *Vorwärts* as evidence of German recognition of German guilt. However, Trotsky asserted that Plekhanov's use of the German newspaper was on the same level as German exploitation of Russian socialists' struggle against Tsarism:

> From *Vorwärts*'s forewarning about German diplomacy Plekhanov sophistically justifies Russian diplomacy ... as a defence of Serbia and of 'rudimentary laws of morality and law.' What distinguishes Plekhanov from the *current Vorwärts* which exploits our struggle against Tsarism to justify German imperialism? Absolutely nothing! The same aim and the same method![18]

During April 1915 Trotsky complained several times of Russian social-patriotic slander of *Nashe Slovo* and its allies. The first shots of this particular battle were fired in Iks's report of Trotsky's paper 'Pan-Germanism and the War', delivered to the Society of Russian Engineers. Trotsky was cited as asking: 'Is it absurd to assert that Pan-Germanism is exclusive to a few Prussian Junkers?', to which Iks replied that perhaps it would be less absurd to assert that Pan-Germanism was shared by N. Trotsky and a small group of Russian Social-Democrats who were 'so obliged to German Social-Democracy' and German political science.[19] Trotsky responded by calling *Novosti* a 'gutter newspaper' and ridiculed the notion of *Nashe Slovo* as a Pan-Germanist publication: 'a suspicious light really shines in our window. Writing articles which do not humiliate the German people and ... which denounce lies and reaction irrespective of national origin ... It is clear: Pan-Germanists!'[20]

Trotsky had also received a letter from a certain Mr Bek-Allaev who had accused *Nashe Slovo* of publishing itself on German money and of having a Jewish editor. Allaev's evidence was *Nashe Slovo*'s thesis that recent Russian success at the Austrian fortress town of Przemysl did not give it a strategic advantage.[21] Trotsky dismissed a tactical discussion with Allaev. However, the charge of a Jewish editor could easily be refuted as the author of the aforementioned war report had a more Russian name than Allaev himself and, in any case, the *Nashe Slovo* war correspondent was a former officer in the Russian army. Trotsky reminded Allaev, or those behind him, that despite the war 'slander is still a criminal offence'.[22]

If Trotsky hoped that a threat of legal action would end the matter, he was soon to be disappointed. *Novosti* carried two rejoinders.[23] In a short letter   L. M. Glezer, announcing that he was Iks, labelled Trotsky's article 'unworthy', and stated that it would be beneath his dignity to refute its 'fictive insinuations'. *Novosti*'s editorial board added that it would not lower itself to the language of Trotsky's 'gutter press' accusation, and that it would not enter into such polemics.

Trotsky responded to Glezer and *Novosti* in a short note. He denied that he had made-up any insinuations. After all, 'Iks wrote that the Engineers' Society had organised a Pan-Germanist talk.' As to Glezer's revelation of his true identity, it was 'the exchange of one political and literary nonentity for another'. He then addressed *Novosti*'s hurt at being called a 'gutter newspaper'. How else could one classify a publication which had, first, in war time France published an 'account' of Trotsky's Pan-Germanism and, then, permitted the 'informer' to write of N.T.'s 'fabrications' when the latter had refuted charges of Pan-Germanism? Trotsky concluded, 'Nasty beginning Mr Social-Patriot! Worrying about European democracy while covering-up dirty tricks.'[24]

The acrimonimity between Trotsky and the Russian social-patriots continued into the next dispute. This arose when Aleksinskii, welcoming *Novosti*'s new editor, indirectly labelled *Nashe Slovo* a defeatist publication:

> during such an important event as war, it is extremely important that Social-Democrats and Social-Revolutionaries who do not share the profoundly mistaken ... ideas of *Zhizn* and *Nashe Slovo* etc, engage in mutual support and cooperation. This cooperation is even more necessary given that in Russia the majority of peasants and workers support our anti-defeatist position.[25]

Trotsky denied that *Nashe Slovo* had ever recommended German domination to the Russian people.[26] On the contrary, he asked Aleksinskii if defeatism would not be better applied to him. After all, did the Russian social-patriots not urge the German people to support Russia's war effort? Trotsky acknowledged that Aleksinskii had included *Nashe Slovo* in the defeatist camp for the sake of simplicity, but there were two sorts of simplicity; one useful and another worse than stealing. Aleksinskii's simplicity was the latter since he had invented *Nashe Slovo*'s 'defeatism'. The reputation that Aleksinskii was earning for himself was that of a 'falsifier'.

A final outburst of hostilities of April 1915 once again brought Trotsky into dispute with Aleksinskii, with polemics concerning Trotsky's evaluation of Rakovsky's visit to Italy. In 'A Sytinist "Little Man" on Rakovsky', Trotsky defended the Romanian socialist from a charge that Rakovsky was in Italy to spread German propaganda.[27] Trotsky pointed out that Amfiteatrov made the charge despite asserting to the contrary that Rakovsky could not be entrusted with an 'official mission'. Trotsky informed the reader that Rakovsky had gone to Italy as a socialist, to convince other socialists to oppose Italian and Romanian intervention in the war, a mission which well suited Rakovsky's character:

> Rakovsky is well known to the International. He has served the revolutionary cause for two decades. He has close connections with Russian, French, Bulgarian and Romanian socialism. He devotes his exceptional energy and – we will allow ourselves to say this also! – makes donations to the cause of the liberation of the proletariat. Amfiteatrovshchina's glue does not stick to Rakovsky.[28]

Aleksinskii, however, took exception to Trotsky's portrayal of Rakovsky. A letter in *Nashe Slovo*, published with a reply from Trotsky,[29] said that Trotsky was guilty of two factual errors. First, Rakovsky was not closely connected to Russian Social-Democracy as he was not, and never had been, a member of either the RSDLP or the S-R Party. Second, the only donations which Rakovsky had made to Russian socialism was to Trotsky's Viennese *Pravda* and to *Nashe Slovo*, hardly sufficient grounds for the beneficiary, Trotsky, to claim a special relationship between Rakovsky and Russian socialism. Indeed, the latter could not be held responsible for Rakovsky's Italian 'mission'.

Trotsky's thoughts on Aleksinskii were clear from his rejoinder, 'To the Slanderers!', which called Aleksinskii to account for his 'facts'. Trotsky denied writing that Rakovsky had made donations to Russian socialism. Indeed, his original statement (quoted above) was that Rakovsky had given money to 'the cause of the liberation of the proletariat'. Moreover, Rakovsky's biography clearly illustrated his history of close cooperation with Russian socialism: membership of the Liberation of Labour Group which pre-dated the RSDLP; work as a Marxist propagandist in 1890s St Petersburg; exiled from Russia as a foreigner he participated in the Foreign Section of the RSDLP and wrote for *Iskra*, etc. Aleksinskii had falsified the biography of one of the first Russian socialists out of 'base "patriotic" slander'.[30] Hoping that some of the mud thrown at Rakovsky was still sticking, Aleksinskii had avoided the central issue of why Rakovsky had gone to Italy. In insinuating that *Nashe Slovo* received money from the German treasury via Rakovsky, shamelessness and cowardice had guided Aleksinskii. A particularly merciless conclusion condemned Aleksinskii as a man who had joined Russian Social-Democracy on the high wave of 1905 and then deserted it, leaving him to the fate of all turncoats:

> socialist turncoats disgrace themselves morally and in search for self-belief they are forced to reach for the most poisonous and dishonourable tools of our class enemies. Aleksinskii's 'Announcement' is far from being the final word in this story ... From slander to degradation and from degradation to slander he will move along a preordained orbit as irrefutable evidence of the fact that the cause which he serves is not only rotten, but also without hope.[31]

The next dispute between Trotsky and one of the Russian social-patriots, with Plekhanov, also had slander as a dominant theme. It followed the appearance of the collection of articles *Voina*, which prompted Trotsky to write an 'Open Letter to Comrade Plekhanov'.[32] Despite being addressed to Plekhanov, it polemicised primarily with Aleksinskii.

In his contribution to *Voina* Aleksinskii poured scorn upon *Nashe Slovo*'s claim to represent majority opinion among Russian workers.[33] How could a majority gather around a newspaper whose contributors could not agree with each other or, indeed, with their own self? On the key issue of German Social-Democracy's vote for war credits there was at least three opinions in *Nashe Slovo*: Larin refused to condemn German comrades, Trotsky condemned and condoned, whereas M.K. rejected any attempt to forgive German Social-Democrats and considered Larin a Germanofile. Martov accepted the idea of Russia's defeat before rejecting it. Voinov and Trotsky conducted a struggle against patriotism in *Nashe Slovo* while soul mates Lunacharsky and Antid-Oto (Trotsky's pseudonym) were writing heart-rendering accounts of 'German atrocities' and of the heroic exploits of Entente soldiers in *Kievskaya Mysl*. Finally, there were some examples of Russian publicists, most notably K. Zalewski, who wrote one thing for *Nashe Slovo* and something else for patriotic newspapers.[34]

In his 'Open Letter' Trotsky limited himself to what he found most offensive in Aleksinskii's article. Aleksinskii had accused him of writing for *Nashe Slovo* 'as an internationalist and irreconcilable opponent of social-patriotism but in the legal press, under a different name, as a patriot'.[35] Indeed, in a footnote to his contribution to *Voina* Aleksinskii had included Trotsky's name in a list of hypocrites who tailored their articles to suit the particular ideological leanings of different publications. Aleksinskii had rejected in advance an argument that the censor could be responsible; a censor could remove sentences but not force a comrade to write something contrary to his true beliefs. Aleksinskii blamed editorial boards for lowering standards: 'I am interested not so much with the people involved – Zalewski, Voinov and Trotsky – as with the editorial boards who *knowing* of their indecent hypocrisy open their pages to contributors' literary somersaults. Previously such things were impermissible in the Russian radical press.'[36]

Trotsky said that he would ignore Aleksinskii's revelation of the real identity of pseudonyms which made his article an 'informer's piece', the lack of any evidence, as well as the charge of hypocrisy itself since this had come from Aleksinskii, who had slandered Rakovsky and Romanian Social-Democracy, who had spread rumours about *Nashe Slovo*'s sources of funding, and who had misquoted Martov. For Trotsky, 'One cannot even begin to speak of seeking common ground in questions of political morals and literary honour with this professional.'[37] Trotsky then turned to Plekhanov and challenged him to declare openly and directly whether he agreed with Aleksinskii. Should Plekhanov support Aleksinskii then he, Trotsky, would publish evidence for readers to decide what they had in front of them: 'political hypocrisy on the one side or shameless slander on the other.'[38]

Plekhanov did not reply to Trotsky's 'Open Letter' and he continued to publicise his view that socialists were duty bound to support the war against the Central Powers. In late September and October 1915 Trotsky touched several times upon his disagreements with Plekhanov.

A report of Rakovsky's analysis of the Russian social-patriots afforded another opportunity to criticise Plekhanov's views.[39] Trotsky presented extracts from Rakovsky's introduction to a new French edition of his brochure *Socialism and the War*. Rakovsky discussed Plekhanov's belief that Balkan socialists who urged their governments

to remain neutral were aiding the Central Powers. Plekhanov illustrated this by a simple analogy: passivity while one man strangles
another shows at minimum no solidarity with the victim and at
maximum helps the strangler. Furthermore, the Plekhanov camp had
censured socialists of neutral countries for condoning their governments' use of neutrality to serve class ends. Countries were exploiting
neutrality to conclude outrageous trade deals. Rakovsky answered this
point first, distinguishing between government neutrality, passive
and provisional, and socialist neutrality, principled and conclusive.
Government neutrality was based upon greed and self-interest. If this
government then participated in the war, this change would also be
for selfish reasons, not a concern for a country's independence. War
was a bourgeois means for bourgeois ends. Rakovsky therefore rejected
Plekhanov's argument that neutrality assisted the Central Powers. Did
the father of Russian Marxism not realise that in the war to save
Belgium, Galicia and Turkey could be brought under Russian control?
Belgium had a right to independence, but this had to be achieved
through socialist means. Urging the working class to join bourgeois
armies in bourgeois wars exposed the working class to the danger of
becoming a tool in the hands of the bourgeoisie which could only
weaken socialism. Plekhanov had clearly forgotten his earlier lectures
on the nonsense of bourgeois wars of liberation. The pupil, Rakovsky,
had learnt the lesson better than the teacher.

Gustav Hevré's demands for a fourth assault on Bulgaria's Black Sea
shores prompted Trotsky to write an amusing retort.[40] According to
Trotsky, Hevré recommended that the attack should be led by Russian
soldiers carrying icons. Trotsky wondered whether Hevré had been
inspired by the the Russo-Japanese War, in which the Russian army
had marched into battle bearing icons. In an unsuccessful campaign,
the icons had not reached the hearts of the Japanese soldiers, but
Trotsky was sure that it would be different with the Orthodox
Bulgarians. Enough icons appealing to the Bulgarian soul should
make-up for any shortfall in ammunitions. However, the liberating
aspect of the war should also be stressed. The French army should be
headed by the Declaration of the Rights of Man, the British army by
Magna Carta and, finally, a volunteer section of Russian social-patriots should be armed with Plekhanov's appeals to Bulgarian
Social-Democrats. For Trotsky, this peculiar mixture of icons, republican declarations and Plekhanovised Kantanism would not only bring
forth the skilful combination of arms which was the essence of current
warfare, but also fascinating results!

Trotsky soon returned his attention to what should lead the Russian army into battle. He reported that Clemenceau had rejected the idea of icons and put forward the notion that Nicholas II should issue the 'charge' call. Thinking nothing of Nicholas II's military prowess, Trotsky teased the Russian social-patriots with the following challenge: 'The question, in our opinion, is very serious: icons or Nicholas II? We consider *Prizyv*'s further silence on this matter absolutely inadmissible. Its voice should be heard at this critical hour!'[41]

In between his deliberations on the Russian army, Trotsky appealed to Plekhanov with a request to 'Leave us in Peace!'[42] This illustrated how Plekhanov's war-time politics condraticted all of his previously held views. The deluge of Plekhanov's recent writings sought to achieve two aims. First, they should bring as much harm and confusion as possible so that his spiritual downfall would be less noticed. Second, the ever increasing unruliness of Plekhanov's pronunciations on the war would smother the protest of his own weakening political conscience. For Trotsky, Plekhanov was prepared to go to any lengths to gain solace by converting others to his point of view. A recent demand that the Russian Social-Democrat deputy Bur'yanov oppose the rest of the fraction and vote for war credits as any other vote would constitute a 'betrayal' was typical of Plekhanov's counter-attack: 'when Social-Democrats accuse you of abetting those forces which caused the war you do not defend yourself but bring forth your own accusations of betrayal!'[43] Moreover, the willingness of bourgeois proprietors to publish Plekhanov was not because he was an original and brilliant thinker. Rather, platitudes from the elder statesman of Russian Marxism served several useful bourgeois ends.

To begin with, Plekhanov had retained some of his reputation and influence as the leading representative of Russian Marxism and was therefore an effective tool in gathering workers' support for the war: 'what confusion sown in the minds of young workers only just coming to socialism!'[44] Furthermore, those people who had previously abandoned socialism could now celebrate the arrival of the most famous convert to date: 'what a victory for all those ... who even at the beginning of the counter-revolution sold their swords and for those turncoats of the latest "patriotic" levy.'[45] Finally, the liberal and democratic intelligentsia could compare themselves to Plekhanov and conclude that they were not such bad people after all, since 'they are not so spiritually meagre, not so morally base for they would never be brave enough to demand that socialists betray themselves and then slander them for ... betrayal.'[46] According to Trotsky, Plekhanov's fall from grace served as a useful moral lesson. Faced with the revolting sight of a founding father intoxicated from chauvinism and spiritually drained, those remaining true to socialism should send the same message to Plekhanov: 'It is all the same to us whether you are at peace. But we ask you now and for always to leave us in peace!'[47]

The last conflict of 1915 concerned Belorussov's distribution of a fund for Russians residing in Paris. Trotsky felt compelled to pen a rejoinder to Belorussov after reading that the Russian social-patriot had refused money to 'unpatriotic' Russian artists. How, he asked, had Belorussov discovered their political allegiances? Had he conducted an opinion poll or had he relied on hearsay? Had the money been donated on condition that only patriots would receive it? For Trotsky, 'It is enough to ask these questions to realise that Belorussov did not care about justifying his actions. He compounded moral cynicism with such incredible stupidity that one can only remark: it's unbelievable!'[48]

In a follow-up piece, his last of 1915, Trotsky reported that Belorussov had turned the management of the fund over to the editorial board of *Russkia Vedomosti*.[49] Afterwards, monies had been granted to artists considered in need by the artistic community itself. Trotsky posed three questions. Did recipients not feel that they were insulting the dignity of the whole artistic community? Should there not be a general meeting of all artists to resolve matters? Finally, should not the Literary Society, chaired by V. K. Aganov, censure Belorussov? In this way Trotsky hoped that the scandal would be concluded, and Belorussov's social and moral standing undermined.

Trotsky began 1916 with a 'New Year' analysis of several Russian social-patriots.[50] This piece was very sarcastic, with Plekhanov and Aleksinskii among the main targets. In his most recent writings Plekhanov had interpreted Marx's relation to Kant. Marx had underpinned a just proletarian foreign policy with 'simple laws of morals and justice',[51] one of which, according to Plekhanov, was the right of nations to self-determination. In the current war, Plekhanov concluded not only that socialists had to fight against those who had broken Marx's laws, i.e. Germany and its allies, but also that socialist revolution would be impossible if socialists did not uphold morality and law:

> the proletariat ... cannot liberate itself from the capitalist yoke without recognising the right of each nation to self-determination. The precondition for the overthrow of this yoke, the unification of

the proletariat of all countries, is possible only if the right of each separate people to self-determination is recognised … German professors love to 'lecture' on 'Kant and Marx,' but not one of them has lectured on how the *economics* of the new society was united with the 'foreign policy of the proletariat' as recommended by Marx … international socialists should campaign more energetically than anyone else against the oppressors and they should insist more energetically than anyone else on a 'foreign policy' based on simple laws of morality and law.[52]

For Trotsky, Plekhanov's use of Kant to justify Tsarist diplomacy was 'a real discovery',[53] made just as Russian soldiers were expected to seize Kant's birthplace, a fact which 'could not but inspire Russian social-patriotic thought'.[54] But, Trotsky argued, tsarism was turning its gaze from the Balkans to Persia, and it needed to seek a suitable ideological prop. Would Plekhanov come to its rescue? 'We await from the Plekhanov school the elaboration of the theme that the occupation of Persia is necessary for world moral equilibrium to counterbalance the occupation of Belgium.'[55] Trotsky helpfully suggested that Vladimir Lyakhov (1869–1919), a colonel who in 1906 had crushed a democratic uprising in Northern Iran, could now be represented as the guardian of 'Rights and Justice'.[56] One paragraph of Trotsky's article was devoted to Aleksinskii, who stood at the opposite end of social-patriotism since, unlike Plekhanov, he held the same regard for moral laws as the Tatars had held for the criminal code. Despite this distance from Plekhanov, Trotsky considered Aleksinskii a permanent fixture of social-patriotic literature, for 'without him all Russian social-patriotic literature would appear insipid, like a Petrushka without its own special smell'.[57]

In early February 1916 Trotsky returned to the last of his three suggestions regarding the 'Belorussov' affair, reporting that the Literary Society had censured Belorussov. However, a current rumour was claiming Aleksinskii as a member of the Literary Society. Trotsky dismissed the rumour as a misunderstanding:

A Society that welcomed Liebknecht would not have accepted Aleksinskii. It is impossible that in censuring the non-member Belorussov, the Society would not have first swept-out the rubbish from its own ranks. This is why the rumour of Aleksinskii's continuing membership of the Society is a simple misunderstanding.[58]

Later that month, Trotsky's commentary upon Plekhanov's writings touched upon Russian domestic politics. Writing in *Prizyv*, Plekhanov considered Khvostov's, Russia's Minister of Internal Affairs, utterance that Russians should 'produce shrapnel, prepare ammunition, but be spared from involvement in government'.[59] For Plekhanov, Khvostov, speaking at the War-Industries Committee, displayed an arrogance typical of the Russian government. Khvostov clearly expected loyalty and service but was not prepared to concede anything by way of political reform in return. Plekhanov was clearly disgusted, and looked forward to the day when Russia would liberate itself from its reactionary political order. He worried, however, lest Khvostov's indifference might lend credibility to defeatist agitation.[60] If the workers followed the defeatists' advice, Russia would be more likely to suffer a military collapse. But who, asked Plekhanov, would benefit from Russia's defeat? Not, he replied, those wanting a democratic Russia but reactionaries of Khvostov's persuasion. A policy based upon a free Russia issuing from defeat in the war was deeply mistaken:

> From the very outset of this current war I did not cease believing that our reactionaries did not wish to defeat Germany because its Emperor was the most trusted supporter of European reaction. Events have shown that I was right ... Victorious over Russia a mighty Germany would instal a government in Russia that would be the most advantageous to Germany. What government could be more advantageous than a government of the Black Hundreds?[61]

Thus, concluded Plekhanov, only the extreme right would welcome *en masse* desertion of the War-Industries Committees by Russia's workers. The duty of all those interested in the introduction of politically progressive measures was therefore clear: to remain firmly in support of Russia's war effort.

In his rejoinder Trotsky doubted that Khvostov and his cohorts would rejoice at the sight of workers abandoning Russia's defences. After all, argued Trotsky, it was Khvostov who had recommended distribution of Plekhanov's manifesto calling upon the workers to elect representatives to the War-Industries Committees, and it was the Russian Minister of the Interior who had helped Kuz'ma Gvozdev to falsify the will of the Petrograd workers. For Trotsky, Plekhanov accepted the appointment of right-wing candidates to ministerial posts as this signified the defeat of the revolutionary internationalists, but was not prepared to go along with their more extreme statements: '"Walk apart but live together!" – this is the strategic principle which Plekhanov transfers into his new period when he helps reaction be revolutionary.'[62]

V. Buslaev's enthusiastic account of a recent session of the State Duma, published in *Prizyv*, provoked a critical response from Trotsky. Buslaev highlighted the Progressive Bloc's demands, put forward in an elaborate programme which called, among other things, for a political and religious amnesty and Polish autonomy, as evidence of 'what a mighty lever healthy patriotism is in Russia's political awakening'.[63] He recounted how the Progressives had stuck to their guns in the face of harsh criticism from Goremykin and soothing noises from Stümer; sufficient grounds for Buslaev to claim 'how quickly the bourgeois opposition in Russia matures under a general optimism'.[64] The most striking feature of recent political events, according to Buslaev, was the support given to the opposition by right-wing, previously pro-government thinkers: 'We are not used to Milyukov's criticism receiving constant support … from Purishkevich and for the right nationalist Polovtsev to speak against the government.'[65] He fired a shot at 'sad doctrinaires and spent revolutionaries [who] rashly declared that under imperialist economies national revolutions are impossible'. Historical progress clearly did not follow the rules of newly-born Marxist cosmopolitans: 'Russia is on the eve of great events … a great people … cannot be restrained by the chains of this cosmopolitanism's reactionary schemas … Russia is liberating itself and it calls upon all those who are alive!'[66]

In a reply to Buslaev Trotsky gave a very different evaluation of the Russian bourgeoisie. The Russian social-patriot's hopes upon the bourgeoisie as a political force were misplaced, wrote Trotsky, because it did not want to take power: 'the central tenet of this bourgeoisie, as the recent Kadet conference once again confirmed, is a *victory in the war and not a will to power*.'[67] Its obsession with victory derived from its connections with imperialism and the military-monarchical regime. According to Trotsky, the bourgeoisie wanted the Prussification of the Russian state order and it was this which lay behind its opposition to Nicholas II: 'Its opposition … is limited by the objective position of the bourgeoisie, to pressurising the bureaucratic monarchy into … pulling itself together, purifying itself, putting its affairs in order … in a word, *Prussification*.'[68] For Trotsky, only the proletariat could wrest power from the old régimé. If the proletariat went for power 'the bourgeoisie would go over to the side of the old order'.[69] Buslaev had claimed that history had a shock in store for Marxists, Trotsky foresaw history preparing a special surprise for Buslaev: 'the historical mission of our social-patriotic Germans is to help the Russian bourgeoisie reach – alas! alas! – the German state order when its radical destruction is being prepared in Germany itself.'[70]

Trotsky stressed the links between the social-patriots in Paris and the old order in Russia in his May Day reflections of 1916. He cited Khvostov's approval of Plekhanov's Autumn 1915 'Manifesto to the Russian workers' as evidence of a Khvostov–Plekhanov Bloc. For Trotsky, 'the combination of Khvostov and Plekhanov (and think of this for one minute as a fresh fact!) is one of the most fantastic aspects of the whole contemporary Russian fantastica.'[71] While even Kadets were complaining about censorship of their speeches, Trotsky reported that the Russian authorities broadcast *Prizyv*'s calls for a successful defence of Russia as freely as the outpourings of the police department. He praised the Russian social-patriots in Paris for having the musical ability of turning the tune of the International into a hymn to Khvostov, even if 'it is impossible to compose anything more loathsome.'[72]

If Trotsky thought the Plekhanov–Khvostov alliance was holding up well, despite its rocky patches, 'Two Magnitudes, Separately Equal to a Third ...' discussed Plekhanov's difficulties in building an International. The elder statesman of Russian Marxism could claim allies in France (Hevré), Britain (Hyndman) and Italy (Mussolini), but what, asked Trotsky, of Germany? This could be sidestepped if Plekhanov followed advice that the International should be drawn from the free countries of the Entente, excluding Hohenzollern Germany. Of course, Plekhanov would avoid the difficult task of defining freedom to include Tashkent but exclude Berlin. However, a possible solution had been offered by Hevré, recently promoted by Plekhanov to 'comrade' after the French socialist had rejected his earlier unpatriotic views to support France in the war.[73] According to Trotsky, Hevré was arguing that the future for socialism in western Europe lay in national socialist parties. In Germany Hevré thought that Südekum should head this party, since 'it should unite with the left bourgeois parties and with their help establish a parliamentary régimé in Germany'.[74] For Trotsky, because Plekhanov had named Hevré his comrade one could follow the mathematical principle that 'two magnitudes separately equal to a third are equal between them-selves' to conclude that Plekhanov's German comrade would be

Südekum. This could only infuriate Plekhanov, who had criticised Südekum as a German-Austrian Social-Democratic imperialist.[75] However, Trotsky could take pride that a previous guess had now been confirmed by mathematics.

The attitude of *Prizvy*'s editorial board to high-level diplomatic links between France and Russia formed the background to Trotsky's 'Why we did not mention Plekhanov'.[76] In a *Prizyv* editorial on Albert Thomas's visit to Nicholas II, the censor had removed all but a reprint of the official communiqué of Thomas's trip to Russia.[77] Five days later an unsigned article in *Nashe Slovo* ridiculed *Prizyv*'s annoyance – deduced from the censor's intervention – at the French minister's presence at the Russian court. *Nashe Slovo* pointed out that the republicans Avksent'ev, Lyubimov, Argunov and Bunakov had revealed their political allegiances by printing 'his majesty the emperor' in lower case letters. However, it also asked the editors if their advanced years had really taught them so little. After all, *Prizyv* supported the Entente and urged socialists to join war time ministries. Did the social-patriotic publication really think that republican ministers would avoid meeting their autocratically governed allies when common war aims had to be discussed? Moreover, *Nashe Slovo* claimed that the censor had rendered *Prizyv* a useful service: the headline and the editorial board's signature remained as testimony of republican disquiet at the French government's contact with the Tsar, but they had been spared from making their specific grievances public. Finally, a popular proverb was offered to *Prizyv* by way of advice: 'one has to take the rough with the smooth.'[78]

In 'Why We Did Not Mention Plekhanov' Trotsky noted that several attentive readers had said that Plekhanov was not listed in *Nashe Slovo*'s naming of *Prizyv*'s republican-minded editors. In an imaginary dialogue conducted between two *Nashe Slovo* readers Trotsky illustrated a hidden motive which may have lain behind the omission. One reader claims that Plekhanov was not named out of a desire to protect a fellow Marxist:

> It is true that they ... named Lyubimov who is also a 'Marxist', but this is safe for if he compromises something it is only him himself. But Plekhanov was not named. And Aleksinskii was not named. At this point our perspicacious Philistine (and that is exactly what we are dealing with) immediately feels jubilant: one has caught *Nashe Slovo* harbouring Plekhanov!
>
> But this is pure rubbish, exclaims, say, another reader ... When

has *Nashe Slovo* indulged Marxist social-patriots? When has it harboured Plekhanov?

Yes ... but about Plekhanov not a whisper. This is not easy ...[79]

Trotsky cut the conversation short and resolved the point at issue. Aleksinskii had been omitted as part of a general policy of avoiding his name out of considerations of a 'literary-sanitary nature'.[80] The silence surrounding Plekhanov was due to more profound reasons. When *Nashe Slovo* had surmised *Prizyv*'s hurt republican feelings it had decided that Plekhanov was not offended, for 'he is not inclined to invent a conscience-stricken republicanism; his "trade" is straight-forward patriotism.'[81] Trotsky concluded that there was an important moral for the wise Philistine: 'Political criticism, like so much else in our complex life, demands differentiation. And if it is necessary to discover unity in variety then one has to be able to observe variety in unity. So there, Mr. wise Philistine!'[82]

Russian military success on the Austrian front brought a jubilant response from Boris Voronov. Writing in *Prizyv*,[83] he argued that the heroic efforts of the Russian soldiers had refuted recent declarations hostile to Russia's cause. The supposition underpinning Zimmerwald's call for the cessation of the war, no side would emerge victorious from the general stalemate, was false. The Menshevik Organisational Committee's prediction that Russia would collapse after one year of hostilities had similarly been disproved. Furthermore, the German General Staff's confidence that Russia would not be able to launch an offensive attack had evaporated, the Central Powers had lost the military initiative. Voronov looked forward to the fall of the German monarch which would pull the symbolic ground from under the tsar's feet. A Russian victory would signal the death-knell of Tsarism: 'Breaking the Austrian front and breaking the Zimmerwald front Russian soldiers bring us closer to our desired outcome to the war and to Russia's internal freedom.'[84]

Trotsky responded to Voronov's analysis in 'Arguments from the Hoof'.[85] He did not name Voronov, but stated that *Prizyv* was quite wrong to claim that Zimmerwald connected its politics to the strate-gic manoeuvres of the warring nations. Zimmerwald rooted its tactics in the interrelation of forces between the revolutionary proletariat and capitalist imperialism, and the fortunes of Russia's soldiers could not undermine this approach. *Prizyv*'s damning conclusion about Zimmerwald was dismissed as 'clearly absurd'. Trotsky explained the social-patriotic newspaper's willingness to discuss socialism with reference to the biographies of its contributors, several of whom were former socialists. However, the conclusions reached on the basis of a past interest in socialism obviously exceeded their authors' intelligence. For Trotsky, if the whole intellectual baggage of the Russian social-patriots could be placed upon a Cossack horse, Zimmerwald's position 'cannot be shattered by an argument from the hoof'.[86]

If the articles surrounding Thomas's visit to Russia gave cause for Trotsky to express his low opinion of Aleksinskii, the 'Dmitriev affair' provided the best opportunity to date for a resounding dismissal of the Russian Social-Patriot. In May 1916 a campaign had been launched by Yakovlev and Belorussov to remove Dmitriev from his post as chairman of the Foreign Press Syndicate.[87] The main rallying call of the campaign was Dmitriev's Germanophilism in view of his editorship of *Parizhiskii Vestnik*, which, according to Yakovlev and his supporters, had conducted pro-German propaganda on the eve of the war. On 10 August 1916 the Foreign Journalists' Society met to discuss the case against Dmitriev and dismissed it. This was then confirmed at meetings of the Society of Russian Journalists in Paris and the Foreign Press Syndicate. The Society of Russian Journalists in Paris highlighted Aleksinskii as having played the most dishonourable role of all in the Dmitriev affair.

Trotsky retold the events surrounding the Dmitriev affair in 'A Story with a Moral', which was concerned most of all in pinpointing the leading and supporting players in the drama. Trotsky claimed that Yakovlev and Jean d'Arc (*Russkia Vedomosti*) were the 'real organisers'. Bateaut, a French journalist, was recruited 'so that in the eyes of foreign correspondents the affair would not have been immediately laid bare as Russian intrigue'.[88] Aleksinskii had been instructed to make the accusations broad so that Dmitriev could be kept under suspicion of Germanophilism for as long as possible. Meanwhile, Trotsky pointed out that Belorussov had written for *Parizhskii Vestnik* so when Aleksinskii said that this journal had been financed from German funds, 'Belorussov had to quickly inform himself: I myself received German money from Dmitriev'.[89] For Trotsky, the classification of the social-patriot scandal mongers into generals and foot-soldiers was instructive as it showed how they were prepared to do dirty work if it served their cause. In his concluding paragraph Trotsky sprung what was perhaps the most scandalous aspect of the whole business upon the reader. Why had Dmitriev not raised a clamour in his employer's newspaper *Rech* against what was, after all, groundless slander? According to Trotsky, Dmitriev's silence was due to his willingness to subordinate himself to the same patriotic cause which had motivated Aleksinskii:

> for the cause which *Rech* serves, Milyukov, Dmitriev himself, and Aleksinskii are all essential. And if in a common cause there falls upon them some secondary harm which corresponds to the objective nature of the business and to the subjective nature of the participants, then they all consider this an inevitable scar in the process of holy cooperation. This is the main moral of the story.[90]

In 'Vandervelde, *Nashe Slovo* and *Vorwärts'* Trotsky defended the accuracy of his newspaper's informants after D.S., writing in *Prizyv*, had questioned the veracity of an earlier *Nashe Slovo* scoop. The origin of this exchange was an earlier short note in *Nashe Slovo*, reporting an incident which had prevented Emile Vandervelde from making a speech at the front.[91] *Nashe Slovo* claimed that the Belgium minister had been so confused by a Belgium soldier's reference to the contradiction between Vandervelde's current and pre-war views that he abandoned his platform without having uttered one word. This story was then picked-up by other newspapers. *Prizyv* commented on the story only after one of the newspapers published a disclaimer. D.S. quoted *Vorwärts* which stated that information received from Amsterdam had shown that *Nashe Slovo's* story was 'devoid of all basis in fact. We regret that we have been misled by this usually well-informed source.'[92] D.S. then challenged *Nashe Slovo* to carry a corrigendum.

Trotsky took up this challenge, but not in the manner dictated by D.S. On the contrary, he asked why *Vorwärts* had taken its Amsterdam source at face value. In order to refute *Nashe Slovo's* article one would have to have done two things: conduct a survey among Belgian soldiers and question Vandervelde. The first option was impossible, but Trotsky stressed the good credentials of the Belgian soldier who had given the story to *Nashe Slovo*: the soldier shared Vandervelde's views on the war and would not want to embarrass his minister by making something up. Moreover, he claimed that it was most likely Vandervelde who was hiding behind the anonymous informer from Amsterdam. Vandervelde himself could not be seen to have contact with a German newspaper. Furthermore, in his final paragraph Trotsky highlighted a reprint of one of Vandervelde's speeches in the previous day's *Le Petit Parisien* as further evidence for *Nashe Slovo's* version of events. In his address Vandervelde spoke of the high personal qualities of the French soldiers. For Trotsky,

> Vandervelde ... was recommending Belgium soldiers to be like the French, modest and satisfied with the bread, wine and meat supplied by King Albert's quartermaster. One wonders whether among his enforced listeners was the socialist who advised the former chairman of the International to limit his future oratorical excursions to back alleys.[93]

Nashe Slovo resurrected the Dmitriev affair in early September 1916, publishing the resolutions of the three aforementioned societies.[94] On the following day Trotsky submitted the first of two articles in which he focused upon Aleksinskii's actions in the Dmitriev affair.

In the first, '*Prizyv* and Its Aleksinskii', Trotsky pointed out that Aleksinskii's contributions to a German journal before the war had not prevented him from levelling a similar accusation at Dmitriev.[95] Indeed, Aleksinskii's articles were so powerful in their pro-German stance that 'the censor has not permitted us to cite even one passage from them'.[96] Moreover, Trotsky claimed that it was Aleksinskii who, after being co-opted as a leading actor in the Dmitriev affair, had carried the accusations to such a level that the 'evil-blackmail character of the whole campaign became clear to all'.[97] The extent of Aleksinskii's disgraceful behaviour was clear as it was his fellow bourgeois-journalists who had condemned him. But, Trotsky noted, *Prizyv* had not uttered one word: 'The slanderous Aleksinskii continues his work as the most trusted brother-in-arms of Plekhanov, Avksent'ev, Bunakov, Voronov, Argunov and Lyubimov.'[98]

In the very next issue of *Nashe Slovo*, Trotsky examined the Dmitriev affair from the point of view of 'Aleksinskii and his *Prizyv*'.[99] Trotsky wondered why Aleksinskii, more than one month after the three press societies had censured him, had not written a self-defence in *Prizyv*. The answer lay in his editorial colleagues' desire to avoid implicating themselves. After all, if they permitted Aleksinskii to conduct his counter-attack in *Prizyv* they would be exposing themselves to charges of abetting. It was their refusal to back him which, claimed Trotsky, prevented Aleksinskii from issuing his own appeal. But, then, what could Aleksinskii say in such an appeal, apart from 'his closest friends Avksent'ev, Voronov, Bunakov, Lyubimov, Argunov and Plekhanov had refused him support and refuge on a matter upon which a man's political life and death normally depends'.[100] For Trotsky the heart of the matter was clear. Aleksinskii and *Prizyv* were united in a common, though hostile, 'agreement with an ineffaceable censure'.[101]

These were to be Trotsky's last words on the Russian social-patriots in Paris before *Nashe Slovo* was banned. His disagreements with Plekhanov and his supporters were clear. Trotsky condemned the war, wheras the social-patriots accepted that, for some, the war was justified and just. The polemics which raged between the two sides were rooted in their different approaches to the war, but they often descended into trading insults. The Dmitriev and Belorussov affairs were of local interest and left no lasting consequences. Recounting them today may seem a dry exercise in exposition. However, they provide an insight into the atmosphere in which Trotsky lived and worked. That the exchanges sometimes approached the level of 'gutter journalism' is also indicative of the passion which each side invested in the debates, and of how much they thought was at stake. In short, Trotsky and the social-patriots were fighting for influence over the workers. According to Trotsky, the Social-Patriots could only lead the masses into the class enemy's camp. It was for this reason that, as a revolutionary socialist, he thought the propaganda war against *Prizyv* and *Novosti* to be of supreme importance. His urgent concern to oppose social-patriotism will also feature in the next chapter, which deals with Trotsky's analysis of Russian domestic politics in his Paris writings.

7
Russian Politics

The late Russian historian Dmitrii Volkogonov has presented Trotsky as becoming increasingly indifferent to his homeland while in exile.[1] This view is wrong if we judge by Trotsky's Paris writings of World War One. Although he subsequently explained his acceptance of *Kievskaya Mysl*'s invitation to be its war correspondent in Paris as a chance to learn more about French politics, developments in Russia were a constant source of attention. This chapter will examine Trotsky's writings on his homeland thematically, i.e. liberalism, the government and, finally, the battle between Social-Patriotism and Social-Democracy among the workers. Each section follows Trotsky's thoughts as they developed chronologically. Although the material has been divided in this way for the purpose of exposition, the connections which Trotsky traced between these various political strains will be stressed; most notably, how social-patriotism, through liberalism, was a link of a chain tying workers to tsarism and the war. In criticising each link of this chain Trotsky hoped he could break the chain itself, in this way fomenting the revolution.

Liberalism

Russian liberals were given an opportunity to respond to Germany's declaration of war at a one-day session of the Duma. At this 'historic' sitting the respective leaders of the Octobrists, Progressists and Kadets in, for most, a sharp reversal of recent policy, declared their allegiance to the Russian government at a time of national need. The Kadet leader, Professor Pavel Milyukov, for example, had opposed a European conflict as late as mid-July.[2] However, motivated by a mixture of patriotic sentiment and self-interest the liberals helped make the Duma session what Milyukov described as 'a grandiose expression of national unity'.[3]

Trotsky went onto the offensive against Russian liberalism in only his fourth contribution to *Golos*.[4] He ridiculed Milyukov's view of the war as a battle for the destruction of militarism and the strengthening of democracy, an idea repeated many times and by people of various political persuasions. Speaking with irony, Trotsky stated how comforting it was to hear Milyukov's confirmation of Russia's preparedness, in spite of financial difficulties, to join the struggle for democracy at a time when parliamentary Britain and republican France were too weak to do so. After expressing confusion over whether the perception of Russia's liberating role belonged originally to Milyukov or to Nicholas II, Trotsky asked how the programme to end militarism and establish democracy would be implemented? Milyukov's statement that 'victorious democracy will bring universal disarmament' could only be understood as an invitation to France and Britain to declare war on Russia. Or, teased Trotsky, was Milyukov including Russia on the list of victorious democratic countries as Sobakevich counted Elizabeth Vorob'ya as a man? It was this uncomfortable conclusion which, Trotsky speculated, forced the Kadet leader to turn to the deficiencies of Russia's internal political order.

According to Milyukov, Russians were dissatisfied with existing political structures, a dissatisfaction expressed on the war's eve by mass strikes and most recently in the war against Germany. For Trotsky, this was reaction's use of the war as a diversion to cover its own weaknesses, even if the government had not been able to fool all of the people. Social-Democratic workers and deputies were attempting to expose the government's camouflage. Indeed, *Golos* itself had not sprung out of a vacuum, but represented views held by many inside Russia. However, it was clear that Milyukov supported the government swindlers, a reflection of 'the modest historical role of Russian liberalism [which] consists precisely of this!'[5]

There was however some agreement between the Russian revolutionary and the Russian liberal. Trotsky conceded Milyukov's argument that a country conducting a war in the name of democracy was obliged to pass democratic reforms. The problem for the *Golos* correspondent, however, was that Russia was not battling for democracy: 'Undoubtedly the conquest of Galicia, Persia, Armenia, Constantinople and the Straits spurs on the development of Russian capitalism. But, on this basis, it is not democracy but rapacious imperialism which triumphs.'[6] Milyukov's trump card – the assertion that victory over Germany would abolish drunkenness – was rejected as Russians were currently drinking 'methylated spirit and varnish'.

At this point Trotsky reported that he had not exhausted Milyukov's views but he already felt uneasy after holding the reader at Russian liberalism's political level for so long. According to Trotsky, future historians would write of World War One as a time not only of barbarism and foolishness but also of stupidity and hypocrisy. Since the true nature of tsarism was so obvious, Russian liberalism had to expend so much energy on hypocrisy and stupidity in presenting Russia's 'liberating mission'. Trotsky expressed his disdain for Milyukov by drawing a parallel between the Kadet leader and Gregus, a secret police agent who had tortured prisoners in Riga after the 1905 revolution:

> Previously he managed the torture chamber and burned the heels of imprisoned democrats with state candles. And now ... with the same state candles in hand he is called upon to play the role of the torch bearer of democracy. The people have a right to peace and freedom from militarism. Gregus will give them both, murdering by the democratic list.[7]

In the summer and autumn of 1915 the Russian government, faced with shortages of weapons and ammunition and demands for an increased role for society in the administration of the war effort in the wake of a series of military setbacks which started with the retreat of May 1915 from Galicia, established a series of committees which included lay members. The first of these new organisations, the Special Commission on Defence of the Country, was introduced in July 1915 and was responsibile for mobilising the nation's industrial economy for war. Pressure soon mounted for similar committees to be established elsewhere. Trotsky commented that the tasks, composition and powers of these proposed bodies were as yet undefined. Nevertheless, the idea of encouraging society to play a more active role in directing the war already formed the 'politics of "the rear"' of the bourgeois opposition, a strategy supported by social-patriots:

> as far as the bourgeois opposition shows signs of life it remains completely patriotic. Given that the exceptionally weak mobilisation of society's forces takes place in the name of a firmer 'national defence', one could have said that Guchkov and Milyukov were plagiarising their politics from Plekhanov, if only Plekhanov's

whole position was not a sad borrowing from Guchkov's and Milyukov's fund.[8]

Trotsky pointed out that the idea of the Special Commission had been taken from Britain, but there were good reasons why one could not expect much benefit from its application in the Russian context. Britain had a mighty and modern capitalist economy combined with a flexible democratic state structure, but even in this favourable environment not much had been achieved. What hope then the Russian variant, which included plans to build a railway network, new factories and educate new technocrats? For Trotsky this programme, as the Russian government knew-well, was a 'pure Utopia'. Why then take this initiative? According to Trotsky, the government wanted to transfer direct economic responsibility for the war effort to the propertied classes. In return the propertied classes had neither demanded nor been promised political power. In actual fact what was occurring was an artificial coming together of the propertied classes and the government, with the former talking of trust as though the disappointments of the post-1905 constitutional experiments had never happened.

Following on from this analysis Trotsky issued several warnings to the liberals, including an aside which once again linked liberalism and social-patriotism. First, the ministries had handed responsibility to 'committees of national defence' only as a ploy to better protect the concentration of power in the ministries' hands, i.e., the committees could be blamed for any mistakes while the ministries continued to take the decisions. Moreover, tactically, the liberals had tied-up their hands. Milyukov could not demand a new session of the Duma since he could not call the government to account, rather, Milyukov himself would be questioned for his trust in the government. On the other hand, the Kadet leader could not insist that the military-society committees should replace the ministries, for 'the Kadet Party would lose its final opportunity for opposition: between the policies of the state and its material-technical resources and methods. This is the very same position in which Plekhanov and other social-patriots attempt to bury the politics of the party of the proletariat.'[9] In this situation the tasks of opposing the governmental regime lay more heavily upon the Russian proletariat than at any other time.

Highlighting the hopelessness of the liberal programme was the intention of a piece which examined the links between the Russian liberals and the French republicans.[10] According to Trotsky's report, the Russian democrats were inspired by Clemenceau's and Hevré's view that republican democracy guaranteed the triumph of the people over both stagnant bureaucracy and selfish capitalist cliques. He argued that the Russian liberals were so enthused by their French counterparts that they had forgotten to call for ministerial responsibility, a basic principle without which parliamentary control is meaningless. Moreover, Trotsky highlighted several reasons why the Russian liberals should not be so enamoured with the French experience. The result of France's 1792 revolution had not been the victory of democracy over capitalist imperialism, but the use of the former to check the excesses of the latter, an outcome to which even tsarism would not object. However, even the French 'democratic' order could not be achieved in Russia through the war. Russia had had no '1792' and no democratic institutions when tsarism entered the imperialist age. In this sense, 'Russian imperialism came too early, or Russian parliamentarianism too late'.[11] Whatever the case, for Trotsky, the Western liberal democratic option was not available for Russia. Milyukov and Guchkov had worked in governmental committees for several years and had not had any influence. Milyukov had accused the War Ministry of tricking the Duma and threatened court action, but this was nothing more than an 'oratorical gesture'. For Trotsky, the social force of the coming revolution was the Russian proletariat, and it did not link its fate with victory in the war. And since the Duma was a 'convent of confusion and impotence', for progress to occur 'the rulers' confusion will have to be overcome by the decisiveness and strength of those who are ruled and those who are fooled'.[12]

The increasing failure of liberal politics was analysed in the aptly named 'Events are proceeding by their own course'.[13] On 22 August 1915 the newly formed Progressive Bloc issued a statement which, among other things, called for the establishment of a government of national unity to lead Russia to victory.[14] Right-wing groups and publications immediately protested against the Progressive Bloc and called upon the government to disperse the Duma. The Tsar, urged on by his conservative prime minister Goremykin, duly complied, closing the Duma in early September 1915 because of the prevailing 'state of emergency'. According to Trotsky, the government had organised right-wing opposition, Black Hundread congresses, etc. to the Progressive Bloc, so as to give itself a pretext for shutting the troublesome Duma. The call should come from 'society' since a government-led initiative would arouse too much liberal opposition. In actual fact, Trotsky pointed out, the government need not have worried itself. The liberal coalition had disintegrated at the first sight of the Black Hundred meetings: 'the "centre" bloc in the State Duma – and forming this centre was Milyukov's greatest victory! – immediately moved to the right and after the Black Hundred Congresses issued ambiguous statements from which only one thing was clear: the residents of Peterhof could sleep peacefully.'[15] For Trotsky, the liberals had capitulated so quickly that a whole number of Black Hundred meetings, organised by the bureaucracy, had nothing to do. Instead they became arenas for sacked ministers to plot against their successors. In the meantime events were progressing by their own course: the national economy had lost millions of good workers to the war effort, the war was dislocating the economy and transport, prices were rising and the printing presses were working flat out, and the government was corrupt. For Trotsky, this sorry state of affairs was leading to revolution, not liberal reform: 'if today the Progressive Bloc is pacified by the government, tomorrow is preparing a rude awakening for them.'[16]

In May 1916 Trotsky had the chance to take a closer look at Milyukov when he visited Paris.[17] A sarcastic and critical account of Milyukov's programme duly appeared in *Nashe Slovo*. Trotsky belittled the status of the Russian liberal's trip. Milyukov was in Paris to strengthen ties with the Allies only a few weeks after Russia had been embarrassed by its exclusion from an Allied economic conference. It was because Russia's standing was low that Milyukov's first interview appeared not in the official *Temps* nor even in the semi-official *Matin*, but in the 'reactionary-radical-anti-Semitic-blackmailing *Œuvre*'.[18] Trotsky then discredited Milyukov's views, partly through portraying Milyukov's performance in the interview in the worst possible light. The *Œuvre* reporter apparently embarrassed the Kadet leader when, in response to Milyukov's assertion that the Russian army was ready for attack and only awaiting orders, he asked why such orders had not been given? After all, in view of the Austrian attack on the Italian front was not the time ripe for a counter-attack? Trotsky pointed out that Milyukov felt no need to respond, merely asserting that the French government would no doubt be delighted to hear of the Russian army's healthy condition, something the French government would hardly deny.

Milyukov became much more animated when he spoke of his hopes and desires for Russia's spoils from the war, including open access to the Straits. This would spur on the Russian economy and resolve the Eastern Question for Britain and France. Milyukov was asked how these very practical reasons related to the struggle for national self-determination and the rule of law? He dismissed this question as based upon a 'romanticism ... [which] disappeared from politics long ago'; anybody who considered the war 'defensive' did so out of ignorance. Trotsky could have argued that Milyukov had encouraged such 'ignorance'. After all, in December 1914 he had criticised Milyukov's then view of the war as a struggle for democracy. However, Trotsky only hinted at this contradiction between the Kadet leader's former and current position by inserting an exclamation mark in the following citation from the interview: 'They fooled themselves (ils s'imaginaient!) that the war had a purely defensive character ... '[19] The explicit line of attack that Trotsky adopted was an unflattering comparison between Milyukov and Bethmann-Hollweg. Milyukov's anti-romanticism sounded very much like Bethmann-Hollweg's justification for Germany's march through Belgium on its way to the sea: 'We have forgotten about sentimentality'. However, wrote Trotsky, the Russian liberal need not concern himself with sharing the same ideological ground as his German opponent, one important feature differentiated Milyukov from Bethmann-Hollweg. The former did not know when to shut up. For example, Milyukov suggested that British phlegmatic determination to withstand the war derived from the fortunate psychological effects of the German Zeppelins. For Trotsky, this stupidity was evidence enough that Milyukov had understood that romanticism had indeed disappeared from politics, but Milyukov had not understood that realism does not consist of making such admissions.

Milyukov arrived back in Russia just in time to participate in the remaining few days of the latest Duma session. Trotsky analysed the gap between expectations of a more powerful and active Duma and its supplementary role in 'Disappointments and Worries'.[20] He began by outlining why one could have expected a more influential Duma. Did Milyukov's recent trips to the Allied countries not signify the Kadet leader's seniority? Surely such a vital mission could only have been entrusted to a leading state actor. Given that Milyukov represented the Duma, was this not a reflection of its importance? Finally, the Russian army was successfully advancing on the Galician front, and it was the liberal's view that victory brought democratic reforms in its trail. When the War-Industries Committees were being praised for their role in recent Russian victories, should one not expect liberal policy to begin to pay dividends? Perhaps, but Trotsky argued that the reverse was happening.

The government had preceded the opening of the Duma with laws relating to the management of the war economy, measures which *excluded* a role for society's representatives. The right wing had been mobilised to call for the Duma to be closed, as it was irrelevant. The reaction of the liberal member of the War-Industries Committees, Guchkov, was to complain that times were hard. The liberal forecast of greater democracy following victory was being falsified. However, for Trotsky, the liberals were not so much dumbfounded by the obvious failure of their strategy, but were helping the government. Three hurriedly prepared pieces of social legislation (sickness payments for workers fulfilling ministries' orders, inspectors for female factory labour, and rest periods for goods workers) were evidence of the liberals' and the government's desire to pacify the workers. In response, Trotsky called upon Social-Democrats to urge the workers to have no confidence in liberal social reformism and to organise revolutionary activity.

Trotsky presented one of his most damning critiques of Russian liberalism in 'Lessons of the Last Duma Session' which, it claimed, reeked from the Progressive Bloc's politically decomposing bodies.[21] To illustrate Trotsky focused upon the limited nature of the Progressive Bloc's demands on the peasant question. According to Trotsky, the peasants had been so squeezed by the war effort that the government feared peasant discontent. In these circumstances winning concessions for the peasants should have been relatively easy. However, the Progressive Bloc had merely suggested that certain legal inequalities be repealed, on the basis that this was all that the Tsar would approve. For Trotsky, this was typical of the Progressive Bloc's general approach of tailoring demands to suit the monarchy, the bureaucracy and the nobility. This was why the liberals had not seized upon the peasants' legal inequalities to attack a whole series of similar cases, national, religious, and Jewish. It was a failure to capitalise upon government weakness that made the bankruptcy of liberal politics all too obvious:

If Russian history of the past decade has shown anything beyond all doubt it is the absolute futility of placing one's hopes and trust on the strengthening of Russian liberalism's democratic-opposition. Standing openly and demonstratively for imperialist cooperation and basing all its policies upon this cooperation, liberalism only completed the whole of its preceding evolution as prepared by the national and international conditions of its development. The liberal opposition is just as unable to abandon its imperialist foundations as it is unable to generate an energetic opposition.[22]

Milyukov's trips to the Allied countries once again drew Trotsky's attention in August 1916,[23] after Milyukov's foreign impressions appeared in the Russian liberal newspaper *Rech*. Trotsky claimed that despite the fact that Milyukov's work bore the usual hallmarks of a liberal pen, mainly impudence and stupidity, his remarks were worth analysing for their curious facts and generalisations.

A first instalment focused upon Milyukov's account of his conversations with the French socialists Renaudel and Longuet, in which the Kadet tailored his remarks to reassure his co-conversationalists. For example, when Renodel asked about Russian pretensions on the Straits, Poland and Persia he was not reminded of his 'naiveté'. Rather, Milyukov played to the French Socialist Party's pacifism to stress that Russia was not an imperialist country. After all, had not Milyukov propogated pacifism before and during the war, against which the issue of Russian expansion paled into insignificance? Evidently not so for Trotsky.

Trotsky also thought that Milyukov's duplicity slipped out in a discussion of whether tsarism would survive a Russian defeat. Milyukov separated the two issues. Reaction could be changed over the short-term whereas the war's outcome would determine Russia's long-term fate. How one viewed tsarism need not be connected in any way with Russian military success. The war could be supported because the fate of future generations depended upon it. Tsarism could be dealt with in a relatively short time following victory. Furthermore, the failure of defeatism in 1905 had revealed the flaws in this tactic not only to the liberal, but also to the Narodnik and Marxist intelligentsia. Similarly, the problems of Poland, Persia and the Straits were the product of a long-standing foreign policy, solvable only in the long term. Trotsky was not impressed by Milyukov's distinctions. The Russian liberal had constructed an argument for revolutionary action against Tsarism and Russia's defence only to please his left-wing company. After all, Milyukov had expressed his real view of the relation between defeatism and revolution in the State Duma, where he had pronounced that if victory could only be achieved through revolution then he would renounce victory. So much for the concerns of future generations! For Trotsky, Milyukov understood that an overthrow of Tsarism which guaranteed victory, strengthening the bourgeoisie, would soon develop into a full-blown proletarian revolution and the death of liberalism. This was why Milyukov would do anything to avoid revolution: 'Twelve years ago Milyukov called for defeatism as it spurred on revolution. Now he would accept defeat if only to avoid revolution. The Russian liberal said nothing of this historical U-turn to his French company.'[24]

A second instalment of 'The Generalisations and Impressions of Mr Milyukov' examined Milyukov's account of the Zimmerwald Conference. According to Trotsky's report, Milyukov claimed that Longuet had first to be defeated before French left-wingers could call for an internationalist socialist gathering. Syndicalists had then joined up with the official Italian Socialist Party and had attracted the support of minority groups in Paris and London. The aim of an international gathering was finally achieved through the auspices of German Social-Democracy. Trotsky pinpointed several inaccuracies in Milyukov's version. The left-wing in French politics began their activities while Longuet was still a minister. Zimmerwald had not taken place through the efforts of German Social-Democracy. The German party, like the French, was split. In both parties the right opposed Zimmerwald as an initiative of the revolutionary left. In referring to German Social-Democracy's important role Milyukov, according to Trotsky, was trying to damn Zimmerwald as 'Pan-German intrigue', relying upon 'ignorance and stupidity'.

Trotsky was more impressed by Milyukov's understanding of the fractions within French socialism: the right majority, the Longuetist minority and the Zimmerwaldists. Milyukov noted that the minority had recently abandoned the majority, asking the International Socialist Bureau to investigate the possibility of renewing ties between the various sections of the Second International. However, Milyukov stated that there was no need for concern over the apparent fall in the right's support. The minority still voted for war credits and served in war cabinets. Moreover, the Zimerwaldists had been forced to vote for the minority, lacking sufficient strength to put forward their own demand of an immediate recall of all sections of the International to purge them of nationalism.

For Trotsky, Milyukov had correctly analysed the dangers of Longuetism. By voting with the minority the Zimmerwaldists had defeated themselves; Longuetism had acted as 'a fresh link in a complex chain attaching the working masses to the existing regime',[25] the French equivalent of social-patriotism in Russia. However, credit for Milyukov's acumen could not be laid at the Kadet leader's door. In Paris Milyukov had received *Golos* and *Nashe Slovo* and his analysis of fractions in French socialism was taken straight from their pages with, however, one notable exception. Milyukov had not mentioned that Longuetism had been created as an attempt to contain a growing revolutionary mood among the workers. And, continued Trotsky, Milyukov had good cause to conceal the real origins of Longuetism. He could not expose the anti-proletarian, pro-government nature of Longuetism for 'he was afraid of weakening the pedagogical force of his French impressions upon the Russian workers' movement ... '[26]

In his final contribution about Russian liberalism in *Nashe Slovo*, Trotsky analysed the Kadet moderate Chelnokov's remarks on which political force was best suited to implement the liberal reform programme. According to Trotsky, Chelnokov, the chairman of the Moscow All-Russian Union of Towns, thought a conservative government could pass liberal reforms while retaining the trust of society and leading political circles, whereas a liberal administration attempting to pass the self same reforms would soon be swamped with requests that it would be unable to fulfil. For Trotsky, it would not be difficult to show the flaws in Chelnokov's logic: a conservative Cabinet would be conservative by nature and act accordingly. However, such an illustration would be pointless if one thought that by it one could convert Chelnokov to opposition to Russian conservatism. The Moscow city politician had constructed his case not out of ignorance, but from an awareness of the common imperialist interests of the liberal bourgeoisie and the bureaucratic-monarchical state. Chelnokov and his ilk knew that the monarchy was incapable of defending its imperialist interests, but it would not surrender its hold on power. Russian liberalism was prepared to help the monarchy acquire the new skills it needed without demanding political power. Hence Chelnokov's insistence that the reins of government were best left in the hands of the traditional bureaucracy. Of course liberals would protest if their conservative allies took them too much for granted. However, liberal protests were not a genuine attempt to overthrow the government. Illusions on this score only helped prop up the old regime. A chain linked liberalism and, through its acceptance of 'liberal opposition', social-patriotism, to Stürmer's conservative ministry:

> Creating (not so much for himself as for others) 'illusions' on Stümer's account, Chelnokov continues to serve the basic interests of his class in the current epoch. Creating illusions for themselves on Chelnokovists' (*Chelnokovikh*) account and for tomorrow's

'struggle for power', opportunists in the workers' movement betray the working class to the bourgeoisie.[27]

Although Trotsky's critique of Russian liberalism ranged from its bogus commitment to democracy to its leaders' hypocrisy, it was its role in the above chain that was of utmost concern to Trotsky. If the workers were to stage a revolution liberal illusions had to be exposed and dispersed. The two links of the chain not looked at thus far, the government and social-patriotism, will now be examined.

The government

From the war's outset Trotsky condemned the Russian government as imperialist, opposed to the interests of the international proletariat.[28] However, it was only in April 1915 that he devoted a full article to the war-time regime in Russia, in which he placed the suspension of the constitution in an international setting. The countries of age-old parliamentarianism had taken this step, but, he argued, one could single out Russia since, unlike other countries where political parties had voluntarily declared allegiance to 'national unity', in Russia the government itself had put an end to the unrestrained functioning of political groups. Having freed themselves of parliamentary criticism Trotsky claimed that all governments were regulating economies for the war, breaking the market rules normally governing economic life. The Russian government also stood out in this sense since it had caused more dislocation and more disruption than elsewhere. This did not bode well either for the Russian economy or for continuing social acquiescence:

> the government's war economy feverishly undermines itself and the longer the war lasts the more it disappears into a blind alley … But the longer the war lasts and the more uncertain its outcome becomes, the more often the rulers need to dip into the state coffers and the more anxiously the propertied classes … ask themselves: does the bureaucracy really know why and where it is leading the country?[29]

However, Trotsky concluded that faced with such questions and criticism the government would not relinquish its newly discovered freedom from parliamentary and societal control.

If Trotsky could not be optimistic about the possibility of a new regime in Russia, he was able to write a humorous account of a recent ministerial reshuffle, part of the government's 'liberalisation' measures in response to recent military setbacks. Nicholas II had sacked the Minister of the Interior, Nicholas Maklakov, and replaced him with Nicholas Shcherbatov. Among a number of other new appointees Katenin was given responsibility for the press. Trotsky assessed the likely course events would take under Shcherbatov and Katenin, based upon the two men's biographies. The new Minister of the Interior had previously occupied the post of Director of the State Stud, which gave grounds for optimism. After all, horses demanded regularity and order in the provision of food and water. Perhaps Shcherbatov's skills acquired among horses were transferable to Russia's larger human stable, although Trotsky declined to make a precise forecast. Katenin, unfortunately, did not have Shcherbatov's sound training and experience, evident from how he had responded to questions concerning his approach to the press. Katenin freely admitted that he had no knowledge of the press but would protect the honourable publications and discard the rest. But how would he differentiate the honourable from the dishonourable? He would, he replied, 'treat the press as the press treats me'.[30] It was this answer, Trotsky claimed, which revealed the difference between the two new ministers. Shcherbatov knew that horses are treated not as they treat you but as horses. The lesson was clear: 'one went through the serious stable school, but the other obviously needs to be sent to the stables for the completion of his state service.'[31]

Trotsky's next commentary upon developments in Russia was a political profile of Alexander Khvostov, appointed Minister of the Interior to replace Shcherbatov after the tsar had weathered the political storms of August 1915.[32] For Trotsky, the latest reshuffle showed that Nicholas II was digging trenches at home after the German advance on the Eastern front had ground to a halt. Khvostov, a well-known reactionary, made a mockery of recent liberal calls for a ministry enjoying popular support. After all, he had crushed worker uprisings in 1905 and it was expected that he would deal with any unrest similarly. Hardly a promising prospect for the vast majority! In turn, liberal acquiescence in the face of Khvostov's appointment revealed how little the government need worry about them. Indeed, for Trotsky, Khvostov's promotion would enter the history books as 'a symbol of the relationship between the monarchy and the patriotic bourgeoisie'.[33]

Trotsky discovered further confirmation for a strengthening of

Russian reactionary forces in the wake of military successes, most notably at the Turkish fortress city of Erzurum, when he examined the appointments of Boris Stürmer as Prime Minister and Makarov, the former Minister of the Interior sacked in the spring of 1915 during public outcry at the German army's rapid advance, as Minister of Justice.[34] He placated French worries that Stürmer, who had also taken over the post of Foreign Minister from Sazonov, would pursue a different Russian foreign policy. Despite his German name, Stürmer would pursue the battle until the Germans had been routed. The most recent cabinet reshuffle was due to domestic concerns. Sazonov, unlike Stürmer, liked the Duma, if only as an additional source of information and influence. True Stürmer had called the Duma before dispersing it and, in a letter to the Tsar, leading figures had accused the new Prime Minister of conspiring with the left to overthrow the monarchy in the name of national defence. But, Trotsky claimed, such accusations were clearly exaggerated. Stürmer's premiership was a swing to the right of the political pendulum, enabled by several victories for the Russian forces led by General Brusilov on the Austrian front. The view that Russia's 'internal Germans' would be defeated along with Germany had been dealt another blow.

Trotsky's appraisal of Stürmer soon underwent a rapid change. In 'Two Telegrams' Stürmer appears not as a die-hard monarchist, but as a politician willing to sacrifice absolutism.[35] Contrary to expectations, Stümer had not begun his government service by calling a press conference or by receiving Entente envoys. To date, Stürmer had exchanged telegrams only with Briand, his French counterpart. This correspondence confirmed that both countries were engaged in a 'great task' without however defining it. In trying to fill this lacuna Trotsky brought two facts to the reader's attention. The Petrograd correspondent of the French newspaper *Journal* had been told by the Ministry of Foreign Affairs that Stürmer had been appointed Prime Minister and Foreign Minister since a Peace Conference would connect Russia's external and internal affairs, a task eased if one person had overall responsibility. Second, the Russian Finance Minister, Bark, had recently visited Western Europe in a quest for financial aid. He was told that loans were to be had in America, but at the price of a more enlightened Jewish policy. The reason for Stürmer's occupation of the two top governmental posts was now obvious, as was his deal with Briand in carrying-out of their 'great task'.

When Trotsky next wrote about the Russian government he was under an order to leave Paris. *Nashe Slovo* had been banned two weeks earlier. However, in the six weeks it took to find Trotsky a new home, *Nashe Slovo* was able to reemerge as *Nachalo* and Trotsky contributed several attacks on the Russian government.

The first of these, written under his new pseudonym En, assessed the corruption which permeated the Russian administration through an examination of several leading state officials' careers. The recently deceased General Dumbadze (1851–1916), as governor of Yalta, had terrorised local residents until complaints about him became so common that he was sacked in 1910. However, a friend of Nicholas II, Dumbadze was reappointed and reigned until 'he was worn out by administration.'[36] More recently, General Komissarov had been sacked as governor of the Rostov region after local people had complained about him to the Ministry of the Interior. Trotsky advised Komissarov to take comfort from the life of the infamous I. I. Vostorgov (1867–1918). Vostorgov was well known as a priest and corrupt officer of state who, nevertheless, was tipped to become a bishop. From these case studies it was clear that being sacked for corruption was no barrier to subsequent promotion. Trotsky concluded with one further peculiar history. Mansevich-Manuilov (Maska) had been hired as a collegiate assessor and was currently in prison for embezzling 100 000 roubles.[37] V. Burtsev, a former Narodnik, was now an ardent patriot. With support from Entente governments he was allowed back into Russia where he was working in museums. Trotsky wondered what he might be doing in that branch of the state service; 'perhaps he is studying the deposit from Manusevich-Maska's trousers'.[38]

In a final, partly censored, contribution on the Russian government, Trotsky disputed Gavas's (official telegraph agency) view of a rapid growth of liberal influence in the Russian administration.[39] In response Trotsky asked how a Cabinet which was considering hiring V. M. Purishkevich (1870–1920), a monarchist reactionary and member of the Black Hundreds, could be classified as liberal. Furthermore, Stümer was attempting to crush the influence of the liberal Chelnokov by enfranchising the clergy for the upcoming elections to the Moscow City Duma. After establishing the 'firm course' adopted by the current regime, Trotsky noted ambiguity. Ministers were proposing conflicting solutions to price rises and shortages of basic necessities. The Agricultural Minister, Bobrinsky, calling for no government intervention to lower prices, was opposed by the War Minister, Shuvaev, who wanted the army to be supplied with cheap bread. When Shuvaev won rumours circulated that Bobrinsky would soon be replaced but, Trotsky pointed out, conflict in the Cabinet was harmful for the 'firm course'. In the meantime, calls were being made for the immediate convocation of the Duma. Trotsky's writings on the Russian government ended with an analysis of another looming Cabinet crisis, the mechanics of which he had outlined in his first article on the Russian state order of April 1915.

The workers' movement: social-patriotism versus Social-Democracy

In the third and fourth instalments of 'The Military Crisis and Political Perspectives', Trotsky outlined why the Russian proletariat would determine Russia's future political order. For Trotsky, this was revealed by the failed 1905 revolution, in which 'the main moving force of the revolution had been the proletariat'.[40] In the intervening years the proletariat's position had only been reinforced. A period of economic boom had enriched the large-capital bourgeoisie while killing off its petty- and middle-counterparts. The proletariat had grown in numbers, was more concentrated in the newer and larger factories, and more advanced in consciousness and organisation. The peasantry remained a culturally backward and dispersed mass, only proletarian and semi-proletarian elements could be won over from the country-side. The further polarisation of the Russian social structure between 1905–15 also carried consequences for politics. The bourgeoisie had abandoned its opposition of 1905 and was backing the government's victory campaign. Similarly, the liberal press, whose ambiguous stance in 1905 had encouraged the masses' revolutionary feelings, was urging the proletariat into an alliance with the ruling orders. In this way the bourgeoisie, Trotsky argued, formed a buffer between the monarchy at one end of society and the proletariat at the other. Given that a Russian revolution depended upon the proletariat, the crucial question for Trotsky was, 'Who would exert most influence over the masses?' The bourgeois message was clear, but two main strains of Social-Democratic thought one could also be distinguished.

Some socialists, social-patriots, thought that the petty-urban bourgeoisie, the intelligentsia and the peasantry could play a revolutionary role. Their programme approved the war and participation in 'organisations for victory', to create a broad alliance which, after the war, would press for radical political change. In the Duma the social-patriots were represented by Man'kov and Kerensky. However, other socialists, revolutionary internationalists, agitated among the prole-

tariat for peace and revolution. For the revolutionary internationalist
the Russian revolution was part of a wider European phenomenon:

> only the international socialist revolution can create the right envi-
> ronment and advance the forces with whose help the revolutionary
> struggle of the Russian proletariat will be conducted to a successful
> conclusion. And the converse: the revolutionary struggle of the
> Russian proletariat ... is an important factor in the interrelation of
> European social forces and gives a mighty filip to the revolutionary
> advance of the European proletariat.[41]

Trotsky did not have to wait too long before having an opportunity
to comment on the battle between social-patriots and revolutionary-
internationalists. In late 1915 he wrote two articles about the election
of worker representatives to the recently formed War-Industries
Committees, organisations concerned with war production.[42] The
first, appearing six weeks after the first elections of September 1915,
claimed that the revolutionary internationalists were strongest. In
writing of a 'rout' of the defencists, Trotsky no doubt had in mind
figures which had already appeared in *Nashe Slovo* showing that
workers at 90 large factories had voted against participation in the
War-Industries Committees, with 81 for.[43] Given the advantages
enjoyed by the social-patriots – the continuing German advance was
encouraging the mood of defence and the bourgeois press was raging
about the 'Teutonic danger' – the Petrograd workers had emerged
from a difficult political test 'with honour'. However, he did not forget
that between one-quarter and one-third of Petrograd's workers had
voted for participation in the War-Industrial Committees. Trotsky
asked 'Why?'

He pointed out that the social-patriots themselves were surprised:
'without an organisation, without traditions, almost without Duma
representatives, without the authority of a party. And suddenly:
several hundreds of thousands of votes! Where from?'[44] For Trotsky
the social-patriotic vote was composed of several elements. Workers
under the spell of bourgeois ideology had united under the banner
hoisted by Plekhanov, *Prizyv* and *Nashe Delo*. To these one could add
the unemployed, indifferent workers who, when threatened by external danger, would support national defence, and some qualified
workers who were earning more money than usual under the 'mobilisation of industry'. In short, the social-patriot constituency was
made-up from opportunistic elements most likely to take the line of

least resistance. It had turned to social-patriotism, a completely new political phenomenon, because the state machine and the bourgeois press had been at its service, or rather, claimed Trotsky, the former had come to the service of the latter: 'Social-patriotism turned-out to be the most handy political instrument in the hands of the ruling classes and the state power for the ideological-political subordination of the backward workers.'[45] Alone the ruling cirlces would have been able to win-over thousands, not tens of thousands of workers. Trotsky insisted that only one conclusion could be drawn: 'an all-out struggle with social-patriotism'.[46]

Following election, workers' representatives had to decide whether to nominate individuals to serve on the central organs of the War-Industries Committees. This second round of voting took place toward the end of November 1915, and Trotsky published his commentary of these debates roughly one month later. He described what had occurred as a new chapter in the history of social-patriotic shame, most notably Gvozdev's behaviour at an electoral meeting of 29 November. Gvozdev, leader of the social-patriotic bloc, naturally wanted workers' representatives to proceed with the nominations. Opposed by a majority of ninety revolutionary internationalists, Gvozdev attempted to overcome this opposition by declaring that one deputy was attending under false pretences. When the revolutionary internationalists abandoned the hall in protest at this 'informer's act', Gvozdev organised the election of ten workers' representatives to the Central War-Industries Committee and a further six to supplementary committees. For Trotsky, this was a falsification of the will of the Petrograd proletariat, whose election of the ninety Trotsky obviously felt amounted to a mandate not to proceed with further elections to War-Industries Committees. The social-patriot's 'evil form of political strikebreaking' permitted only one of two responses: 'either fellow-travelling and empathy, or an implacable and immediate organisational rebuff'.[47]

An advert in *Nash Golos* promoting an edition of social-patriotic essays provided the pretext for Trotsky's next writing on Russian social-patriotism. *Nash Golos* announced that there would be over nineteen contributors, each of whom supported the idea of self-defence. Trotsky reproduced this information in *Nashe Slovo* before adding several comments. The proposed publication showed the social-patriots' energy. Second, L. Sedov's participation belied the notion that there was a left-wing group within *Nashe Delo*. If there was such a group Sedov would have opposed self-defence. Third, An's contribution was illustrative of how new disagreements had replaced the old. Previously, An had rejected his current co-contributors as 'opportunists'. This was a blow since as the analysis of the War-Industries Committees elections had shown, there had to be a propaganda war against social-patriotism: 'The more An has served the workers' movement ... the greater his authority and the more decisive the struggle with An and the social-patriots should be.'[48]

When *Self-Defence* appeared copies must have circulated outside Russia. Trotsky reviewed the book in two articles, intending to discredit social-patriotism and its calls for an alliance with the liberals.[49]

L. Sedov's chapter, 'Yesterday – Today – Tomorrow', may not have appeared 'due to circumstances beyond the editors' control',[50] but, Trotsky claimed, Sedov's spirit was still apparent. After all, a Foreword did say that the authors, despite differences of opinion, were united in their belief that internationalism and Russia's defence were not mutually exclusive.[51] In actual fact, claimed Trotsky, the authors disagreed not only among themselves but even in themselves. Before examining each chapter by way of a series of brief extracts, 'so that the reader can grasp the book's overall "spirit"', Trotsky characterised the arguments put forward by all as 'banal and superficial ... united by capitulation before the bourgeois nation and the class state'.[52]

Self-Defence was introduced by Vera Zasulich's essay 'On the War'.[53] In the light of her undoubted contributions to the Russian workers' movement, Trotsky wished he could pass over her in silence. However, now she was 'a political enemy against whom one has to conduct an irreconcilable struggle'.[54] He recreated Zusulich's argument as desiring as total a defeat of Germany as possible, not only out of feelings for her homeland but also because of a concern for Western democracy. Germany's merciless pursuit of victory had aroused in her indignation and disgust. Trotsky had not reproduced Zasulich's arguments faithfully. Thus, for instance, her desire for Germany's defeat was not caused by a concern for Western democracy as Western democracy *per se*, but because the 'destruction or even weakening of Western democracy by a mighty country, led by semi-absolutist Prussian Junkers, would be a huge blow for the present and a threat to the future order to which the proletariat aspires'.[55]

Trotsky described the next contributor, A. Potresov, as the 'Gvozdev' of the whole collection. He said that Potresov saw the appeal of the homeland as having caused the collapse of the Second International. At the same time, Potresov was not counterposing the homeland to internationalism. The proletariat was merely protecting the riches created by it in its 'homeland'. Russia still had to reach the stage of 'patriotism', citizens laying down their possessions at the homeland's alter, after which it would become a part of Europe. The exposition of Potresov's article ended by citing the social-patriot's final sentence: 'Through patriotism – there is no alternative – into the kingdom of brotherhood and equality!'[56] What Trotsky did not do, however, was to report either why Potresov considered patriotism a precondition of internationalism, or the distinction Potresov made between bourgeois patriotism and proletarian patriotism. According to Potresov, capitalist development not only brought with it an ever-increasing social polarisation, it also transformed each individual into a citizen. In turn, it was a feeling of citizenship which underpinned patriotism, i.e., one is part of a society, irrespective of one's hatred for other social classes:

> we do not always consider another aspect of capitalist develop-
> ment, that the stratification of society is accompanied not only by
> ever-increasing class struggle but also by ... the transformation of
> the ordinary person into a citizen ... the more active hatred to a
> section [of society] is, the more one feels love towards the whole,
> an active love which is patriotism.[57]

Furthermore, since capitalist development is uneven and since 'citizenship' is concomitant upon capitalist development, various nations will have different degrees of citizenship and hence of patriotism. Moreover, as it develops patriotism takes various forms, an 'aggressive bourgeois patriotism', prepared to interfere in another country's interests in pursuit of its own, and a 'proletarian-democratic patriotism', espousing freedom so long as no harm is inflicted upon others. The Second International had collapsed because 'proletarian-democratic-patriotism' was, as yet, too weakly developed. However, Potresov was confident that internationalism would grow out of patriotism:

> internationalism is the further development of patriotism ... The
> war is not only the expression of the citizenship accumulated by
> centuries of development in national-state boundaries, it also
> causes the first serious fisures in this bounded citizenship, simulta-
> neously laying the foundation stones upon which aware and
> conscious masses will build ... aided by the creative power of inter-
> nationalism.[58]

Trotsky focused on the emotional aspect of Ivan Kubikov's 'The Working Class and National Feelings',[59] which had cited of a line of poetry, 'If kind, though poor, the homeland will cry'. However, there was another side to Kubikov's analysis which went unreported in Trotsky's review. For Kubikov, the proletariat of each country did not, as Marx claimed in 1848, have nothing to loose but its chains. In the sixty-plus years since Marx and Engels penned the *Communist Manifesto*, the European proletariat had made significant material, cultural and organisational gains, achieved, moreover, in the nation-state. Hence the desire of each country's proletariat to defend its gains from possible seizure by foreign forces.

For P. Maslov, advanced capitalist countries exploit the less well advanced through trade policies. For instance, Ireland and India became markets for Britain's industrial goods and not competitors not by political oppression, but through Britain's trade policy. This was why, to achieve economic independence and develop domestic industry, the United States had to overturn Britain's trade policy. Maslov claimed that pre-war Germany had a trade surplus with Russia, despite Russian protectionism. However, German capital wanted to make super-profits, via the imposition of an economic order after victory: 'At whose expense will these advantages be gained? Clearly, at the expense of the defeated country. It is also clear that the extraction of this super-profit will impact on the economic development of the exploited country.'[60] Maslov looked at German-occupied Poland to illustrate how indigenous industry was being stripped not only to satisfy Germany's war needs, but for the 'demands of German industry'.[61] Moreover, the German government was pressurising Polish workers to emigrate to Germany to fill the demand for labour power. The Polish bourgeoisie, anxious to protect its property, and the Polish workers, concerned about their jobs and rights in Poland, had a common interest to repulse German aggression. Socialists who insisted that the outcome of the war was a matter of indifference were poor defenders of the interests of the Polish working class.

Although Trotsky did not mention why, for Maslov, control over trade policy was so important, he did give an accurate summary of Maslov's views: 'the Germans threaten the Russian trade system and hence Russian industry and hence the Russian proletariat.'[62] He then correctly quoted a section of Maslov's chapter which regretted that leading German socialists had supported the attempt to destroy Russian industry which could be saved only by defeating Germany. Maslov's insistence that democrats were obliged to ensure that any peace should include 'mutual concessions in economic relations, so that one country does not exploit another',[63] however, went unreported.

K. Dmitriev examined the special demands faced by backward countries during World War One.[64] For example, whereas an advanced country can redirect resources normally spent on repairs and reinvestment, a backward country is forced to reduce consumer output: 'This is why the rear is now facing goods shortages: industry and in part agriculture cannot keep up with normal demand plus the rapidly growing demands of the army.'[65] In Russia the effect of the war on the consumer was being aggravated, according to Dmitriev, by the government's financial policy. By printing more money the rouble had devalued by one-third, the cost of which was to be met by consumers, especially the workers. For Dmitriev the hardships of war at the rear had to be minimised because of the close connection between home and the front: 'the rear's material and spiritual hardships are transmitted with lightning speed to the front and affect the army's morale.'[66] The problem for backward Russia was how to meet the overwhelming production demands of World War One without diverting too many resources from the home market. Dmitriev's solution was the rational use of the country's resources, only achieveable if democrats organised the war effort. The intervention of democratic forces was all the more urgent for Dmitriev, since only in this way could democracy influence the post-war settlement. Hence his conclusion, ripped from its context and quoted without comment by Trotsky: 'Through the country's defence to the free world, a mutual guarantee of all interests – such now can be the only slogan of Russian democracy.'[67]

From An's essay, 'Marxism and Radicalism', Trotsky cited the following extract, which he ridiculed by inserting an incredulous '(listen!)':

> Each European Marxist party approached the war from the point of view of economic development, i.e., they remained Marxists. But (listen!) since each considered their country to be defending itself, naturally, they all, in line with the International's regulations, took up arms;[68]

and then by using An's nationality to throw the question of Russia constituting a 'country' into doubt:

And since An considers his country to be defending itself (To An, who hails from the Caucasus, it is absolutely clear that neither in Persia nor in Armenia has Russia's 'defence' been carried through to the end), he 'follows the International's regulations' and issues a call to arms.[69]

In the first instance Trotsky's critique rests upon an apparent flaw in An's logic. After all, why should concerns about economic development lead Marxists to support the war effort for those acting in 'self-defence'? An had answered this question. As societies emerge from feudalism they experience two different stages of development, first general political liberation and then an era of social struggle. In the first stage the proletariat will unite with the bourgeoisie to throw off the feudal yoke, in the second the two classes will oppose each other. At the outset of World War One Western Europe was in the second 'social' stage while Russia was still in the first. This explains social-democrats in the West for whom, 'victory or defeat means the strengthening or weakening of the proletarian movement, for military destruction of the economic base which conditions a nation's history destroys the basis of the class struggle and retards the whole economy.'[70] However, An went on to say, and Trotsky omitted this from his report, that not all social-democrats in the West could call their country 'defencist': 'A mistake was committed: a section of the International imagined its state to be defencist whereas it was aggressive, the war's initiator.'[71]

In the second instance, when An's call to arms was declared to be part and parcel of a link between defence and economic development, Trotsky simply distorted An's meaning. In actual fact, An connected the Russian proletariat's support for Russia's war effort to the Russian bourgeoisie's linkage of its political demands with Russia's defence:

the advocates of 'using' propagate victory, making converts out of previous opponents, with the usual results – the political and organisational inactivity of the proletariat which is not able to connect its political demands with the demands of the moment. Political leadership goes to the bourgeoisie whose awakening opens a new era in the Russian liberation movement. Only the bourgeoisie connects political renewal with the necessity to defend the country from foreign invasion, gaining support from all sections of society. Even the proletariat begins to stir under the sound of the bourgeois alarm-bell and responds to its speeches.[72]

If Trotsky had presented a more accurate reconstruction of An's views, he would have opened the more complex can of worms of the political and social stages of a move away from feudalism and the implications of this for one's political programme for war-torn backward Russia.

For Vladimir Vol'skii the homeland was the only possible form in which both culture and the workers' movement could develop. For him the slogan 'the proletariat has no homeland' meant that the proletariat should not, for example, organise a seizure of power in the homeland, a proposition which 'has nothing in common with Marxism.'[73] According to Vol'skii the Stuttgart Conference of 1907 recognised the nation as the 'treasure store' of human progress, and that each nation had an inalienable right to self-defence. Trotsky chose not to review Vol'skii's thoughts on the homeland. Instead, he focused upon the social-patriot's critique of a left-wing deputy who, in the Duma, had asked the following questions: 'What do you, supporters of self-defence, demand of the working class? Does it not tire itself out working in the factories, does it not bear all the war's hardships and does it not die on the battlefield?'[74] Trotsky summarised Vol'skii's response thus: one also has to give one's mind and soul. This set up Trotsky's punch-line, which rests upon a disbelief in the social-patriot's cheek: 'In other words, for us it is not enough that the proletariat sacrifices its life – it should also give its soul.'[75]

However, in order to achieve this effect Trotsky had to distort Vol'skii's argument. The latter had not called upon the proletariat to give its mind and soul because its physical courage was lacking. It was foolish to frame the question in this way. For Vol'skii the left-wing deputy's questions were premised upon a view of the proletariat as cannon-fodder. In actual fact the proletariat is more than its body, it has an intelligence and a heart which were of crucial importance in organising the country's defence: 'If a force of four to five million fighters forms a firm and long wall stretching from the Baltic to the Black Sea then it expresses the collective will and strength of the whole nation. If the fighters quiver then this is a sign that the nation is weak.'[76]

Trotsky dealt with the next two authors, Evgeniy Maevskii and V. Levitskii, in one paragraph. Of these he said they were destined to write of 'general-national' tasks to their dying days. For Maevskii, in World War One Russia had to guarantee its independence and democratise, possible only by an alliance of democratic workers and the bourgeois opposition. However, the bourgeoisie and especially its leaders, Milyukov and Chelnokov, thought that it could act independently, repeating the tactical mistakes of the advanced workers in 1905. Then, the workers, rejecting the bourgeoisie as weak, had viewed themselves as the only effective political force. And, of course, the 1905 Revolution failed. The urgent task for Maevskii was to bring the workers and the bourgeois opposition together. The bourgeoisie's current policy of isolation from the workers was 'the bourgeoisie in a blind alley'.[77] Trotsky began his appraisal at this point in Maevskii's argument, labelling it as 'the freshest of his discoveries'.[78] Maevskii concluded that the proletariat should lead the bourgeoisie out of its blind alley; a conclusion which Trotsky ridiculed by inserting an exclamation mark in the following quote: 'Workers' democracy, and this is in its interest for (!) this is in the interests of the country's defence, should also save the bourgeois opposition from its errors.'[79]

Trotsky did not report Levitskii's view that only a worker-bourgeois alliance could save Russia and reform its political system, nor did he retrace Levitskii's account of how the proletariat and the bourgeoisie had progressively organised themselves in the face of political, economic and military failures, and how these two as yet uncoordinated organisations would inevitably merge into one. He did, however, quote from Levitskii's final paragraph; making no comment other than informing the reader that the emphasis was not his: 'Only a movement of an *all-national* character, which embraces *different* social classes ... can lead Russia out of its external and internal difficulties'.[80]

In his contribution A. P. Bibik imagined a Russian proletariat dressed in Hamlet's cloak as it resolved the question 'to be or not to be', and invented an imaginary dialogue to illustrate how Hamlet's cloak was discarded as the decision to fight for Russia's victory was reached. Trotsky exposed two aspects of Bibik's article to his humour and his doubts. First he recounted Bibik's assertion that once it was clear that German Social-Democracy had backed the Prussian Junkers, French and Belgium workers resolved to meet the German army 'without olive-branches.'[81] Trotsky showed his scorn by adding '(As is well known the Prussian Junkers offer all Bibiks a choice of outfit, white or 'defensive' and arming themselves according to taste, olive-branches or rifles)'.[82] Then, in response to Bibik's claim that workers' meetings had closed ranks and conclusion that 'Russian workers also have a Homeland and this Homeland is in danger',[83] Trotsky asked, 'When were these workers' meetings which gathered around a Homeland with capital letters?'[84] After all, Bibik had provided no evidence. Moreover, the Menshevik Organisational Committee had recently remarked that: 'Comrade Bibik is a leading worker of the Menshevik wing, and his conversion to "defencism" will be influential',[85] i.e. Bibik had tried to convince the workers to throw off Hamlet's cloak rather than workers discarding Shakespearean clothing of their own accord.

The twelfth and final essay in *Self-Defence* was V. L'vov-Rogachevskii's 'How It Was Then',[86] which compared the current 'Patriotic War' with its predecessor of 1812. For L'vov-Rogachevskii 1812 started a period of national rebirth and renewal which unfortunately did not last. However, he was convinced that the current national awakening would prove more permanent, leading to the 'total Europeanisation and democratisation of Russia, for this is in the interests of the whole of democratic Europe'.[87] In his review Trotsky did not reconstruct L'vov-Rogachevskii's historical analogy. He simply quoted the social-patriot's call for each 'peaceful man' to 'Stand up in the name of the country's saviour!'[88]

Trotsky summed-up his review of *Self-Defence* partly by poking fun and partly by being serious. He claimed that after reading *Self-Defence*'s wealth of literary sources – 'some foolish, some formal' – one could not help sensing 'a wave of condescension to the phraseology of the French social-patriots';[89] and he quoted from a speech made by Hevré to illustrate that 'political acoustics ... do not take offence'.[90] On a more serious note Trotsky recalled Potresov's and L'vov-Rogachevskii's calls for sacrifices to be made for the defence of the homeland. He threw their belief of Russia's democratisation following a successful defence effort into doubt by conjuring up the silhouette of a policeman informing the social-patriots: 'You are honourable although a bit pushy, but don't shout in vain, we ourselves shall do the awakening!'[91]

Trotsky soon returned to these themes in 'Self-Defence: Training to be a Patriot'?'[92] He criticised Maslov and others for accepting the pro-war stance adopted by the socialist parties of Britain, France, Australia and Belgium.[93] However, the main target of Trotsky's attack was Potresov's assertion that 'internationalism is the further development of patriotism',[94] which Trotsky interpreted as a pattern of historical development from a stupid parochialism through patriotism to international socialism. And, wrote Trotsky, it would follow from Potresov's schema that Russian Social-Democracy had arrived too early, 'a historical abortion'. After all, Potresov himself had said that Russia was just entering the second 'patriotic' stage. In order to refute

Potresov's understanding of the historical process Trotsky reformulated the social-patriot's stages as a production chain, 'from supply through manufacture to the factory'.[95] He argued that, viewed from this perspective, the peculiarity of Russia's development became clear, for

> European factories began to conquer Russia sooner than Russia's 'natural' development had reached not only manufacture but also European supply. Following on from this Russia's industrial backwardness – in current world economic development – is expressed ... in the extremely concentrated character of Russian industry.[96]

Furthermore, Trotsky claimed that this peculiarity of economic development had political and social consequences. The Russian worker was dragged out of his state of 'stupid parochialism' not via patriotism but by exploitation in the work place, acquiring class consciousness, not patriotism: 'sharpening class antagonisms in the very first stage does not permit further acquaintance with the homeland map painted in patriotic colours.'[97] For Trotsky, Potresov was merely repeating the slogans put forward at an earlier time by Peter Struve. However, he highlighted one important difference. Struve had attempted to win over the Marxist intelligentsia to the liberal opposition which was taking its first timid '"non-class" steps', whereas 'Potresov issues his call in 1916, at a time of European war, to socialist workers to join the camp of the patriotic opposition which is led by imperialist capital'.[98] The Marxist intelligentsia had rejected Struve, and revolutionary workers should respond similarly to Potresov.

Indeed, several days later Trotsky praised the Social-Democratic fraction in the Duma, represented by Chkheidze, for exposing a social-patriotism as 'rubbish'. In Russia at that time Trotsky viewed the Duma as 'the only place from which one can clearly and unambiguously put the masses on guard against social-patriotic seduction, broadcast in numerous legal publications.'[99] The social-patriotic newspaper *Prizyv* also reported Chkheidze's speech but in a way that did not please Trotsky. According to Trotsky, *Prizyv* had claimed that the Social-Democratic deputy had not supported Zimmerwald in the Duma.[100] Trotsky disputed this, pointing out that Chkheidze had both welcomed the call of 'struggle for peace' issued by the Zimmerwald Manifesto and had denounced social-patriotic war slogans as 'lies and hypocrisy'. On the other hand, he did criticise Chkheidze for not completely unfolding the Zimmerwald banner, but nevertheless insisted that 'one cannot equate Chkheidze's moderate anti-militarism with *Prizyv*'s social-militarism'.[101] For Trotsky, the biggest flaw in Chkheidze's speech was its refusal to declare open hostility to the War-Industries Committees out of a concern for colleagues participating in the organs of 'self-defence'. This timidity, he wrote, seriously weakened the rebuff to social-patriotism.

However, a continuation of this article noted a recent development which could only help demarcate social-patriotism from revolutionary socialism. The social-patriotic deputies Bur'yakov and Man'kov, recently elected to the Duma and both social-patriotic 'turncoats', had attacked Chkheidze using quotes from Aleksinskii, Avksent'ev and other leading social-patriots. For Trotsky, Chkheidze should take up the challenge and make clear that social-patriots were one link in a chain tying the proletariat to its class enemies:

> Comrade deputies! ... You would be able to ignore Bur'yakov but behind him stands Gvozdev and behind Gvozdev stands Potresov and Plekhanov and behind them the imperialist bourgeoisie. You should openly declare to the Russian proletariat that social-patriotism is the deadly enemy of its historical mission. You should advance slogans not only flowing directly out of Zimmerwald but also [slogans] clearly formulated at the last Zimmerwald meeting: 'Abandon the War-Industries Committees!' You should throw to one side all obstacles which hamper you from openly opposing Gvozdevism with Zimmerwald. This is the only way to break the disbelief accumulating in the advanced workers to you ... This is the only way in Russia to concentrate the proletarian struggle under the banner of the Third International![102]

Trotsky issued the above call on May Day 1916. His tone became even more urgent in an article published just nineteen days later. On a positive note, he claimed that the Duma Social-Democratic fraction had not become social-patriotic. However, out of two tactics, a 'revolutionary mobilisation of the proletariat against the war' or a 'passive wait-and-see' policy, the Duma fraction was moving 'between the two alternatives with a clear tendency towards passive internationalism'.[103] It was an unclear grasp of international-revolutionary perspectives, of the dependence of the Russian proletariat's struggle against bourgeois imperialism upon the correlation of class forces across the whole of Europe which, wrote Trotsky, explained 'our fraction's vague speeches and the passive wait-and-see character of its internationalism'. Given Trotsky's emphasis upon the Duma fraction as the main disseminators of revolutionary socialism, his concluding words of advice were quite in place: the Social-Democrats in the Duma had to break all ties with the social-patriots, otherwise they faced a 'totally hopeless situation'.

When, however, Trotsky next took up his pen to write of Chkheidze he was not able to say that his advice had been followed. 'Deputy Chkheidze's Tour' reported how the Social-Democratic deputy, on a trip to Georgia and sharing a platform with a priest and a colonel, had advised the local population to form self-help groups and cooperatives to soften the impact of rising prices in the countryside. The meeting then unanimously passed a resolution calling the local population to order. Trotsky said that there was nothing objectionable in Chkheidze's advice to increase self-help and not to seek solutions to the economic crisis in episodic acts of violence. However, he also pointed out that the dreaded Khvostov had issued similar advice. Chkheidze had merely repeated official slogans and this was not the responsibility of a Social-Democratic orator! For Trotsky, Chkheidze should have explained that the disorganisation caused by the war could not be overcome by seeking refuge in cooperatives, only by revolting against the basic cause of high prices. An opportunity to propagate Zimmerwald had been lost. Trotsky asked whether Chkheidze had spoken along these lines but the bourgeois press, from which he had taken his information, had falsified the Social-Democrat's arguments. Unfortunately, claimed Trotsky, several facts said 'no'.

Chkheidze had spoken alongside a priest and a colonel, which would not have been possible if he had polemicised against the war. Second, after a revolutionary-socialist speech the crowd would hardly have approved a resolution calling the people to order. Finally, Chkheidze would not have been allowed to make further appeals in places suffering from high prices if had really acted as a revolutionary socialist. No, said Trotsky, Chkheidze had played the role of a kind-hearted liberal, attempting to calm a situation before the governor calmed it by other means. Once Chkheidze had welcomed Karl Liebknecht's parliamentary opposition to the war. But, Trotsky pointed out, Liebknecht had not recommended cooperatives but the slogans 'Down with the War' and 'Down with the Government', for which he had been sentenced to prison. Trotsky said that not everyone was obliged to match Liebknecht's decisiveness and bravery. However, he concluded that 'those with Liebknecht's and

Zimmerwald's banner are not able to compromise this banner with impunity'.[104]

In what was to be his last article on the battle between social-patriotism and revolutionary-socialism in the Russian workers' movement while in Paris Trotsky could not have been in good spirits. At the same time as he was writing of the disgrace of Russian social-patriotism in Paris through Aleksinskii's antics, he was forced to report of Chkeidze's increasing espousal of social-patriotism. Social-patriotic practice in Russia was obviously proving to be made of sterner stuff than its ideological counterparts in the French capital.

*

In his writings on Russia from Paris, Trotsky noted a chain, from social-patriotism through liberalism to the government, which tied the proletariat to the war. He considered the liberal strategy of democratic reforms following military success mistaken. Contrary to liberal expectations, military advances brought a shift to the political right. Trotsky's articles on the government attempted to show how the monarchists were increasing their influence, even if to the detriment of efficiency and coherence of policy. Furthermore, for Trotsky the liberals were not serious contenders for power. Despite carrying an opposition mantle, the liberals wanted a more efficient authoritarian political system to answer the needs of capitalist development in Russia, i.e., the Prussification of the state order. Faced with a revolutionary situation the liberals would back the old regime.

Given that he thought that the proletariat was the only class which could transform Russia's political system and given that he dismissed Russian liberalism as an ideological prop of the monarchy, Trotsky was most concerned that the social-patriots, who accepted the liberals' tactics and called for a worker–liberal alliance, should be opposed in their attempts to win support among the workers. This concern explains his constant focus on the social-patriotic-liberal-government chain so that it should be clear to all, and to criticise the outpourings of the social-patriots to alert the workers. To achieve these goals, Trotsky was willing to distort social-patriotic writings and ridicule social-patriots.

However, by the time of his expulsion from Paris his urgent calls to Chkheidze to adopt a firmer stance against the social-patriots had not been heeded. On the contrary, it looked as though Chkheidze, who as leader of the Social-Democratic fraction in the Duma headed the most important medium for the dissemination of revolutionary propaganda among the workers, was moving towards social-patriotism. Nor can we say that *Nashe Slovo* made any impact upon Russian workers.

By the autumn of 1916 the following picture of Russian domestic politics, constructed from Trotsky's journalism, emerges: a government in disarray, a bankrupt though vociferous liberalism and leading Social-Democrats taking up social-patriotism. It was not a scenario that Trotsky himself would have welcomed. If socialists were to take advantage of Russia's permanent political crisis, they would have to become revolutionary-internationalists and assert ideological hegemony over the proletariat. Ironically, the February Revolution of 1917 took place without the conditions laid down by Trotsky and with the liberals playing a more revolutionary role than he would have predicted. However, these developments lay in the future. The next chapter will ask whether Trotsky discovered more promising developments in the European workers' movement.

8
European Social-Democracy

German Social-Democracy

In German Social-Democracy Trotsky discerned the same split between social-imperialists, passive centrists and revolutionary internationalists which characterised his analysis of Russian socialism. The vote of the largest socialist body of its day, the German Social-Democratic Party, for the war credits crushed any hopes that a united Second International would put a rapid halt to imperialist hostilities. For Trotsky, the Second International lay in ruins, and he looked for signs of international solidarity, i.e. a Marxist analysis of the war from socialists of all nationalities. Such unity would provide not only a basis for the rebirth of the International on new and firmer foundations, but also inspiration for revolutionary activists of the Trotsky mould. It is not surprising, therefore, to find Trotsky again and again emphasising the activities and growing influence of the German revolutionary left.

The title of one of Trotsky's first pieces on German Social-Democracy, 'There Are Still Social-Democrats in the World', was taken from a lead article in the February 1915 issue of *Lichtstrahlen*. That Trotsky borrowed from the radical German publication in this way is not accidental, it expressed the overriding concern of all wishing to overcome the recent socialist 'disgrace'. Trotsky's article was composed mainly of extracts from the *Lichtstrahlen* editorial, which praised Russian socialists for their stance on the London Conference: socialists should not realign according to military divides but, on the contrary, reveal the war's imperialist nature. Trotsky returned *Lichtstrahlen*'s compliment:

Never before ... have the activities of socialists in one country depended to such a degree upon socialists elsewhere. The rise of international solidarity and the struggle for peace can develop only parallely in all countries sucked into this bloody whirlpool ... Russian revolutionary Social-Democrats support not German imperialism ... but its deadly enemy, the internationalist wing of German Social-Democracy. In turn, the struggle of the latter is for us vital in our struggle against 'Entente' reaction.[1]

Trotsky's review of the first issue of Rosa Luxemburg's and Franz Mehring's journal *Internationale* was a further commentary upon the battle between social-nationalism and internationalism in the German workers' movement. Trotsky reported Luxemburg's critique of Kautsky's passive waiting for the war to end, as well as her response to the idea that the International engages in class struggle during peace and defends the nation when it is at war, i.e., bourgeois oppression increases during wars and this makes class struggle more necessary. After all, reasoned Luxemburg, how else was one to interpret the military dictatorship? Was not the socialist duty to oppose oppression? Furthermore, one could not abandon class struggle for class reconciliation without harming the movement: 'either the International remains a heap of ruins post-war or its restoration begins on the basis of class struggle.' The first step towards the latter, for Trotsky and for Luxemburg, was 'a struggle for a quick end to the war'; i.e. international socialist agitation *during* the war. In the course of 1915 the annexation question became central in German politics. German military advances increasingly brought the possibility of a 'German peace' into general discussion. However, the German Social-Democratic fraction's support of the war was premised upon Germany conducting a defensive war, and it restated its anti-annexationist stance in the Reichstag. For Trotsky this was not enough and he approvingly reported Rosa Luxemburg's view that social-imperialism had to be rejected outright. From Karla Zetkin's contribution Trotsky reproduced her call for a struggle for peace. Finally, he recounted Franz Mehring's view that the pro-war SPD leadership, despite attempts to underpin this policy with quotes from Marx and Engels, had abandoned scientific socialism in the pre-war era. The review ended by underlining the central message:

Against this self-deception, against this sad, cowardly and fraudulent method of scientific socialism for aims which are its deadly enemies, Franz Mehring calls for a merciless struggle under the banner of Marxism. One has to clearly show that we and they are made of a *different spirit!*[2]

In the pre-war years and beyond, Karl Kautsky was one of German Social-Democracy's leading theoreticians. Although not a Reichstag deputy, he attended the meeting of deputies of August 13 1914 which discussed tactics for the following day's vote on the war credits.[3] *Golos* readers were acquainted with Kautsky's views on the war from the October publication of his article 'Prospects of Peace'. Here Kautsky investigated what a good and lasting peace would look like. His response, national independence and a further spread of democracy, was based upon a particular view of the relationship between production, politics and the nation. From one direction, 'the more citizens speak the same language, the more intensive economic, political and spiritual life develops,' from another, the 'participation of the lower classes in spiritual and political life grows as a result of contemporary production'; processes which strengthened each nationality so that they could develop peacefully only within the nation-state: 'In the nation-state both these tendencies unite and strengthen one another. In a state of nationalities inter-ethnic conflict grows and retards economic and political development ... Hence it would be harmful if in the present war nation states used victory to annex other states, turning themselves into states of nationalities.'[4]

Polish, Baltic, and Finnish independence following Russia's defeat were, for Kautsky, examples corresponding to the requirements of democracy and progress. The German Social-Democrat was also optimistic about the post-war world order, in which the arms race that had caused the First World war would be eliminated. Kautsky envisioned disarmament as a staged process: the defeated countries would be disarmed and reap the economic benefits of disarmament, and the victors, faced with this economic evidence and an absence of military threat from the economically successful disarmed states, would not rearm. Social-Democracy in the victor countries would be given a 'solid basis for a successful struggle for disarmament'. Kautsky foresaw opposition to disarmament coming only from the military-industrial complex, but he predicted that even it, swamped with orders for the reconstruction of a ravaged infrastructure, would be won over. However, Social-Democracy would have to wait for the war to end before discovering how it could best secure a desirable peace. He was, though, still optimistic: 'Under the pressure of war we can achieve the unattainable ... even superpowers have to take public opinion into account. In peace negotiations the ruling classes often disagree. Public opinion can have an unprecedented influence.'[5]

It was not until June 1915 that Trotsky commented upon Kautsky's war-time position, in a lengthy review of Kautsky's review of Plekhanov's brochure *On the War*. At the outset Trotsky adopted a somewhat favourable tone, noting that Kautsky had given a healthy corrective to Plekhanov's statement that the German Social-Democrats had advocated proletarian action to prevent a war in the pre-war era. On the contrary, 'The German Marxists, and above all Bebel, at all national and international congresses rejected outright the idea of a general strike in response to mobilisation orders as utopian.'[6] But Trotsky and Kautsky soon parted company. Trotsky stated that Kautsky's defence of Haase's reading of the declaration in favour of war credits as that of the fraction and not of Haase himself had been demolished by Haase's recent refusal to read the latest patriotic declaration of the Social-Democratic Reichstag fraction.[7] The first instalment concluded with a critique of Kautsky's contention that *Vorwärts* changed from an anti-war to a pro-war stance because of the censorship. While he did not offer his own explanation for *Vorwärts's* U-turn, Trotsky said that the censor was blameless.[8] Since the fatal days of August 1914, however, Trotsky reported that both Haase and *Vorwärts* had moved to the left. Against this background, Kautsky's defence of outdated 1914 behaviour could only belittle this shift and confuse the international proletariat.

The second part of the trilogy of articles on 'Kautsky on Plekhanov' focused upon the German socialist's analysis of the war. Trotsky mentioned that Kautsky rejected the social-patriotic belief that victory of their homeland was in the best interests of international socialism. For Kautsky, all of the warring countries were economic and moral equivalents. There was no reason to suppose that the victory, or defeat, of any one country taken separately would be the most advantageous outcome. Nationalism among the workers had forced Social-Democratic parties across Europe to support the war, but, since the war was unlikely to progress beyond a stalemate, Kautsky declared that an immediate peace should be concluded on social-democratic principles, i.e., mutual agreement, not force. Kautsky expressed the hope that Plekhanov would join him in his call for peace.

The final instalment claimed that Kautsky's theoretical position was not as sorry as Plekhanov's but the latter's political position was clearer, and belittled Kautsky's lack of critical acumen. For example,

Trotsky contended that patriotic workers did not condition the behaviour of the Social-Democratic parties at the war's outset, rather the policy of national reformism, 'which characterised the whole proletarian class movement in the preceding epoch,' had to be examined. Of course, the mood of the masses could not be omitted, but nevertheless Social-Democrats should not capitulate to the workers. The urgency of this last point was becoming more and more apparent for Trotsky since, as even Kautsky himself had recognised, the proletariat was increasingly aware that the war was stuck in a stalemate. Workers would increasingly turn their anger on those responsible for the war, and Social-Democracy would be able to exploit this anger only to the extent that it had an independent revolutionary policy. This led Trotsky to Kautsky's greatest crime: he acknowledged that the ruling classes were becoming more and more isolated but refused to advocate proletarian action until the war had concluded. For the impatient Trotsky this was not good enough:

> The preservation of civil peace or a decisive break with the raving bourgeois 'nation'? ... This is the question which, as previously, Kautsky does not answer in his article on Plekhanov ... we want to struggle during the war so as not to appear bankrupt after the war ... in a situation unique for its drama, when the whole future of socialism is at stake, Kautsky does not give one piece of advice or one statement which we could approve.[9]

By the end of 1914 Liebknecht, hoping to provide a rallying-point for anti-war forces in Germnay, decided to break party unity in the Reichstag and vote against the second war credits bill of 3 December. In May 1915 the 'Left Opposition' issued its own manifesto, 'The Chief Enemy Is at Home', which *Nashe Slovo* reprinted. This decried German attempts to depict Italy's entry in the war as a betrayal. Did Germany not know Italian displeasure at Austria's ultimatum to Serbia, which had brought antagonism between Austro-Germany and Italy over supremacy in the Balkans to a head? The manifesto claimed that in the war-hysteria manoeuvres of the Italian imperialists, the German and Austrian regimes were merely observing the mirror image of their own recent behaviour. For the German Left Opposition, it was international imperialism which carried responsibility for the war, against which the international proletariat should struggle. Italian anti-war socialists were applauded for their bravery and for setting the appropriate example.[10]

'The Chief Enemy' also contained a damning description of German war aims: 'In March of this year a real chance for peace was spurned. Britain extended its hand – but greedy German imperialists turned it down. Attempts to conclude peace were totally dashed by German imperialists interested in colonial acquisitions, and in annexing Belgium and French Lorraine.'[11] In the context of German politics of World War One this statement had the makings of a political scandal. After all, in August 1914 Haase, representing Social-Democratic Reichstag deputies, had declared: 'We need to secure our country's culture and independence ... As soon as security concerns are met, the war shall be ended by a peace which will enable friendly, neighbourly relations ... On this basis we agree to the proposed loan.'[12] If the German radicals were correct, the party leadership would have to abandon any pretence of Germany's 'defensive' war, and perhaps lose control of the party.

In 'The German Opposition and German Diplomacy' Trotsky reported on the political fallout of the German radicals' Manifesto. The official newspaper *Norddeutsche Allgemeine Zeitung* denied that the German government had rejected peace negotiations to make new conquests, claiming that there was no wish for peace in Paris or in London. To refute this, Trotsky cited three sources. A letter in *Berner Tagwacht* outlined no less than three separate sets of secret peace negotiations, each of which had foundered because of the German government's insistence that it make territorial gains; *Norddeutsche Allgemeine Zeitung* of 24 April claimed that it would be folly for Germany to abandon its advantageous military position to conclude an inappropriate peace; and Bethman-Hollweg had asserted that Germany's Eastern borders should be extended and that Belgium should join a German customs union. It was Trotsky's hope that if warring governments could be shown to have aggressive war aims, if 'defencist' propaganda which formed the basis of 'civil peace' between socialist parties and their national governments could be proven false, then internationalist opposition to the war in socialist parties and among the proletariat would grow.[13] It was this self-same hope that would later underpin Trotsky's 'No Peace, No War' strategy when he headed the Bolshevik delegation in peace negotiations with Germany.

German Social-Democracy's 'centre' issued its own response to the 'annexationist' question in 'The Demand of the Hour'. Signed by Bernstein, Haase and Kautsky the manifesto made clear the centre's dissatisfaction with the Bethmann-Hollweg's annexationist demands. The centre's support for the statement of 4 August 1914 continued, and the SPD was urged to conduct a (non class-struggle) campaign for a peace of understanding. For Trotsky, as for the German Left, the centre's rejection of class struggle made it, objectively, a bulwark of the right 'social-imperialists'. Class struggle, in Trotsky's eyes, was *the* defining feature of Marxist strategy. In this sense the German centre was comparable to the 'passive internationalists' in Russian politics.[14] At the same time Trotsky acknowledged that the centre's critique, signed by leading figures, was worrying for the right. Indeed, the government was so disturbed that *Leipziger Volkszeitung* was suspended for publishing 'The Demand of the Hour'. Credit for the centre's shift leftwards was given to the German radicals who had 'raised Kautsky from his tranquillity'.[15] However, according to Trotsky, the centre was more destructive than constructive, and had to be defeated:

> the left's struggle with the centre in Germany is far from over. The working masses will increasingly break out from under the tutelage of the unprincipled centre, taking many leaders with them, the more decisive and principled the left conducts its critical and agitational work.[16]

A dispute between *Nashe Slovo* and a Central Committee of the Bund member, Vladimir Kosovskii (1868–1941), prompted Trotsky's next commentary on German Social-Democracy. The conflict arose out of two of Kosovskii's articles of May 1915, particularly a piece in the Bund's *Informatsionnyi Listok* on how to reestablish the Second International. Unlike Trotsky, Kosovskii had not written off the Second International for good. The errors committed by social-patriotism in August 1914 were perfectly understandable in the context of unprecedented difficulties. Kosovskii foresaw that 'the further course of the workers' movement' would correct mistakes in war time tactics. In this way, 'the International ... [will] ... be reestablished from the elements which have always composed it.'[17] He highlighted German Social-Democracy's continual shift leftwards as an example of self-criticism correcting a party's programme. He also noted that this was an uneven process. While the German party was abandoning the 'German' myth of the war as a war of liberation from Russian aggression, French socialists remained bound within the long established (and mistaken) view of the French Republic liberating Europe. Indeed, pro-war hysteria had grown in France since August 1914: French socialists were using growing anti-war sentiments in Germany as evidence of its internal disintegration to spur French soldiers on. Kosovskii urged French socialists to follow the example of their German comrades. The gulf of distrust which had opened-up between socialists after the outbreak of hostilities had to be overcome, not through London Conferences, but by uniting socialists of all countries in opposition to the war: '*Our task* is an immediate end to the war and a *peace without annexations*. All socialist parties could unite around this.'[18] The final myth dissected by Kosovskii was that of the Russian Social-Democrats themselves who thought that they could 'save the "rotten" ("social-chauvinist") West'. He argued that the slogan advanced by Russian 'real' socialists, i.e., 'new splits and new unifications', was simply the application of a long-standing Russian policy of splits on an all-European scale. The notion that a new International could be formed from 'Social-Democratic internationalists' was a nonsense because nobody knew what a 'Social-Democratic internationalist' was. Indeed, for Kosovskii, this definitional deficiency was not accidental because it lay at the heart of the policy of splits:

> Splitting everywhere, once and for all turning their backs on those who do not wish to turn the International into a sectionalist clique, they cannot but end up with a unification formula which is not worth tuppence ... This is how the Russian splitters think of the 'Third' International. If they achieve anything at all, it will be only a sad clique, a sect, a caricature of the International, devoid of all influence and significance.[19]

In the light of the Third International's subsequent history we may wish to praise Kosovskii's prescience. *Nashe Slovo* responded differently to this direct attack upon its campaign to unite socialist internationalists in a new, Third International. It denied that the *whole* of German Social-Democracy had abandoned the 4 August policy. Was not Mehring and his supporters calling the party leaders and press the 'corrupters'? By painting an over-optimistic picture of an anti-war mood gripping German Social-Democracy, *Nashe Slovo* claimed that Kosovskii was 'drawing a veil over the disgraceful behaviour of the German Social-Democrats'. It disputed Kosovskii's characterisation of the Russian socialists, pointing out that *Nashe Slovo* was not for splits, but winning old organisations from within by internationalists:

> Kosovskii's organisational fetishism (unity at all costs) is the obverse of organisational nihilism (splitting at all costs).

Organisational fetishism is not our option. Without internationalism the International will not be restored.[20]

Kosovskii defended himself in *Nashe Slovo*, which published his
letter to the editorial board. Kosovskii reiterated that German Social-
Democracy was being self-critical in a way that French socialism was
not. In turn, he accused *Nashe Slovo* of overstating its case. It was
wrong, for example, when it claimed (issue 47) that German Social-
Democrats were calling the war a war of liberation for the Poles while
defending Junkers who burned Polish villages. According to Kosovskii,
Nashe Slovo's scaremongering about the Second International could
bury all hopes for socialism:

> To say, without just cause, that the main parties of the
> International are in disarray and that social-imperialism and social-
> chauvinism reign everywhere, is also to say that the masses have
> been corrupted and that our cause is hopeless, for the official
> parties express the mood of the masses. We discredit international-
> ism and put off people who would otherwise come over to our side.

Kosovskii also denied that he had ignored ideology. On the contrary,
his point was that the 'old socialist parties ... cannot abandon
Marxism. This is guaranteed by the further class struggles of the proletariat. What will unite these parties and what will preserve socialist
unity is precisely Marxist ideology.'[21] This brought Kosovskii to the
nub of his disagreement with *Nashe Slovo*: he thought that one could
restore the International on its old foundations while the Paris publication did not.

It was at this point that Trotsky resolved to add his polemical skills
to the debate. 'Without Measure' ridiculed Kosovskii's misunderstanding of what constituted an internationalist policy:

> if voting for war credits ... and renouncing class struggle, desolving
> one's policy into the policy of the leading Junker national bloc, if
> all of this, in Kosovskii's view, is not rendering a political service to
> imperialism, then in general we are speaking different languages.

He agreed with Kosovskii that self-criticism was under way in the
German Social-Democratic Party, but he accused him of having no
analysis of its *dynamics*, of *why* self-criticism was occurring, i.e.
because the internationalist left-wing was struggling against the

centre and the party hierarchy. The vital issue was: 'Who do you support?' If Kosovskii thought that *Nashe Slovo's* case against him was harmful to socialism, for Trotsky only an internationalist policy, abandoning the reactionary features of the Second International's ideology, could guarantee a future for socialism:

> national blocs will come crashing down on the heads of those who created them. The task is to arm the proletariat with a clear consciousness of its revolutionary aims. This is our task, the left wing in the International. If we seek unification then it is not to form 'sects' ... but in order to internationalise our struggle with nationalism in the 'old' parties and proletarian organisations.[22]

Trotsky liked to pen biographical sketches. In 'Haase–Ebert–David' he charted the state of German Social-Democracy by following the handing-on of the reading of the SPD's declaration in favour of war credits during successive sessions of the Reichstag. For Trotsky, that men of decreasing stature fulfilled this demeaning task was evidence of a certain 'equilibrium ... established between people and ideas'. Moreover, David's leadership would have two beneficial consequences. The 'small skinny chap with the manners of a provincial diplomat' clearly illustrated the depths to which German Social-Democracy had sunk. Second, and more importantly, revolutionary internationalism could not be compromised by David's headship since he was a known reformist. Indeed, according to Trotsky, 'David's *political* triumph is our *ideological* triumph, for the symbolic sequence of German Social-Democracy's leaders in the Reichstag gives a personalised, physical expression to the idea that the principles of an independent class policy of the proletariat are incompatible with social-nationalism.' He bemoaned the left's inactivity, but predicted that Liebknecht's lone voice of opposition would one day 'have the last laugh'.[23]

One of Trotsky's Zimmerwald reports focused upon the German delegation, highlighting the important results a consistent application of Internationalist principles could bring. He stated that the German delegation consisted of abstainers in the war credit votes, i.e. people who had so far not joined Liebknecht. Ledebour's justification for abstaining, the preservation of party unity, was recounted, but Trotsky labelled abstaining as a 'passive reconciliation with "civil peace" ... [which] demoralises the proletariat'.[24] After reiterating his favoured tactics, the take over of the SPD by the left through an internal campaign, Trotsky reported that the abstainers conceded some ground during conference debates on German Social-Democracy. Ledebour abandoned his insistence that the SPD should not be censured for its votes on the war credits. Trotsky claimed a victory that was all but complete. The German delegation would not accept a formal obligation to oppose the government in future budget votes, but it did see that it was morally correct to do so.

Bukvoed's four-part 'Mehring on War' prompted Trotsky to write a rejoinder on the state of affairs among the German left. The final three of Bukvoed's contributions examined Mehring's analysis of pre-nineteenth-century wars. Trotsky had no major disagreements with the exposition's main conclusions: war is intrinsic to class societies and that war is a double-edged weapon upon which social-democrats cannot build their tactics.[25] However, in the first instalment Bukvoed set the scene for his subsequent pieces by outlining various responses which socialists had taken to the war, including the 'offensive/defensive' distinction and calling for the defeat of one's own government as the 'lesser evil'. He pointed out that even Liebknecht had initially supported the war, and claimed that the left opposition which had eventually crystallised against the policy of 4 August was disintegrating.[26] It was this claim that Trotsky found objectionable. Notwithstanding philosophical-historical and tactical disputes which are 'possible and even inevitable', the German left opposition *was* united around a programme of 'political action'. He regretted that Liebknecht had not immediately adopted a revolutionary-socialist stance in August 1914, but 15 months later Liebknecht's name was 'synonymous with socialist bravery'. After distinguishing the revolutionary left ('conducting in Germany a brave struggle against "civil peace", disrobe the hypocritical ideology of "national defence", break down the barriers of legality and call the masses against the war and the ruling classes') from the passive-pacifists (Kautsky, Bernstein, Haase), Trotsky issued the following battle cry: 'Hand in hand with those [left] elements we have begun and will conduct further work towards the creation of a Third International!'[27]

In December 1915 the Social-Democratic deputy Scheidemann met the German chancellor to discuss Germany's war aims. This meeting resulted in Bethmann-Hollweg's most annexationist statement to date, backed by Scheidemann. The left-centre in German Social-Democracy was appalled. In a re-run of a dilemma that was to plague the Russian Provisional government of 1917, the left-centre was willing to support the war only as long as it was fought for defensive aims. Faced with openly annexationist pronouncements from the government and the SPD leadership, in December 1915 20 left-centre deputies broke party unity on the war credits, rather than abstaining as they had done in March and August. Rosa Luxemburg was not ecstatic by the left-centre's shift leftwards. For her, its opposition was because what had begun as a defensive war was now aggressive, whereas the left opposed the war as an imperialist war. Trotsky's analysis of the declaration of the 20 followed Luxemburg's critique, declaring it not 'sufficently principled',[28] and regretting that French social-patriots could only gain ammunition for France's war of 'self-defence' from the declaration's evaluation of Germany's strategic advantages. However, Trotsky found good cause for revolutionary optimism in his explanation of the left-centre's shift leftwards. According to the *Nashe Slovo* correspondent, it was Zimmerwald, the pressure issuing from the masses and the logic of events which had pushed the 20 from abstention to open opposition. The tide had turned and was clearly flowing in the direction of Zimmerwald. The vote was not a single 'episode' but an 'important date in the rebirth of socialism.'

Two special events of very different natures gave Trotsky reason to pen hagiographies of Franz Mehring and Rosa Luxemburg, two of the leading figures on the German left. Franz Mehring was 70 on 27 February 1916, and Trotsky paid tribute to his talents as historian and publicist of the German workers' movement. However with no doubt an eye to, among others, Plekhanov, he stated that it was not for past services that he was now raising his hat to Mehring. The 'old man' of the German movement had opposed the policy of 4 August in the journal *Internationale*, 'providing invaluable support for the growing left opposition which is now the genuine bearer of the German proletariat's honour'. Rosa Luxemburg had been arrested on 18 February 1915 for anti-war activity. She was released on 22 January 1916, commenting, 'I have returned to "freedom" with a tremendous appetite for work.'[29] Trotsky welcomed her back to the 'new class struggle' and ended his tribute on a political point, expressed emotionally: 'In the persons of Franz Mehring and Rosa Luxemburg we greet the spiritual kernel of the revolutionary German opposition with which we are linked by an indissoluble brotherhood in arms.'[30]

At the beginning of April 1916 Trotsky commented upon the most recent vote on the budget, at which the centre for the second time voted against the government. In the previous months the German left had further defined its position as a separate fraction. On New

Years Day 1916 a group of left delegates approved Luxemburg's Zimmerwald Manifesto as part of a campaign, in Liebknecht's words, 'to recapture the party upwards through mass rebellion.'[31] Liebknecht thought that the centre would either have to go over to the left or join the right or be crushed in the clash of the two extremes; a fate which Trotsky assigned to the centre of Russian politics.[32] In 'On the Split in the Reichstag Social-Democratic Fraction' Trotsky affirmed his critique of the centre as 'socialist pacifists', and reviewed the significance of the centre vote from a new standpoint. He began by claiming that in the decade preceding 1914 Europe had experienced two parallel processes: a massive development of the productive forces and an equalisation of the forms and methods of struggle of the workers' movement in Britain, Germany and France, i.e. a growth of parliamentarianism and centrally organised trade unions. The most notable consequence of the equalisation of the conditions and methods of workers' struggles was the formation of a single psychology, namely limited, national-reactionary responses from proletarian organisations, which did though take various forms in different countries. In Germany, for example, the workers were hypnotised by workers' democracy within their organisations, whereas in France the proletariat was hypnotised by the French Republic and the traditions of 1789. Nevertheless the rapid appearance of social-patriotism in workers' organisations in all the warring countries grew of the shared psychology, rooted in the nature of the previous epoch. Trotsky noted that Russian, Italian and Balkan socialists had remained truer to internationalism, but their efforts would be for nought unless German Social-Democracy threw off the heritage of 'organisational fetishism':

> Only a profound internal upheaval in German Social-Democracy can guarantee the creation of a centralised revolutionary International, just as only the capture of power by the proletariat in Germany, the mighty citadel of capitalism and militarism, can secure the victory of the European socialist revolution.

It was from this perspective, the importance of German Social-Democracy, that Trotsky interpreted the splits in the Reichstag fraction, including the pacifist centre, as an important step towards a genuine rebirth of international socialism:

> Before the German proletariat there henceforth stands two fractions, forcing it in the fire of events to make a choice and freeing it

from automated discipline, a tool of imperialist reaction. Only through a rupture in organisational routine will the German proletariat move to the unity and discipline of *revolutionary activity*. The split in the fraction is an important stage on this path.[33]

Issues concerning the International were central to Trotsky's next contribution on German Social-Democracy, examining 'K. Kautsky on the International'. This article translated in full Karl Kautsky's letter, published in *Berner Tagwacht*, in which the German socialist replied to a left-radical critique of his war time positions. Kautsky reasserted that the International was weaker during wars than during peace, but emphasised that this did not mean that the International had to lie low until peace was concluded.[34] For Trotsky, Kautsky's position could only lead social-democrats into a blind alley. In order to overcome militarism the International would have to be at the height of its powers. Why, then, ask the organisation of the international proletariat to struggle for peace at a time when it was at its weakest? Trotsky then focused upon another flaw in Kautsky's case, i.e. limiting a struggle for peace to calls by socialist parties for a peace without annexations. Trotsky pointed out that the resolutions of the Copenhagen, London and Vienna conferences followed Kautsky's advice, but had been impotent because their demands had not been connected to a programme of action. Trotsky turned Kautsky on his head – the Second International, formed during peace, had proven itself to be weak whereas, during the war, a new International was taking shape that would show itself to be an instrument of revolution. After labelling Kautsky's opposition to outright social-patriotism a 'half-way house' which alerted the workers to official falsehoods while not taking them to the logical conclusion of revolutionary action, Trotsky urged the left radicals to continue their campaign against Kautsky's 'procrastinating pacifism'.

Thus far Trotsky's analysis of the struggles between the social-patriots, the centre and the left in German Social-Democracy had focused upon the balance of forces, their likely future development and the consequences of this for the workers' movement. In 'Höglund and Liebknecht' he reported on the response of the ruling classes to the ever-increasing crystallisation of the left. On May Day 1916 Liebknecht was arrested for shouting anti-war slogans in the middle of the Potsdamerplatz in Berlin. Trotsky placed this arrest in the context of a series of similar measures taken against revolutionary internationalists in several countries. In Sweden Höglund, member of parliament, was arrested along with two other members of the Swedish left opposition, Heden and Oljedund, for calling upon workers to stage a general strike if Sweden abandoned its neutrality; John MacLean received a long term of imprisonment in April 1916 for his anti-war activity in Scotland; and, finally, in Ireland the seven men who signed the declaration of Irish independence during the 1916 Easter rebellion were shot. For Trotsky, all these measures were but a foretaste of the 'future policy of the whole European bourgeoisie in the approaching epoch of revolutionary upheavals'.[35] In the meantime Höglund and Liebknecht were the heroes of the forming Third International.

Trotsky examined Liebknecht's trial from another perspective in 'Karl Liebknecht'. He noted that the German socialist had received the minimum sentence possible for his 'crime', but rejected in advance any thought that the court had been lenient. Liebknecht had agreed with all the charges against him and had even attempted to antagonise the court. What then explained the minimum sentence? According to Trotsky, the state did not wish to make a martyr out of Liebknecht: 'in Germany, where the awakening of the mightiest of social classes is at stake, one has to dole out repression in doses so as not to hasten the process of hightening revolutionary passion.'[36] However, pointing to the political strike which had been called as response to Liebnecht's sentencing, Trotsky declared that Liebknecht's imprisonment could not divert events from taking their 'natural course of development'. The name on the banner of the workers' movement was now Liebknecht, whom Trotsky claimed as his 'closest ally'.

Trotsky's final report on the German Social-Democracy before he was exiled from France was a reprint of an article which had appeared in the second issue of the Bremen publication *Arbeiterpolitik*. 'Amongst the German Opposition' serves as a convenient concluding summary of Trotsky's views on developments in the German workers' movement.[37] It outlined the different nature of the centre's ('pacisfist', 'half-hearted') and the left's ('revolutionary', 'principled') opposition to Scheidmann's support of Germany's war efforts. Trotsky warned the left not to join up with the centre which, due to its uncertainty, would always remain within the orbit of the right. Dismissing accusations of 'sectionalism' that had been levelled against the left, Trotsky reemphasised his basic position: strict adherence to principles was necessary for firm action which would win the day, and the organisations, from below and from within.

Austrian Social-Democracy

From 1907 until 1914 Trotsky, after being refused right of settlement in Berlin, set up home in Vienna. There he met with the leading lights of Austrian Social-Democracy, Victor and Fritz Adler, Rudolf Hilferding and Otto Bauer. At the outbreak of the war the behaviour of the Austrian party could have been no less disappointing to Trotsky than that of its German counterpart. It immediately approved the SPD's vote of 4 August. Nevertheless, he for long remained silent on the Austrian SPOe, publishing his first article on this party in May 1916. His quiescence can be put down to several possible reasons. Just as the internal contradictions besetting Austria could have been seen as secondary to Germany's mightier and faster developing economy and society, the SPOe could have been viewed as an adjunct of its 'big brother'. Another and more prosaic possibility is that there was little material for journalistic accounts of Austrian developments. The Austrian parliament was prorogued in the spring of 1914 and was not summoned until May 1917. Hence there was no crisis on war credits, the focus of much of Trotsky's reportage on German Social-Democracy, in the Austrian party. Furthermore, the party press supported the German SPD vote *en bloc*, *Arbeiter-Zeitung* declaring 4 August 'a day of the proudest and most powerful exaltation of the German spirit',[38] and Trotsky loved nothing better than a clash of fractions before entering the fray. Indeed, it was a shift in outlook of *Arbeiter-Zeitung* that prompted him to write a report for *Nashe Slovo*.

'In Austria' gives a brief account of the first two issues of *Arbeiter-Zeitung* of May 1916. As background information Trotsky sketched the newspaper's pre-war politics, the most 'German national socialist newspaper ... [which] ... was always prepared to defend the "German" interests and the German character of Vienna from Czech "encroachment"'. Now, though, the newspaper was devoid of triumphant German nationalism. A lead article of 2 May spoke of a hopeless military situation for both of the warring camps, and reported a widespread desire for peace. A further contribution painted a sorry picture of the economic situation, claiming that only time would tell whether capitalism would survive the dislocation caused by the war. While reports of this kind were obviously welcome to Trotsky, he derided the Austrian party for not constructing a political programme of action centring on a struggle for peace. Passiveness was tantamount to social-patriotism which meant support for the ruling classes, and the Austrian party's crime was that it was the 'most passive' of all social-patriotic parties: 'it would be hard to think of a policy so intent on neutralising the proletariat, suppressing any initiative, dampening all protest, as that of Austrian Social-Democracy.'[39] Trotsky concluded in typical fashion with a call to the Austrian opposition to liberate the proletariat from the shackles of official party policy.

The link between analysis and practice also featured in Trotsky's next piece on the Austrian Social-Democrats, praising them for their theoretical ability which 'approached Marxism'. Two recent articles from *Arbeiter-Zeitung* had illustrated how the war was preparing the ground for a future socialist order. The ravage caused by the conflict had placed socialist goals of peace and labour on the agenda; the dislocation of war had knocked parochialism out of people, ushering a new internationalist spirit; and, finally, the might of military technology had revealed what a centralised, mass organisation of production could achieve. In short, *Arbeiter-Zeitung* predicted that the post-war order would be an 'epoch of social spirit.' Of course Trotsky could agree with much of this analysis. He approvingly summarised *Arbeiter-Zeitung*'s view of the war as 'forming in its entrails a revolutionary generation and bringing it face to face with the tasks of a socialist organisation of society'. However, he regretted the fact that true to the traditions of the Austrian party, the leadership retained an outdated and reactionary policy.[40]

In his next writing on the *Arbeiter-Zeitung* Trotsky had not a hint of praise for the Austrian publication's strong approval of Italian socialists who, right up to Italy's entry, had urged their country to remain neutral. Trotsky reasoned that sinister motives lay behind *Arbeiter-Zeitung*'s new found 'internationalism'. *Arbeiter-Zeitung* had done nothing less than use Italian socialist opposition to Italy's entry as evidence of the Italian ruling class's 'aggressiveness', a crucial plank in the 'defensive' lie propagated by the Austro-German military machine. Furthermore, Trotsky pointed out that such hypocrisy was not limited to Austro-German social-patriotic publications. He highlighted *L'Humanité* as *Arbeiter-Zeitung*'s French soul mate. It was using the radical German newspaper *Leipziger Volkszeitung*'s denunciations of the German ruling class so that its French counterparts could 'shine radiantly before the auditorium of the French proletariat'. This left Trotsky with the rather depressing question: 'which of them is better?'[41]

When opposition to the Austrian government did manifest itself in an open and dramatic way, it came as something of a surprise to

Trotsky. In October 1916 Fritz Adler, editor of *Kampf* and a left radical, demonstrated his hatred of the war and the government waging it by killing the Austrian Prime Minister, Baron Stürgkh. Trotsky wondered why Adler resorted to terrorism. After all Adler, as a Marxist, did not believe that a 'well-directed bullet can cut the Gordian knot of great historical problems'. According to Trotsky, the key to understanding Adler's act lay in Austrian Social-Democracy's internal affairs. Regular readers would know of Trotsky's frustration with the SPOe, able to produce clear analysis but incapable of taking firm political action. How much greater must this frustration have inculcated a radical living in the midst of indifference and inactivity. The son of the 'father' of the Austrian movement knew all too well the bureaucrats and careerists who had risen to dominate the party during the pre-war parliamentary regime. It was they who had rejected Adler's 'Zimmerwald' resolution presented to a meeting of the SPOe's national council in March 1916. The pressure of demanding action to save socialism from bearing responsibility for the war and finding only an indifferent leadership reached such a point that Adler resolved to make a dramatic gesture. For Trotsky one could have nothing but admiration: 'Like a heroic pointsman who cuts his veins and warns of danger with a handkerchief soaked in his own blood Fritz Adler turned his life into a alarm bell for the deceived and inert working class ... The heart of this unhappy humanity still beats if, among its sons, there is such an errant knight!'[42]

French Social-Democracy

Opposition to the war was understandably weak among French socialists. It was after all Germany which had invaded France, 'shared' imperialist guilt did not hold much attraction for a people who accepted that they were fighting a 'war of defence'. This did not prevent Trotsky from using his journalistic powers to argue for a revolutionary programme of action against the war in France.

His first clash with a French social-patriotic publication was in a 'Letter to the Editorial Board of *L'Humanité*'. It was in *L'Humanité* that an adversary familiar to Trotsky, Aleksinskii, had described Parvus as an 'agent-provocateur paid by the German and Turkish governments',[43] claiming that even *Nashe Slovo* had warned others to have nothing to do with Parvus. Trotsky felt compelled to pen a reply not because he was against critiques of the German philosopher. He opposed Parvus's war time position and had described the inspirer of the theory of permanent revolution as 'politically dead'.[44] Trotsky objected to the insinuation that *Nashe Slovo* also thought Parvus to be a German agent, for which there was no evidence. If *Nashe Slovo* advised a boycott of Parvus's institute in Copenhagen, it did so only because Parvus was subordinating socialism to militarism and the class state.

The dispute with *L'Humanité* did little to enlighten readers of Trotsky's greatest worry, that of the *union sacrée*. He seized the opportunity presented by a ministerial crisis to claim a future for revolutionary socialism in France. During 1915 the French army was on the offensive, incurring great losses for little territorial gain. By October 1915 a mixture of growing opposition within and outside the government brought about the fall of the Viviani cabinet. In 'The Essence of the Crisis' Trotsky did not deny that poor military performance played a large role in Viviani's fall. There was though a more important and instructive aspect to this affair, namely 'the basic contradictions ... of French radicalism in the current imperialist epoch'.[45] In brief, the French radicals, made-up primarily of petty bourgeois elements, were powerless before imperialist finance capital. It was the latter, the big capitalists, which decided policy. Indeed, socialist deputies were allowed to occupy war-time ministerial posts out of pragmatic considerations. They served as a useful control lever over the people at a time of great hardships. Conservative dailies continued to appear while the radical press had disappeared or lost its teeth. What further evidence did one need that the imperialists were in control? For Trotsky, France needed to find socialists who would not sacrifice themselves to the *union sacrée* but those who would overcome all obstacles to achieve socialism.

One month later Trotsky stressed the extent to which the ruling class in France did not have control of events. In 'Without a Programme, Without Perspectives, Without Control' he speculated that no programmatic changes would result from Briand's appointment to head the government. In part Trotsky related the inertia of French politics to the condition of its parliamentarianism which had no fresh reserves of people or ideas. Most at blame, however, was the failings of the European ruling classes, of which the French was only a representative example, which had lost any control over events. *Nashe Slovo* readers could at least be comforted by their correspondent's concluding words: 'history is calling other forces to seize control'.[46]

However, when opposition to the war began to be heard with increasing frequency in the French Socialist Party it was not of a sort that pleased Trotsky. It was none other than Karl Marx's grandson, Jean Longuet, who led an opposition group in the parliamentary party. His disaffection with the war issued from pacifist principles, expounded in *Le Populaire*, a weekly newspaper which he also edited. At a meeting of the Socialist Party's national council of April 1916 Longuet and his supporters mustered over 30 per cent of the votes cast. From August 1916 until the time of his expulsion from France Trotsky again and again advised revolutionary Marxists why and how they should wage a campaign against 'Longuetism'.

In his first article on this theme Trotsky examined Longuet's plans to restore the International. The French pacifist had called for a meeting of socialists of Entente countries as a first step towards a conference of socialists of all nationalities. Trotsky asked why such a hopeless scheme had been proposed. After all, the Italian, Russian, British, Serbian and Portuguese parties all supported Zimmerwald and would hardly attend an exclusively Entente affair. For Trotsky, it was clear that the Longuetists were playing a role common to all purely parliamentary oppositions, 'to win time',[47] which at that moment this was tantamount to 'wasting time'.

Following the conclusion of the Zimmerwald conference of September 1915, the French delegates Merrheim and Bourderon organised a *Comité pour la Reprise des Relations Internationales* in Paris. Trotsky had close ties with Merrheim and in August 1916 he sent a draft declaration to the *Comité*, outlining why Zimmerwaldists should have no truck with Longuetists. He pointed out that the Longuetist parliamentary group still voted for the war credits, thus failing a crucial litmus test for internationalism. For Trotsky, the Longuetists were playing such a pernicious role in French politics that he employed conspiracy theory to explain their existence: Longuetism was necessary as an outlet for opposition to Renaudel's uncompromising support of the war while holding this opposition within the boundaries of official party policy. It was for this reason that Trotsky perceived the Longuetists to be the most dangerous species of social-patriots for they attempted to 'soothe the workers' socialist conscience with secondary concessions, in this way diverting them from a real struggle against the war'.[48] Hence the urgent task was to disrobe the Longuetists' lies and to spread real revolutionary language among the workers. Trotsky urged the *Comité* to take these tasks upon itself. Just over one week later he was able to report that, despite objections from some syndicalists, the *Nashe Slovo* resolution was passed by the *Comité*.[49]

Not everyone was overjoyed by the *Comité*'s acceptance of the need to struggle against Longuetism. In an interesting letter published along with a reply from the editors, A. Lozovskii, for example, criticised *Nashe Slovo*'s declaration even though he himself was a left critic of the centre.[50] Lozovskii argued that the declaration made three basic errors. It incorrectly categorised the *Confédération Général du Travail* as the equivalent of Longuetism in the syndicalist movement, in actual fact the *Confédération* clearly backed Renaudel's out and out patriotism. Second, *Nashe Slovo* was wrong to say that the Longuetists were consciously trying to mislead the workers. While he accepted that the centre was not sufficiently internationalist, Lovoskii viewed its shortcomings as an objective consequence of its politics which were sincerely held. By insisting upon the subjective motivation of the centre *Nashe Slovo* was complicating relations between the Zimmerwaldists and the centre when the latter, and especially its left wing, could become tomorrow's ally. Finally, Lozovskii questioned the tactic of sending a resolution to the *Comité* as a means of combating Longuetism. The *Comité* was dominated by syndicalists who would pass as many anti-Longuetist resolutions as were sent, but who were themselves even less revolutionary socialist than the centre. Furthermore, tactical resolutions were not the best way to achieve agitational aims. *Nashe Slovo* should have invited Longuetists to a gathering of socialists to debate its declaration and only then urged the meeting to pass a resolution.

In its reply *Nashe Slovo* accused Lozovskii of committing the worst of political crimes, that of underestimating the enemy. In the case of Longuetism the consequences of this crime were magnified since its tactic depended upon goodwill towards it for success: 'for the Longuetists ambiguity is an important tool in their political struggles; for Zimmerwaldists ambiguity means death or more precisely dissolving into Longuetism.'[51] *Nashe Slovo* announced that it was not against a public debate with Longuetists, but one had to define one's relation to them beforehand, precisely what its resolution had achieved. A clear statement of the shortcomings of Longuetism and the necessity to combat it was now extant. One only had to have the bravery not to be diverted from these tasks.

On the day that Trotsky received his expulsion order from France, the concluding part of his analysis of 'French and German Social-Patriotism' appeared in *Nashe Slovo*. In the first contribution Trotsky was concerned to establish the stable and anti-revolutionary nature of Longuetist politics. He argued that Longuetism's mixture of support for the war while calling for socialists not to accept ministerial posts should not be taken as evidence of a transition to a left position. Rather the Longuetists thought of their strategy as long-term which would accrue several advantages for socialists. They would back their country's war effort but avoid both responsibility for any mistakes and being assimilated into a national bloc. In retaining a distinct socialist identity the ground would be prepared for future electoral successes, and lead to a speedy restoration of the International which would be able to influence a peace settlement. Trotsky not only thought the Longuetists inconsistent – how could one vote money to a government which one considered unfit to join? – he also declared that the Longuetist programme shared the aims of Renaudel and the right: 'Supporting the Socialist Party in the war as a means of disciplining the workers in the interests, and under the control, of the capitalist state by these means strengthening or, at least, preserving the party's parliamentary position – these are the tasks general to Renaudel and Longuet.'[52]

The second and concluding article focused upon the assumptions common to the Longuetists and to German Social-Patriots.[53] According to Trotsky both groups thought the war should be conducted to safeguard their countries' independence and were in favour of a peace without annexations. The Longuetists were even able to point to their German counterparts as an illustration of what French socialists would gain by refusing ministerial posts: Scheidemann had been able to attend the Hague conference because this in no way reflected upon the German government. After pointing out that the Longuetists and Scheidemann also shared antipathy towards Liebknecht, Trotsky outlined two scenarios in which he illustrated why an internationalist perspective was worth retaining. In a pessimistic picture he argued that if the crisis in the workers' movement proved protracted, only revolutionary internationalism could provide workers with a principled explanation of events. Optimistically, if the workers were to arise in anger at their worsening condition, the revolutionary internationalists would immediately be able to occupy a vanguard role. Unfortunately for Trotsky, at the time of writing, there was little sign of revolutionary internationalism dominating French socialism.

British socialism

Trotsky wrote very little about events in Britain, despite the fact that the British socialist movement was beset by the same social-chauvinist-centre-left splits upon which he commented elsewhere.[54] There can be no doubt that although he presented no full analysis of the correlation of forces in the British workers' movement, Trotsky felt that the left wing of the British Socialist Party, John MacLean and associates, and its publications, *Justice* and *The Call*, were his allies in Britain. For example, he noted MacLean's imprisonment of April 1916, and in an article on the 1916 Easter Uprising in Ireland he referred to the Glaswegian socialist as the leader of a revolutionary upsurge in Scotland: 'Scottish soldiers broke the Dublin barricades. But in Scotland itself the coal miners are uniting around the red banner raised by MacLean and his friends.'

Trotsky's only commentary upon the Easter Uprising contained an analysis of Irish class forces and revolutionary perspectives reminiscent of Trotsky's prognoses for Russia. Thus, to the extent that an Irish trade-industrial bourgeoisie had formed since the turn of the century it was 'anti-proletarian' and subordinate to British imperialism; the peasants were backward and isolated, governed by 'stupid farm egoism'; finally, the proletariat, the only revolutionary force, had to be won over to revolutionary internationalism from 'national enthusiasts' and myopic trade unionism. Viewing the events in Dublin as evidence of a transition from feudal agrarian 'national' upheavals to the era of international socialist revolutions, Trotsky welcomed the Easter Uprising as evidence that 'the historical role of the Irish proletariat is only just beginning'.[55]

There are several possible reasons for Trotsky's reticence in commenting upon British developments. *Nashe Slovo* received reports from Britain from, amongst others, G. V. Chicherin, and Trotsky probably agreed with these analyses.[56] Furthermore, he had not been in Britain for many years and felt better qualified, or more stimulated, to write about countries and people of which he had personal knowledge. He had not met, nor would he ever meet, John MacLean, whereas he knew Kautsky, Plekhanov, Adler and so on. Certainly 'personal factors', a friendship with Christian Rakovsky and time spent in the Balkans as war reporter for *Kievskaya Mysl*, were present in Trotsky's writings upon developments in the Balkans.

Balkan Social-Democracy

Trotsky had formulated his solution to the ethnic tensions rife in the Balkans, the creation of a Balkan federative republic, while working as a reporter there during the pre-1914 Balkan Wars.[57] He carried this analysis into his World War One writings and in several theoretical articles attempted to show why transnational state structures would ensure peaceful economic, political and cultural development.

Trotsky thought the nation and the state to be two distinct entities. The former was a lasting source and bearer of culture, most noticeably through language, while the latter was a temporary phenomenon constructed for economic reasons. At some point in history the interests of economic progress brought the capitalist state into existence. However, by World War One economic forces had outgrown the limits of the national state. Hence Trotsky's argument that the real source of the war was not external aggression from one state against another, as the social-patriots and exponents of the 'defence of the homeland' insisted, but a *domestic* demand for economic development. According to Trotsky, even if the war resulted in a European map redrawn so that state structures coincided with ethnic groups, new conflicts would inevitably arise: 'An independent Hungary or Bohemia or Poland would seek a sea outlet by infringing the rights of other nationalities just as Italy seeks it at the expense of the Serbs or the Serbs at the expense of the Albanians.'[58] For Trotsky, the only possible solution to these problems was to guarantee the independence of the nation, vital for cultural survival and growth, and a wider market, essential for economic wellbeing, through the establishment of transnational democratic states. Furthermore these goals could only by reached through socialism:

> Destroying the very basis of the economy the current imperialist war is the most convincing expression of the dead-end in which bourgeois society is foundering. Only socialism, which neutralises the nation in an economic sense, uniting humanity in lasting cooperation, liberating the world economy from the vice of the nation and liberating national culture from the vice of international economic competition – only socialism provides solutions to the contradictions which currently threaten human culture.[59]

In his journalism on Balkan Social-Democracy Trotsky focused upon individuals who shared his analysis as a way of propagating their case. During his sojourns around the Balkans Trotsky met and became friends with the founder of Romanian socialism, Dobrodjanu Gerea. Trotsky celebrated Gerea's 40th birthday with an anniversary article in *Nashe Slovo*.[60] Here he commended the former leader of Romanian Social-Democracy for his theoretical acumen, expressed with particular clarity in the book *Neo-Serfdom*. Finally, Trotsky stressed the connection between scientific socialism and correct practice by noting Gerea's battle against Romanian imperialism and for the establishment of a Balkan democratic federation.

In the two-part article 'In the Balkans' he illustrated the hopeless intrigues both of the Balkan bourgeoisie, who wanted to use the strategic weaknesses of the great powers to aid capitalist development in the Balkans for their own gain, on the one hand, and of the great powers, who wanted to seize territory in the Balkans under the guise of fighting for the liberation of oppressed peoples, on the other. He cited the Bulgarian Social-Democratic publication *Novoe Vremya*, which had highlighted the impossibility of the Balkan peoples deciding which side to back in the war: opting for the Entente would result in domination by Russia and Italy, deciding for the Central Powers rule from Berlin and Vienna. Trotsky called upon his Bulgarian, Romanian and Serbian comrades to continue broadcasting such beliefs, firm in the conviction that one day this would ease the transition to socialism.[61]

As the war dragged on without a sign that the military stalemate would be broken, a struggle to win over neutral countries became increasingly intensive. In October 1915 Germany succeeded in attracting Bulgaria to its side in return for a promise that it would receive territory in Macedonia lost to Serbia during the Balkan Wars. Trotsky examined Bulgarian socialists' responses in 'Bulgarian Social-Democracy and the War.' Once again he found social-patriots who, guided by 'national' interests, supported the intervention. However, Bulgarian social-patriots had had to perform a particular somersault, for they had been forced to abandon their previously held Russophile philosophy. The revolutionary-socialists, on the other hand, had faced no such dilemma. Although their publications had been suppressed they had preserved their belief in socialism and in a democratic federative Balkan republic. In what was very much an article intended to strengthen the spirit of the faithful Trotsky expressed his conviction that

> we do not for one minute doubt their revolutionary bravery and belief in socialism; that together with them – over the trenches which currently separate us – we are convinced in a future revolutionary uprising in which we and they will find our true place![62]

An earlier chapter noted how Trotsky cited Rakovsky's critique of the Russian social-patriots as further ammunition in his battle with this group. On several occasions he also referred to the exploits of his old friend on specifically Balkan affairs. Trotsky received Rakovsky's introduction to *Socialism and the War* in manuscript form. He reproduced several extracts from it in *Nashe Slovo*.[63] These citations made several points, most notably that a federative Balkan republic could only be achieved through the class struggle of the proletariat, and that judging the war with 'offensive' and 'defensive' criteria meant using imperialist categories.

In 1916 Romania came under increasing pressure to join the war. It did so in August 1916 when, in return for a promise of land in Transalvania, it sided with the Entente. Rakovsky's arrest and subsequent conditional release following his participation in strikes in Galicia prompted Trotsky to comment upon developments in Romania.[64] He praised Rakovsky's 'revolutionary internationalism' and presented a brief analysis of Romanian society. Despite the weak development of Romanian industry Trotsky claimed that the 'young and energetic' proletariat was the most strategically powerful class in a country of 'dark peasant masses' and parasitic ruling cliques. He argued that these latter had allowed Romanian socialists to conduct anti-war agitation while they wanted Romania to remain neutral. Indeed for a while the socialists even served as a convenient counter pressure to pro-Entente activists. However, socialist agitation became inconvenient for a government which was considering a more active role in the war. Hence Rakovsky's arrest. The lesson Trotsky drew from these events was the closer governments moved towards declaring war, the clearer the distinction would become between revolutionary socialists, who would be sent to gaol, and social-patriots, who would join war ministries.

*

Trotsky's Parisian journalism on European Social-Democracy sought to make several points. August 1914 marked a significant turning-point, for it signalled the end of the Second International and the epoch of reformism from which it grew. In order to prepare themselves and the proletariat for the coming epoch of revolutionary upheavals Marxist internationalists should propagate their ideas independent of all right social-imperialists and their centrist cohorts. Marxist internationalists, in arguing their own line, should remain within existing parties in order to win them from within. Finally, a Third International would have to be established to guide communists in their struggle to establish transnational federative republics.

We have seen that Volkogonov viewed Trotsky as a cosmopolitan, absorbed with non-Russian affairs.[65] However, if one compares the volume and nature of Trotsky's writings on Russian domestic politics and his polemics with the various branches of Russian Social-Democracy with his articles on pan-European affairs, it becomes evident that he wrote more, and felt on surer ground, when commenting upon the former.

Although Trotsky himself had great faith in the power of the pen and the veracity of his analyses, it would be true to say that he observed and followed events rather than moulded them. It would be difficult to claim any great influence for his journalism upon European developments, even in the socialist parties. His articles stressed a core set of beliefs, as is to be expected from a task which had a predominantly propaganda character. In the circumstances he could hardly do anything else. Faced with a situation in which most socialists supported their countries' war efforts, he was fighting a rearguard battle. Perhaps he would encounter more promising circumstances as he moved from the Old World to the New.

9
From the Old World to the New: Spain and America

The fullest account of the several months that Trotsky spent in Spain appeared in *Krasnaya nov* of July 1922 and January 1926. In these issues the Russian journal published extracts from Trotsky's note-books, in which he kept a record of events from his expulsion from France to his arrival in New York. These extracts were then reprinted in volume nine of Trotsky's collected works, *Europe at War* (1927), and were subsequently used as the basis of chapter 21, 'Through Spain', of his autobiography, *My Life* (1930). In these texts Trotsky recounts the day he spent in San Sebastian, 'where I was delighted by the sea but appalled by the prices'; his rapid departure to Madrid where, after seven days of freedom, he was arrested; his then transfer to Cadiz where, under police surveillance, he was permitted to wander about the town until his fate was sealed: he was to remain in Spain until he could board a boat bound for America. On 20 December he travelled to Barcelona, whence, reunited with his family, on 25 December he set sail for New York.

Trotsky's 'Spanish interlude' was neither the most comfortable nor the most exciting of his life. He could not speak or read Spanish, and several times complained that a Spaniard's knowledge of foreign languages did not extend beyond his 'Parlez-vous français?'[1] He found the pace of life in Madrid 'lazy', the city 'provincial', the people devoid of 'entrepreneurship, just as in their eyes there is no concentration'.[2] His main enjoyment was derived from visits to Madrid's museums, 'temples of art', but in the copy work of the young Spanish artists who also frequented the museums he saw no evidence of any current Spanish artistic talent. From Paris he received the address of a 'French socialist-internationalist Depré', a director of an insurance society, with whom he made contact. Depré found Trotsky lodgings, in general working as his 'agent' in Spain: he informed him of the state of Spanish socialism ('totally under the influence of French social-patriotism. Serious syndicalist opposition in Barcelona'),[3] took Trotsky food in prison and conducted a campaign on his behalf in the Spanish socialist press. In the Madrid prison Trotsky mused upon the cruel blow which fate had dealt him:

> how did I end up in prison in Madrid? I did not expect this. True, I was exiled from France. But I lived in Madrid as a traveller passing through, corresponding with Grimm and Serrati about going to Switzerland via Italy, visiting museums ... a million miles removed from the Spanish police and justice. If one takes into account that this is my first time in Spain ... not knowing Spanish, not seeing anyone apart from Depré, not attending any meetings, my arrest is revealed in all its absurdity.[4]

Trotsky's transferral to Cadiz did not bring about any great reversal in his fortunes. Although no longer in prison he was constantly annoyed by his police escort, of whom he penned a damning characterisation:

> It would be difficult to imagine anything more stupid and rotten than this subject. He reads poorly in Spanish, is inarticulate, smokes, spits, smirks at all approaching women, winks, waves goodbye and does not give me any peace.[5]

He described Cadiz as even more backward than Spain in general, writing in a letter to Depré that 'Cadiz is a town of scientific and literary chastity truly touching – some centuries after Gutenberg!',[6] and requesting that he send him some books. In the local library Trotsky did discover a store of one German and two dozen French books, all of which had been attacked by book worms! He made notes on Spanish history from early nineteenth-century French books, regretting that the masses were prevented from learning of the crimes of the forefathers of the contemporary ruling elites:

> the people learn little from history because they do not know it. It reaches them – to the extent that it reaches them at all – in distorted school legends, national and religious holidays and in the lies of the official press. Historical facts which should enlighten the people become, on the contrary, a method to further mislead them.[7]

Indeed, after emerging from an empty museum and being struck by the noisy behaviour of the 'democratic public' on a pier, he commented that 'gigantic efforts will be needed to raise the culture of the mass'.[8]

Readers of *Nachalo*, the newspaper which replaced the now banned *Nashe Slovo*,[9] were kept informed of Trotsky's whereabouts. It carried, for example, Trotsky's Spanish best wishes to his friends in France.[10] A subsequent short note was completely censored, but from its headline readers would know that 'N. Trotsky is in Cadiz'.[11] Eventually the Paris publication was able to present a fuller version of its correspondent's recent experiences when it translated a piece on Trotsky which had appeared in *El Socialista*, the newspaper of the Spanish Socialist Party.[12] This told of Trotsky's arrest by the Madrid police, and of the efforts of Spanish socialists to attain his release. An editorial supplement to the translation said that Trotsky had spent three days in a Madrid prison before being sent to Cadiz. *Nachalo* noted that it was thanks to the interference of Spanish comrades that Trotsky had not immediately been sent to Havana upon arrival in the Spanish port, allowed instead to await a boat for New York, but warned that *El Socialista* bore all responsibility for writing of Trotsky as a 'pacifist'.[13]

Trotsky was able to maintain contact with his editorial colleagues in Paris, his 'Spanish impressions' appearing in *Nachalo* in early December. Although sent from Cadiz, this article focused mainly upon the events surrounding his stay in Madrid. After hinting that it was the intrigues of international diplomacy that lay behind his imprisonment,[14] Trotsky recounted that when he had asked the Spanish police to explain the cause of his arrest he received the reply: 'Your ideas are too advanced for Spain.' He protested in vain that he had not expounded his views either at meetings or in print. Of the prison regime Trotsky was at first surprised that one could pay for a better cell and conditions, but he soon came to see the sense of this arrangement: 'Why establish a fictive prison equality in a society constructed on class inequality? Moreover, granting privileges to paying prisoners, the wise administration helps the state budget which in Spain, as is well known, is more in need of help than anywhere else.'[15] From prison Trotsky sent a letter to the Minister of Internal Affairs complaining of the injustice he was suffering.[16]

It was on the road to Cadiz that he had earlier suspicions confirmed: the French authorities had telegrammed their Spanish counterparts warning of a dangerous 'anarcho-terrorist' who had entered Spain via San Sebastian.[17] In Cadiz he avoided being sent to Havana, where he was sure he would be arrested upon arrival, through the intervention of the republican deputy Castrovido. There was one further aspect of his meetings with the Prefect in Cadiz which worried Trotsky. In a letter to Depré he said that the Prefect used a translator from the German consul to communicate with him. 'But,' he warned, 'if by any chance my enemies learn of this "fact" they will be able to use it in their own fashion.'[18] In a lighthearted postscript to his article in *Nachalo* he took the necessary preventive action: 'P.S. Because the Cadiz Prefect does not speak in a foreign language he invited some German as a translator. It turned out that this German is a secretary of the German consul. For the information of the agents and chiefs from *Prizyv*!'[19]

Trotsky's concern that he would become the subject of scandalous articles back in Paris because of the 'German connection' was not unfounded. Indeed, his next, and last, contribution to *Nachalo* was a response to a commentary upon his exile from France by the newspaper *L'Action Socialiste*, a translation of which appeared in *Nachalo*. *L'Action Socialiste* objected to the way in which the closure of *Nashe Slovo* and Trotsky's expulsion had received sympathetic treatment in several French publications, and even among some deputies in the National Council. Were people not aware that the 'brave' *Nashe Slovo* had afforded material assistance to the Germans with the aim of bringing about Russia's defeat? Did they not know of Trotsky's true character, most notably revealed in his dealings with Guesde, Sembat and Thomas?

> This person [Trotsky] at the outset of the war wrote an angry brochure in support of the Entente. Then this person was seen roaming about Guesde's and Sembat's anterior, supplied with a letter of recommendation from Plekhanov, in order to receive permission to go to the front as a correspondent of a Russian journal. As soon as this request was granted this person ... poured pure insults over Guesde, Sembat and Thomas.[20]

Articles defending *Nashe Slovo* and Trotsky from *L'Action Socialiste*'s critique subsequently appeared in *Nachalo*.[21] Trotsky's own defence expressed puzzlement at the relevance of some of his adversary's statements: why should a professional journalist not appeal to ministers with a request to visit the front? did journalists not have to visit anteriors in order to seek appointments?[22] However, his main objection was that he had never sent a request of any sort to Guesde and

Sembat. Indeed, he had seen the former only once, from the window of a comrade's flat, and the latter never. He then explained how, when in Zurich, he had requested a letter of introduction from Plekhanov to Guesde should he ever need to turn to the latter for help. But, after discovering the views that both men had adopted after the start of the war, he resolved not to use Plekhanov's letter, even ripping it up and recounting this episode only to Martov and Vladimirov.[23] In conclusion he recommended that people read the extracts of his German brochure which had been published in *Nashe Slovo* to discover what 'material assistance' he had attempted to afford Germany.

Thus, although Trotsky described his Spanish episode as 'non-political' he remained at the centre of controversy both in Spain and in France. In February 1917 *Nachalo* answered readers requests for information about Trotsky and his family by printing short notices of their safe arrival in New York, and the warm welcome given to them by representatives of socialist groups, including the editors of *Novyi Mir*.[24] Trotsky once again found a Russian socialist publication in which he could expound his views.

The boat which carried Trotsky and his family out of Spain pulled into New York harbour in the early hours of 14 January 1917. The Bronstein's arrival was not unexpected. From Cadiz Trotsky sent letters to the editors of the New York émigré socialist newspaper *Novyi Mir*, informing them of the outcome of his Spanish episode. In early December 1916 *Novyi Mir* passed on to its readers the news which it had received from one of Trotsky's most recent communications: he was to be expelled from Spain and was intending to come to New York, America's port of call for many European immigrants.[25] Upon safe arrival, *Novyi Mir* gave him a warm welcome, declaring that 'America has acquired a mainstay fighter of the revolutionary International'.[26] In his autobiography Trotsky described his occupation in the United States as that of a 'revolutionary socialist'.[27] Indeed, 24 hours after he set foot on American soil his first article appeared in *Novyi Mir*.

'Long Live Struggle!' outlined how the war had transformed Europe into an 'arresting company' in which tsarist methods of censorship and oppression reigned on both sides of the trenches. However, alongside this, it noted that, from the point of view of a revolutionary socialist, changes of a more optimistic character had also taken place. Most importantly, in response to the most bloody and shameful war in history, the masses were increasingly becoming discontented and more and more acquiring a critical analysis. The Europe that Trotsky had recently left was, he felt, ripe for upheaval: 'the combination of pure hatred and critical analysis is worrying for the contemporary European ruling class for it means revolution.'[28] One might have thought that a professional revolutionary would be loath to leave this situation behind. Would not landing in America mean the loss both of an opportunity to lead a revolution and of the analysis appropriate to it? But Trotsky's move to the 'sufficiently old New World' did not mean abandoning the views which he had formed in Paris. He assured his American readership that the United States faced the same 'problems, dangers and obligations' to be found in Europe. He could thus enter the fray of American socialism fully equipped to do battle.

One of his first opportunities to enlighten an American audience of what lay in store for them was during a speech of 25 January to an international meeting of welcome, in which he expounded upon the connection between war and revolution. Trotsky delivered many talks in New York, the vast majority of which remained unpublished. We are therefore fortunate that Trotsky included the text of his January lecture in *Voina i revolyutsiya*. He argued that one could now trace several consequences of the outbreak of war which, taken together, were leading to revolutionary upheavals. To begin with, societies had become more and more split into two hostile camps: 'the rich had become richer and the poor poorer.' Added to this, state coffers across Europe were now empty, preventing the ruling classes from acquiescing the masses with further social reforms; 'people are becoming poorer not only materially but also in illusions.' Trotsky discerned a new and, from his point of view, exciting 'mental state'. People, he claimed, were no longer dominated by routine and were prepared to be daring; in other words, they had acquired the qualities of revolutionaries. Finally there was an international group of socialist saviours – Liebknecht in Germany, MacLean in Britain, Höglund in Sweden, Rakovsky in Romania, etc. – which, faced with the hostility of bourgeois institutions and the betrayal of former comrades, had for long been in the minority but would soon be leading the discontented majority to revolution. At the outset of his speech Trotsky compared an America rich in material goods, although sold for 'outrageous prices', with an impoverished Europe, and he worried whether his native continent would survive. His concluding remarks were more optimistic: 'The coming epoch will be an epoch of social revolution. I carried this conviction out of a Europe ravaged, burnt and drained. Here, in America, I welcome you under the banner of the coming social revolution!'[29]

Trotsky wrote a lengthy account of the last two and a half years of his life in Europe which appeared over several issues, spread over several months, of *Novyi Mir*.[30] Published under the subheading 'From a Diary', these articles were a mixture of autobiographical incident, biographical sketches and social and political commentary. The first category included, for instance, a transcript of Trotsky's conversation of August 1914 with the head of the police in Vienna after which he decided to catch the first train to Zurich, being trapped in a street in Paris during a Zeppelin attack, and so on. The figures who found themselves in the second category could not have been flattered by what Trotsky wrote of them. Briand, for example, was described as a 'past master in the art of wire-pulling, a trafficker in the lost souls of the French Parliament, an instigator of bribery and corruption'. The final category, social and political commentary, consisted of Trotsky's thoughts on the effects of the war and on various socialists' responses to it. He mentioned meeting a Serbian revolutionary who had been involved in the plans to assassinate Archduke Ferdinand. He recounted the young man's despair at his country's then fate as a pawn in the diplomatic manoeuvres of the great powers, in this story highlighting the war's imperialist nature. His description of Vienna after Ferdinand's death was full of hatred for the 'bourgeois press' which had 'set about the task of working up the popular mood'. At the same time he regretted that this 'irrefutable proof of the moral degeneration of bourgeois society' had been obscured by influential socialists who supported the war. Unfortunately, Trotsky claimed, the betrayal of socialism by socialists, while a surprise for many, was not unexpected for him. During his stay in Vienna from 1907–14 he had had ample opportunity to acquaint himself with the 'purely chauvinistic nature' of *Arbeiter-Zeitung*'s editorials on international affairs. What shock, then, the Austrian party's patriotic response to its government's war declaration? Although Trotsky said that he did not expect Plekhanov to go so far as an exponent of national militarism, in the pre-war era he already had reason to suspect Plekhanov's internationalism:

> in 1913, when I was in Bucharest, Rakovsky told me that during the Russo-Japanese war, Plekhanov had assured him ... that in his opinion the idea that socialism should ... 'work for national defeat' ... was an importation into the party by Hebrew intellectuals.[31]

In Austria, Switzerland and France Trotsky witnessed the same split between the social-patriotic right, the passive centre which acted as an appendage to the right, and the minority international left. He stressed the wide gulf which separated the latter from the others, writing that 'social-patriotism debases men morally and mentally,' and left the reader in no doubt as to the seriousness of the battle between social-patriotism and internationalism. The war had brought forth hopes which it could not fulfil and the resulting disillusionment of the masses could only be used to the advantage of revolution if socialists remained true to their faith.

Trotsky drew upon his diary, on this occasion written during a train journey across France, for his next contribution to *Novyi Mir*. 'In a French Carriage', a two-part article, was similar in its portrayal of the realities of war to the war sketches which he had written for *Kievskaya Mysl*. The first instalment begins with the train entering Lyon station. Immediately the habits of the trenches were on view for all to see: a group of naked soldiers stood washing themselves on the platform. The reader was then brought into closer acquaintance with life in the trenches through the experiences of a French miner-syndicalist with whom Trotsky conversed *en route*. The miner reported that most soldiers in the trenches were of peasant origin. Industrial workers were engaged in war production, while the petty bourgeoisie became officers or joined organisations in the rear. He then described the psychological difficulties trench warfare brought peasants, used to life above ground with a full horizon in view. The miners, at least, worked below ground even in peace time, and were familiar with the dangers of explosives and poisonous gasses. However, the one aspect of the war which was new to all – whether miners, peasants, soldiers, officers, French or Germans – was the scope and character of battle: 'The most awful thing is the uninterrupted firing of hundreds of different guns. Each sound is terrible after its own fashion and all, devoid of tempo and rhythm, come together in an indescribable and unbearable crashing ... from which one cannot escape ... you are brought to a state verging on madness.'[32]

The second and final section of 'In a French Carriage' focused upon the positive psychological consequences of trench warfare. On the train Trotsky noticed the movement of thousands of people of all nationalities. He contrasted this to the pre-war era in which, on the one hand the industrial workers had come to occupy the most important strategic position in the economies of the advanced nations, and, on the other, old social classes, peasants and the petty bourgeoisie, characterised by a limited outlook and suspicion of all that was new, had retained a leading influence in social and political matters. Since August 1914, however, peasants who had not been in a town for decades had visited several in the course of several months. Trotsky expressed his conviction that this upheaval could not but create a psychological transformation, in which 'traditional fetishisms' would be destroyed.[33] The post-war world would be inhabited by a new human type, full of criticism and daring, ready to introduce rationalism in production, politics and economics. This, of course, meant socialism.

The articles which Trotsky produced from his diary for *Novyi Mir* could not have brought much comfort either to a government considering declaring war or to those who would have to go forth and fight. However, at the time of the appearance of Trotsky's 'war notes' it was becoming increasingly likely that America would enter the conflict. At the end of January 1917 the German government, hoping that it would starve Britain into submission, announced it was going to engage in unrestricted submarine warfare from 1 February. This meant breaking the terms of American neutrality.[34] Interventionists immediately called upon President Wilson to declare war on Germany. In the hope that the Kaiser could be persuaded to change his mind, Wilson at first opted for severing diplomatic relations with Germany, which he announced on 3 February. Several days following this announcement the first of a series articles in which Trotsky examined the growing tensions in America through the prism of his European experiences appeared in *Novyi Mir*.

'A Repetition of Things Past', for example, claimed that America, a country without its own traditions and ideology, had many times provided a home for ideas which had exhausted themselves in Europe. Previously this had involved political and religious ideas, now it was the legend of a 'war of liberation'. Trotsky advised Americans to scan European newspapers of late July and early August 1914, from which they would gain an understanding of the aims of the patriotic campaign that the American press was currently waging. The press barons had to convince the people that its government was concerned about 'freedom' and 'justice' and that it was reacting to aggression. At first this 'preparatory work for war' would hold out the possibility of a peaceful resolution to the crisis, publicising the good intentions of the home government in humble terms. Only when the plans for mobilisation were complete would 'the devilish chauvinistic music' be played to its fullest extent. It was by proceeding in this way that Trotsky claimed the government and the press hoped awkward questions concerning the real reasons for American intervention would be avoided:

> What about the war deliveries which the German submarines threaten? What of the billions of profit falling with a Europe bleeding to death? ... Who can speak of this at a time of great national enthusiasm! If the New York stock market is prepared for great sacrifices (the people will bear them) then, it goes without saying, this is not in the name of contemptible money, but in the cause of a great truth ... how to call it? – morals. It is not the fault of the stock market if, in serving eternal justice, it receives 100% and more in profit![35]

The response he demanded from American socialists and advanced workers was to raise the 'mighty melody of the International'.

One of the main messages which Trotsky had propagated in Europe was that the tune of the International had not only to be 'mighty' but also 'pure'. In other words, socialists had to hold an internationalist position and have no truck with social-patriotism. Trotsky repeated this message to American colleagues through *Novyi Mir*. 'In the School of War',[36] for instance, recounted how the honour of socialism had been saved in Europe by, among others, Liebknecht, MacLean and Rakovsky. Trotsky held up the Italian party as an example of how influence over the masses could be retained and strengthened if socialists occupied an anti-war position. The question facing American socialists was: Would they accept the lessons to be learnt from Europe? In a subsequent article Trotsky stated that the authority of the Second International could not be cited as a justification for socialists advocating the cause of national self-defence. At pre-war meetings Kautsky, described as the 'leading theoretician' of the Second International, rejected national self-defence along with the notions of 'defensive' and 'aggressive' wars in disputes with Bebel. Trotsky admitted that the formal resolutions of the Second International contained contradictory statements. However, the Basel Congress of 1912, called specifically to discuss a proper socialist response to war, was unequivocal: 'preserve inseverable ties during war, fight together for its hasty conclusion and use the growing war crisis and dissatisfaction of the mass to speedily overthrow the capitalist order.'[37] Finally, in 'Two Warring Camps', Trotsky highlighted the pitfalls of Longuetist tactics, i.e. to be 'simultaneously for the capitalist homeland and for the proletariat',[38] to show that social-patriotism and revolutionary internationalism were two mutually exclusive principles.[39]

Trotsky did not limit himself to pointing out the lessons which recent events in the European socialist movement held for American socialists. In New York he actively engaged in polemics with local organisations for the application of a revolutionary socialist perspective. In a commentary upon a recent anti-war meeting held in the Carnegie Hall, for example, he criticised the Socialist Party for organising this with a pacifist group 'The Friends of Peace'. From an 'organisational-political' point of view, he argued, it was not expedient to share a platform with pacifists. After all, pacifists were well-known for publicising their opposition to war until it was declared, after which they would announce their 'patriotism' and encourage the masses to conduct the war to a successful conclusion in the name of 'peace and justice'. By standing alongside pacifists, if only temporarily, Trotsky stated that the masses would be brought into confusion at a time when 'clear class consciousness' was urgently necessary. Moreover, he claimed the mood of the Carnegie Hall gathering, overwhelmingly revolutionary socialist, had been weakened 'both psychologically and politically' as two resolutions, one pacifist and one socialist, were unanimously accepted by the same show of hands; anyone reconstructing the meeting's atmosphere from the resolutions would be led astray. Some good had, however, come out of the meeting. Trotsky welcomed the socialist resolution's insistence that American intervention in the war would 'only serve the egoistic interests of American capitalists ... to feed upon the unfortunate war in Europe', and that the proletariat should 'apply all the means at its disposal against the attempt to involve America in the war.'[40] The duty of Socialist Party leaders to vote against war credits and to call for revolutionary action against the war campaign had now been made clear. For Trotsky, one had to ensure that they carried-out this 'great obligation'.

It was, however, events at the bottom of the Socialist Party's structure which brought forth Trotsky's next rebuke to social-patriotism in the American socialist movement. In a short note he recounted how, while attending a Socialist Party branch meeting, Anna Ingerman cited Klara Zetkin, the German left revolutionary, in support of the view that socialists could join government-led military organisations.[41] Trotsky stated that Ingerman had every right to draw upon Scheidemann, Plekhanov and Vandervelde to achieve her aims, but it would be better if she left Zetkin, currently in prison for anti-war activities, in peace. Ingerman then sent a letter protesting Trotsky's report which, along with his reply, was published in *Novyi Mir*.

Ingerman disputed Trotsky's version of events, declaring that 'in aspiring to show his knightly feelings for Klara Zetkin, comrade Trotsky completely forgot what actually occurred at the meeting.' In actual fact, she claimed, *nobody* had opposed the proposition that it was inadmissible for socialists to volunteer for the army and navy. What was discussed was the issue of whether comrade doctors and medical sisters who served in the Red Cross should be excluded from the party. It was in this context that she had repeated Zetkin's words to her that 'my husband and my son, doctors, will certainly join a medical organisation: this is our duty', not with the intention of throwing Zetkin's internationalism into doubt, but to show that one could participate in the Red Cross and hold party membership. To Trotsky's claim that Zetkin is 'one of us' Ingerman retorted: 'It is possible to disagree with you, comrade Trotsky, and all the same remain a true internationalist.'[42]

Trotsky countered Ingerman's letter with the claim that she had missed the central issue of the status of the Red Cross, which she obviously accepted as a neutral body. However, he advised that if one turned to the source from which Zetkin's view of this organisation could be revealed, the journal of the German left, *Internationale*, a different picture would emerge. This publication clearly stated that socialists should afford assistance to wounded soldiers through their own and not state bodies, of which the Red Cross was one of many.[43] Thus, even if one accepted Ingerman's story, she still had no right to cite Zetkin. In his conclusion Trotsky responded to Ingerman's accusation that he was claiming internationalism for himself. He stated that before this issue could be resolved Ingerman would have to declare her internationalist principles. As matters stood she was an 'intermediary element' which had 'cited a personal conversation with Zetkin in defence of a tendency to which Zetkin herself is irreconcilably hostile'.[44]

If Trotsky viewed the Red Cross as part of the imperialist war machine, one can well imagine the disgust he must have felt for the Council of National Defence and its Advisory Commission. These bodies had been created by Congress in August 1916 to coordinate industries and resources for national security and to prepare for their application in the event of war. The Advisory Commission had a series of sub-committees, one of which, the Labour Committee headed by Samuel Gompers, had responsibility for, among other things, drawing up plans to enrol skilled labour in industrial reserves and to suggest adjustments to employment problems to guarantee uninterrupted war work.[45] Trotsky analysed Gompers and his Committee in 'A Sheep's Constitution'. He condemned Gompers as a social-patriot who was attempting to place a whole generation of the proletariat at the service of militarism. Of course, he pointed out, Gompers claimed that the interests of the workers would be protected by the Council of National Defence – capital would bear the burdens of war and so on. But, asked Trotsky, what guarantee could Gompers offer that these promises would be honoured? Trotsky himself foresaw a very different scenario:

> in the first real collision with the unions the American ruling classes will repeat what the British, German and French ruling classes said in similar circumstances: 'the defence of the homeland, on your own admission, is the first duty of the proletariat and in fulfilling this duty you do not have the right to make demands.'

Gompersism, defined by Trotsky as the 'desire to achieve for the proletariat a 'beneficial' industrial constitution on the basis of the immunity of capitalist exploitation', was labelled the deadly enemy of the proletariat against which each internationalist should struggle with all his might. Fortunately, according to Trotsky, conditions had never been better for winning the workers over from Gompersism, for during war the bourgeoisie would not be able to afford the reforms with which they pacified the workers during peace. He predicted that the gap between expectations of a better life and the poverty which war would bring would create minds receptive to revolutionary propaganda. Socialists could use this to their advantage only if they repeated the following messages: 'No concessions to the state, to militarism and to patriotism. No deals with Gompersism.'[46]

As part of the struggle for revolutionary internationalism Trotsky himself engaged in polemics with the newspapers *Forverts, Russkii Golos*, and *Russkoe Slovo*.

Forverts was a powerful Jewish daily with a circulation of 150 000 by 1917. It was edited by Abraham Cahan and had in its own ten storey high building overlooking the heart of New York's Jewish quarter.[47] The paper gave Trotsky an enthusiastic welcome when he arrived in New York and he contributed four articles to it over the course of January and February. The publication of a fifth piece, ironically enough as it turned out on social-patriotism, was prevented when Trotsky broke with the newspaper at the beginning of March. Joseph

Nedava, basing his account upon a conversation with David Shub in New York in July 1969, gives the following version of the dispute:

> The incident was brought about by the State Department's expo-sure, on March 1, 1917, of a German plot to embroil Mexico in the war against the United States, promising to Mexico the return of New Mexico and parts of California as a prize. The disclosure aroused the wrath of even the pro-German *Forward* [*Forverts*], which then printed on the front page an announcement that 'if Germany can really commit such an idiotic move of diplomacy, then every citizen of America will fight to the last drop of his blood to protect the great American republic.' A few hours after the publication of this statement, Trotsky stormed into Cahan's office on East Broadway, and an angry exchange of words passed between them. Trotsky then severed his connection with *Forward*.[48]

If Trotsky did go to Cahan's office, he left behind his article, for when he opened his campaign against *Forverts* in *Novyi Mir*, he demanded his manuscript's return.[49] He immediately sought to qualify his earlier cooperation with *Forverts*, announcing that he always knew that it was not fully internationalist. He had, he claimed, contributed articles to it as this was appropriate to the discussion nature of January and February and, in any case, colleagues who knew the paper better than he and who translated sections of it for him had advised him to do so. However, the increasing displays of hostility between Germany and the United States, together with *Forverts*'s state-ment that Americans should fight to the last drop of blood, had changed the situation. Trotsky thought that the proletariat should struggle against the imperialist homeland and he therefore stood on the other side of the barricade to *Forverts*. To avoid the impression that he supported *Forverts*, he requested that publication of his piece be stopped and the manuscript returned.[50]

In a subsequent note Trotsky reported that he had received numer-ous letters from Jewish workers approving his stand against *Forverts*. He pointed to these letters, and the anti-'national defence' resolutions of a local party branch meeting, as evidence that *Forverts* had lost touch with its readers. Encamped within its ten-storey headquarters he accused the Jewish newspaper of establishing a dictatorship over its readership, of not reporting the latest party decisions which were obviously uncomfortable for it, and of social-patriotic betrayal. For Trotsky the time had come for a 'cleansing of the ranks'.[51] He urged

Jewish workers to recapture their newspaper and expel Cahan from the party, assuring them that in these tasks they could rely on *Novyi Mir's* complete backing.[52]

During his conflict with the Jewish daily Trotsky several times mentioned his reliance upon friends to translate from Yiddish into Russian. He had no such difficulties in the campaign he waged against the 'non-party' newspapers produced for New York's Russian colony, *Russkii Golos* and *Russkoe Slovo*. His first commentary upon these publications highlighted their differing points of view on the likelihood of American intervention in the war. Ivan Okuntsov (*Russkii Golos*) thought that opposition from Wall Street would keep America neutral, whereas Dymov (*Russkoe Slovo*), thought that pressure from the same source, which had made super-profits from the 'blood of the people', would lead America into battle. Trotsky said that, however comforting Okuntsov's view was, he had to agree with Dymov. This left him with only one 'reader's difficulty'. An editorial of the self same issue of *Russkoe Slovo* in which Dymov's article appeared viewed America's entry into the war not as a desire to make more money, but as a 'guarantee of progress'. 'Why', concluded Trotsky, 'had the editorial and the correspondent agreed to confuse their public?'[53]

When Trotsky next took up his pen to write of his 'non-party' protagonists it was not to accuse them of bewildering their readership, but of 'indecency'. The cause of Trotsky's charge was the appearance of adverts, placed in *Russkii Golos* and *Russkoe Slovo* by the New York Council of National Defence, urging citizens to petition President Wilson recommending American intervention. Previously, he noted, neither of these newspapers, aware that the Russian colony was anti-war, had joined efforts to whip the population into a patriotic fury. What had made the newspapers change their track, Trotsky claimed, was money: 'In such critical moments one gets to know the real value of people, ideas, parties and publications ... when gold was added to the ideological preparation of the people *Russkoe Slovo* and *Russkii Golos* found their place.'[54]

When America eventually officially entered World War One on 6 April 1917 Trotsky had already left America. Before his departure he had, however, written critical analyses both of the reasons for America's intervention and of its likely consequences.

In his address of war to the American people President Wilson declared, 'The present German submarine warfare against commerce is a warfare against mankind. The world must be made safe for democracy.'[55] Seizing upon these words Trotsky stated that if one took them

at face value America should have long ago declared war on Britain for
its blockade of Austria-Germany. What prevented this step, according
to Trotsky, was that it would have resulted in the loss of the Entente
orders for war supplies from which American industry was making
super-profits. In turn, Wilson was so upset by the recent German
blockade not because it violated any principles, but because it effec-
tively put a halt to Entente orders without replacing them with an
equivalent from Berlin. America was now deprived of all war trade and
its profits. This left her in a position of real neutrality which, Trotsky
argued, she could not sustain because since August 1914 her industry
had been increasingly and then finally restructured to serve military
demands. It had, in other words, become a war economy. He then
dismissed the possibility that American soldiers could alter the military situation in Europe, pointing out that if the mightiest (British)
fleet in the world could not guarantee a free passage for goods then
nothing could. For him, it was the bosses of finance capital and their
interests which dictated American foreign policy and this meant war:

> a colossal new market will immediately be opened for American
> ammunition factory bosses in America itself ... they need a
> 'national danger' so as to be able to place the tower of Babel of war
> industry on the shoulders of the American people.[56]

At the same time as laying bare the profit motives which demanded
war, in other articles Trotsky argued that the real winner from
American intervention would not be the capitalist bosses, but revolution. When he summarised his New York experiences in his
autobiography Trotsky mentioned the conveniences in his flat
(including electric lights, a bath and telephone) that Europeans were
unused to.[57] In one of his comments upon daily life in New York at
that time, however, he wrote a moving description of the effects of the
drudgery, out of which American capital built its achievements,
suffered by ordinary people. He noted, during a rush hour ride on the
metro, a humble and depressed crowd whose only solace lay in
chewing gum.[58] The war, he predicted in other writings, would show
the proletariat that only they, through social revolution, could resolve
the problems that beset capitalism and which had led to America's
entry into World War One.[59] He advised all socialists to 'prepare the
soldiers for revolution!'[60]

After Nicholas II's abdication of the Russian throne in March 1917
anyone seeking confirmation of the link Trotsky constructed between

war and revolution had a ready and current example to hand. Events in Russia continued to occupy Trotsky while he was in New York both before, but especially after, the collapse of the monarchy.

He submitted two articles to *Novyi Mir* on Russia prior to Nicholas's fall from power. The first was to commemorate the twelfth anniversary of Bloody Sunday. Calling revolutionary anniversaries days for 'great study' as well as for remembrance, Trotsky enumerated the lessons to be learnt from the events of 1905: the proletariat was the only revolutionary class in Russia and all calls for it to cooperate with the bourgeoisie were a hopeless utopia.[61] In his second pre-revolution piece on Russia he highlighted the Tsar's cynical view of the Duma, and the latters willingness to fulfil its master's needs. He achieved this primarily through an imaginary conversation between a Russian and foreign diplomat, in which the former stated that the Tsar would recall the Duma so as to receive another foreign loan, upon the receipt of which the Russian parliament would once again be closed. 'Thus,' Trotsky remarked without further comment, 'Russian politics marches along the path of progress.'[62]

Three points had for long been part of Trotsky's analysis of the pattern a revolutionary upheaval in Russia would take: it would be led by the proletariat; its policies would be socialist in content; and it would call forth, either by inspiration or by force of arms, a spate of revolutions across the whole of Europe. During World War One Trotsky modified this analysis somewhat, adding that the United States of Europe would be the state form through which the European revolution would realise itself, and that revolution would occur first of all in Germany.[63] News of the fall of Tsarism obviously confounded Trotsky's last prediction, but for the most part he was able to retain his prognoses for interpreting the events taking place in his homeland.

According to Trotsky, it was street demonstrations by the workers, eventually backed by the army, that had brought about the tsar's abdication. The bourgeoisie, led by his old antagonist Professor Milyukov, had not wanted the monarchy's collapse. On the contrary, he claimed, the liberals looked to the Tsar as the most trusted defender of property against the proletariat, and to the institution of monarchy as the form of government best suited to conduct an imperialist foreign policy. For Trotsky, the liberals had been *forced* to form a Provisional Government by two pressures, one external and the other internal. From outside the British, French and American money markets had told the Russian bourgeoisie to assume power because they did not want Nicholas II to conclude a separate peace with Germany, and the bourgeoisie was the only group that would continue the war. Then, the bourgeoisie itself was afraid that its responsibility for the war would be revealed if a workers' government called a halt to the hostilities. However, Trotsky argued that the bourgeoisie could not retain power for long. The fall of the Provisional Government was guaranteed because it could not satisfy the people's demands for peace, bread and land. He noted that a workers' committee had already been formed to 'protest against liberal attempts to misappropriate the revolution and betray the people to the monarchy',[64] and he called upon it to wrest total control in its hands to take Russia out of the war and to resolve the agrarian question. For Trotsky any other outcome would mean that the revolution had failed, since only a 'Revolutionary Workers' Government ... will be able to secure the fate of the revolution and the working class'. In turn he looked to the establishment of a revolutionary workers' government in Russia as an example for the German proletariat to follow. Otherwise, he worried that Wilhelm II would use the Russian proletariat's backing of its bourgeoisie to rekindle the German workers' enthusiasm for war. He raised the possibility of revolution not spreading from one country to another only to dismiss it. Revolution would leap from Russia to Germany either by example or by triumphant Russian workers liberating their German comrades by force of arms; or it would jump from Germany to Russia by the same means. Trotsky was so convinced that the whole of Europe was simmering with discontent, that 'the war has turned the whole of Europe into a powder-keg of social revolution',[65] that he was prepared for all eventualities.

*

It was in this buoyant mood that Trotsky and his family set sail from New York for Russia on 27 March 1917.[66] He could look back upon his time in America with a certain amount of satisfaction. He had argued for a revolutionary socialist analysis of and response to current events in print and at a host of meetings.[67] On the other hand his campaign against social-patriotism had not stopped America entering the war, but Trotsky must have realised that his journalism could not do this. Besides, he now welcomed war as a harbinger of revolution, without, of course, recommending defeatism!

No, Trotsky's biggest disappointments lay in the future. However, prescient his predictions on the fate of the Provisional Government may appear to be, we now know that his hopes for a pan-European revolutionary government in the form of a United States of Europe were not realised. The German workers did not manage to seize power, despite the fact that the Bolsheviks overturned the Provisional Government in November 1917, and despite Trotsky's efforts to reveal the imperialist nature of the war through his 'no peace, no war' strategy during the peace negotiations with the Kaiser's government. It was perhaps quite fitting that the man who had argued that the proletariat needed to halt the war before it could turn cannons against the class enemy should have negotiated Russia's exit from World War One. However, this book has focused upon Trotsky's thoughts and activities while he was a revolutionary in exile and the story of how, why and in what context his association with the 'war to end all wars' came to an end lies beyond the scope of this present study.

Conclusion

For various reasons, World War One can be seen as the most significant event of the twentieth century. Without it no Russian Revolution,[1] without it no Hitlerite Germany.[2] Given the magnitude of the war's destruction and its consequences, Trotsky's revolutionary activities may seem frivolous and even irrelevant. This study has pointed out that some of the localised disputes with, for instance, social-patriots have no long-term significance, however illustrative they are of how Trotsky occupied his time. It is also unlikely that Trotsky's journalism made any great impact on workers and socialists. However, there are reasons to judge Trotsky's work positively, if critically, and for arguing that some of his work remains pertinent to contemporary issues. Furthermore, World War One is an important part of Trotsky's intellectual biography.

Trotsky's programmatic response to the outbreak of World War One was the logical outcome of his analysis of the causes of the hostilities. For him, the war was imperialist, by which he meant an attempt by the leading capitalist powers to acquire dominance on the world market through militarism. He argued that the imperialist powers were motivated by a desire to facilitate the further development of the productive forces which, according to Trotsky, needed to break out of the limits set upon them by the nation state. He thus recognised that, amongst others, Britain and Germany were seeking to fulfil a historically progressive task. However, he rejected the notion that any one of the belligerent capitalist powers could attain its goal. In part the evidence for his view was there for all to see: the war had turned into one of bloody attrition, resulting in thousands of deaths and a massive expenditure of resources, but without any sign that one power would emerge the clear victor.

For Trotsky, it was left to the international proletariat to establish transnational state structures in the form of a Balkan Federative Republic and a United States of Europe, as the first step towards the setting-up of a United World Republic. These transnational governmental institutions were, he thought, the only means by which both the productive forces could develop in a planned, harmonious manner on a world scale, and the needs of different cultural groups for free expression could be satisfied. He thought this programme realistic because, at the time of writing, he perceived the nation state to be an anachronism and capitalism as struggling with tasks which it could not resolve. This left the proletariat, the only class whose common interests spanned state boundaries, as the natural international force able to resolve the productive, political and social problems facing humanity.

If the proletariat did not seize power Trotsky foresaw a period a further capitalist crisis and acts of military aggression. But the whole thrust of his analysis, not to mention his Marxist optimism, led him to reject this possibility. In part he thought the experience of war itself was preparing the masses for revolution, both practically and psychologically. Added to this, he genuinely believed that the war had opened a new epoch in human history, in which the reformism which had polluted the workers' movement pre-1914 would be removed from the tactics of a new and revolutionary Third International. It was this latter body which, he claimed, would provide the necessary slogans and leadership. It was for these reasons, because he perceived a revolutionary situation as current, that propagating a clear and revolutionary policy to the workers remained his central concern. Hence the fervour with which he entered into battle with the social-patriots, i.e. socialists who backed their government's war efforts, in this way encouraging the masses to sacrifice themselves for the class enemy. Indeed, it would be true to say that the struggle with social-patriotism absorbed Trotsky's attention more than any other issue raised by World War One.

Of course, Trotsky suffered many setbacks and encountered strong opposition to his programme, even within the 'internationalist' camp. Most notably, he did not succeed in uniting internationalist elements of all fractions around his analysis of the war. Although the Bolsheviks, Mensheviks, and Trotsky all levelled accusations of fractional intrigue at one another, the fact that they did not join forces is mainly to be explained by reasons other than established fractional loyalties. This is not to deny the importance of the distrust which, for example, Martov felt for Lenin as a result of pre-war disputes. However, in the last analysis Trotsky's call for unification was not realised because the leaders of each fraction held their own position on the war. Thus, for instance, Lenin thought that the imperialist war should be turned into a civil war and he refused to accept anyone who did not hold this view as a member of the internationalist camp. Hence his polemics with, and dismissal of, Trotsky. In turn Trotsky and Martov understood the significance of the slogan struggle for peace in very different ways; the former seeing it as a means to mobilise the masses for the immediate conquest of state power under the leadership of the Third International, the latter as the first step of many on the path to the renewal of class conflict under the auspices of a reunited Second International.

In concentrating upon propaganda work for 'international social-ism', Trotsky continued an activity and drew upon experience which had marked his political life to 1914, and would continue to mark it to his death. In this respect he did not differ from the Russian social-ists against whom he polemicised, Lenin, Zinoviev, Martov, Plekhanov, etc. Trotsky though stands out not only for his unique response to the war. More than any other Russian socialist he wrote from several different countries and from a diverse range of circum-stances. No other socialist's output touched upon so many topics: the nature of trench warfare, the social-psychological consequences of the war, political life in Europe and America, and the politics of socialist movements. It was this scope and depth of involvement that marked Trotsky off from other Russian socialists, and which give him the confidence to pronounce with such certainty upon pan-European revolutionary developments in the inter-war period. This is why, on Trotsky's reading, the Bolsheviks should have despatched him to guide the German revolution of the 1920s; this is why a Third International under his leadership would have responded far more adequately to the fascist threat in Germany. Trotsky was, if nothing else, a man of war.

Trotsky's distinctiveness, however, did not stand him in good stead in post-Lenin's Russia. In actual fact his 'otherness' counted against him. Although he would later falsify his political biography, arguing that he moved closer to Lenin as World War One progressed, we have seen that Trotsky and Lenin were further apart in March 1917 than the autumn of 1914. This serves to emphasise how crucial the revolu-tionary turmoil of 1917 itself was in bringing Trotsky finally into Bolshevik ranks. The conversion was sudden, the product of a unique situation. This should not surprise. After all, sharp swings in political allegiances are common place during great upheavals, including in 1917, a year of great political fluidity in Russia. Only the exigencies of the power struggles of the 1920s demanded that Trotsky should obscure this fact. Myths were created which dominated future historical research. Now that we know the contingent nature of Trotsky's conversion to Bolshevism, his departure in much changed circumstances a decade later is not so peculiar. Rather than ponder why Trotsky was exiled, we may prefer to ask: what kept him so long? It was in disputes of World War One, for example, that Trotsky pointed out that a defeated country was not the best environment in which to begin a socialist experiment. In the excitement of 1917 Trotsky appears to have forgotten his misgivings and his warnings of how economic and social backwardness, both of which featured prominently in his later analysis of Stalinism, would work against a socialist project. If Trotsky was correct to argue that the social-psychological impact of the war would help produce a revolution, we can question his wisdom in joining the Bolsheviks in 1917.

Although relations with the Bolsheviks, and Mensheviks, took up much of Trotsky's war-time output, it was the struggle against social-patriotism that most preoccupied him. Given his assumptions, he was right to prioritise in this way. However, although urging internationalists to make clear the distinction between social-patriotism and internationalism, Trotsky did not realise the extent to which such a fracture did occur and with what consequences for the inter-war European workers' movement. The revolutionary-internationalist parties established after 1919 were not to win majority support among Europe's working-classes. Nor were they able, even when faced with the rise of Nazism, to form united fronts with reformist socialists. The hostility which should distinguish relations of social-patriots and internationalists favoured by the Trotsky of World War One could not be easily controlled and was to sour relations on a permanent basis.

Trotsky was far more perspicacious about the broad political frameworks to which Europe should aspire. Even if we reject Trotsky's explanation of the causes of World War One as 'a revolt of the productive forces against the narrow confines of the nation state', we cannot but be impressed by his solution of a transnational United States of Europe to govern the continent's political and economic life. The goal of a United States of Europe has entered mainstream political lexicon, to the chagrin of Eurosceptics. Of course the goal is still far from being realised. Only time will tell whether the problems of a single currency in a multi-state framework can be resolved within capitalism, but perhaps even Trotsky himself would be surprised by the extent of unity and coordination attained to date. Finally, in the light of contemporary Balkan Wars, Trotsky's favoured Balkan Federative Republic has much to recommend itself. His analysis of ethnic conflict and the need to 'neutralise nationalism' is well taken. It was interesting to read a recent, and presumably unconscious borrowing from Trotsky, which argued that a Balkan Federative Republic was the only sensible political arrangement for Southeast Europe.[3] It is a great achievement that Trotsky's writing of 1914–17 can still have so much to say to us as we leave this most bloody of centuries behind.

Notes

1 Switzerland

1. L. Trotskii, *Voina i Revolyutsiya*, I (Petrograd, 1922), p. 40.
2. Ibid., p. 9.
3. Ibid.
4. Ibid., p. 51.
5. Ibid., p. 52.
6. Ibid.
7. Ibid.
8. Ibid.
9. Ibid., p. 48.
10. Ibid., p. 65.
11. Ibid., pp. 67–8.
12. Ibid., p. 57. In an April 1922 footnote Trotsky explained the failure of this prediction by an underestimation of the role of the intelligentsia which gave tsarism some 'stability'. However, he insisted that its role 'only delayed the disintegration. In essentials our analysis was confirmed by events. The difference was only in time.' (ibid.).
13. Ibid., pp. 58–9.
14. Ibid., p. 53.
15. L. Trotsky, *War and the International* (1971), p. 34.
16. Ibid., pp. 11–12.
17. Ibid., p. 18.
18. Ibid., p. 24.
19. Ibid., p. 39.
20. Ibid., p. 76.
21. Ibid., pp. 28–9.
22. Ibid., p. vii.
23. Ibid.
24. 'In the social production of their existence, men inevitably enter into definite relations, which are independent of their will, namely relations of production appropriate to a given stage in the development of their material forces of production. The totality of these relations of production constitutes the economic structure of society, the real foundation, upon which arises a legal and political superstructure and to which correspond definite forms of social consciousness. The mode of production of material life conditions the general processes of social, political and intellectual life ... At a certain stage of development, the material productive forces of society come into conflict with the existing relations of production or ... with the property relations within the framework of which they have operated hitherto. From forms of development of productive forces these relations turn into their fetters. The changes in the economic foundation lead sooner or later to the transformation of the whole immense super-

structure': K. Marx, Preface to *A Contribution to a Critique of Political Economy* (Moscow, 1970), pp. 20–1.

25. Trotsky, *War and the International*, p. vii.
26. Ibid., p. x.
27. Ibid., p. viii.
28. Ibid., p. x.
29. Ibid., p. 73.
30. Ibid., p. 75.
31. The translation was not, however, completed without difficulties. In a letter to Mandel and Platten of 4 November 1914 Trotsky recounted that Kotsiolek, the main translator of *War and the International*, was demanding that the pamphlet be printed with his name on the title page as translator and that he receive the correct royalties. Trotsky objected to the first request on two grounds. First, Kotsiolek's translation had been far from perfect and both himself and especially Professor Ragaz had had to make many revisions. Second, 'it would look as if I had written and published the brochure in Russian and *for a Russian* readership and Comrade Kotsiolek had now translated it for a German readership. It is clear that if this were the case the brochure would loose much of its appeal for the public and many of them would be put off buying it. It would be absolutely inadmissible to hinder the aims of the brochure in this way.' With reference to the second request Trotsky said that he had already paid Kotsiolek 80 francs, and that he did not oppose Kotsiolek receiving royalties out of any future profits the pamphlet might make. As a compromise solution to the first problem Trotsky suggested that at the end of the text the following reference to Kotsiolek should appear: 'Translated into the German from the original Russian by M. Kotsiolek' ('Pis'mo L. Trotskogo Mandelu i F. Plattenu po povodu intsidenta s M. Kotsiolekom pri perevode broshyury avtora na nemetskii yazyk', RTsKhIDNI, F. 451, O 1, D. 89).
32. See, for example, L. Trotskii, *Moya Zhizn* (Moscow, 1991), p. 236.

2 *Kievskaya Mysl*

1. L. Trotskii, *Voina i Revolyutsiya*, I (Petrograd, 1922), pp. 10–11. (An earlier version of this chapter appeared in *Irish Slavonic Studies*, 14, 1993.)
2. L. Trotskii, *Moya zhizn* (Moscow, 1991), p. 237.
3. Trotskii, *Voina i Revolyutsiya*, I, p. 157.
4. Ibid., p. 158.
5. Ibid., p. 157.
6. Ibid., p. 159.
7. Ibid.
8. Ibid., p. 11.
9. Ibid.
10. Ibid., p. 10.
11. I. Deutscher, *The Prophet Armed* (Oxford, 1954), p. 230.
12. Ibid.
13. For Deutscher's exposition, see, ibid., pp. 227–32.

14. Thus, Deutscher does not refer to the text where Trotsky expounds his view on his contributions to *Kievskaya Mysl*. If Deutscher had been aware of Trotsky's view then surely he would have referred to it. The following Trotsky biographers do not provide an exposition of the *Kievskaya Mysl* articles: J. Carmichael, *Trotsky: An Appreciation of his Life* (London, 1975); T. Cliff, *Trotsky 1879–1917: Towards October* (London, 1989); I. Howe, *Trotsky* (Hove, Sussex, 1978); B. Knei-Paz, *The Social and Political Thought of Leon Trotsky* (Oxford, 1978); R. Segal, *The Tragedy of Leon Trotsky* (Harmondsworth, 1983); and R. Wistrich, *Trotsky: Fate of a Revolutionary* (London, 1979). A recent Soviet biography, by Dmitri Volkogonov, repeats Deutscher's interpretation but without any exposition of the *Kievskaya Mysl* writings as supporting evidence: 'It is true that Trotsky was forced to display maximum shrewdness: *Kievskaya Mysl* was for the war, for war until victory. It willingly published articles critical of Germany and unwillingly, with cuts, those that referred to the Entente': D. Volkogonov, 'Lev Trotskii. Politicheskii portret', *Oktyabr*, 6 (1991), p. 159.

    Pierre Broué, who also provides no exposition of Trotsky's *Kievskaya Mysl* articles, claims that the intervention of the censor meant that Trotsky's war reportage for the Kievan newspaper was not serious: 'his calling as a press correspondent did not absorb him completely, in so far as his employer gave in quietly to the pressures of the censorship and in practice absolved him from the task of writing serious articles which would not have any chance of being published': P. Broué, *Trotsky* (Paris, 1988), p. 147. However, Trotsky never complained that his articles for *Kievskaya Mysl* had been censored.

15. Trotskii, *Voina i Revolyutsiya*, I, p. 10. Yu. V. Got'e's diary of 1918 contains the following interesting reference to Trotsky's gathering of the *Kievskaya Mysl* articles for publication in *Voina i Revolyutsiya*: '7/20 April. Yesterday there appeared in the Museum a person of short height, with a Southern accent and a turned-up nose who, it turned out, was Mrs Trotsky. She wished to receive *Kievskaya Mysl* for 1915 and 1916 for her "husband"; she was very polite. I informed her that certain formalities were necessary to which she agreed. She appeared today, well dressed but tastelessly, in a car with a soldier who stood to attention before her. She received her *Kievskaya Mysl* in return for a letter, "To Citizen Librarian of the Rumyantsev Museum, Professor Yu. V. Got'e" in which, with all the bourgeois conventions such as "I have the honour to request" and "I beg you to accept my assurance", Mr Trotsky asked about the issuing of journals to him (as in the original) for no longer than two weeks': Yu. V. Got'e, 'Moi zametki', *Voprosy istorii*, 11 (1991), p. 151.

16. Trotskii, *Voina i Revolyntsiya*, I, p. 10.

17. Ibid., p. 11.

18. Deutscher, *The Prophet Armed*, p. 228.

19. Trotskii, *Moya zhizn*, pp. 237ff.

20. This version becomes even more appealing when one considers the context in which Trotsky wrote his autobiography. By the end of the 1920s his main concern was to show his Leninist pedigree. His work for *Golos* and *Nashe Slovo* had a direct bearing on this, whereas his writings for *Kievskaya Mysl* did not.

21. L. Trotskii, 'Bosnyak-volonter', *Evropa v Voine, Sochineniya*, ix (Moscow, 1927), p. 17.

22. '"Sed'moi pekhotnyi" v bel'giskoi epopee', ibid., p. 10. See also 'On the North-West', in which the idea that the war was about the right of nations is rejected through a discussion of Italy: 'The nation and the War! But, sir, this is your all-European mistake when you talk of the Italian nation. There is no Italian nation': Na severo-zapad, ibid., p. 23.

23. 'Dve armii', ibid., p. 7.

24. 'Otkuda poshlo?', ibid., pp. 49–58.

25. 'Voina i tekhnika', ibid, p. 190.

26. Ibid., p. 191.

27. 'Vse dorogi vedut v Rim', ibid., p. 20.

28. 'Politicheskii moratorium', ibid., p. 5.

29. Ibid., pp. 5–6.

30. L. Trotskii, 'Zhan Zhores', *Gody velikago pereloma (Lyudi staroi i novoi epokh')* (Moscow, 1919), pp. 128–29. Trotsky also raised the issues of reformism, revolution and internationalism in several other biographical pieces. See, for example, 'Rakovsky and Kolarov' ('Kh. Rakovskii i V. Kolarov', ibid., pp. 60–5); 'Ledebour and Hoffman' ('Ledebur, Gofman', ibid., pp. 78–83); and Trotsky's final contribution to *Kievskaya Mysl*, 'An Epoch has Passed' ('Otkhodit epokha', ibid., pp. 143–51). Given that these articles appeared towards the end of Trotsky's work for the Kievan newspaper, Deutscher's conclusion that 'he [Trotsky] confined himself more and more to reportage and strictly military surveys' (Deutscher, *The Prophet Armed*, p. 228) does not appear convincing.

31. Trotskii, 'French', *Evropa v Voine*, p. 27.

32. 'Dve armii', ibid., p. 8.

33. Ibid., p. 9.

34. Ibid., p. 11.

35. Ibid., p. 13.

36. Ibid.

37. Deutscher, *The Prophet Armed*, pp. 227–8.

38. Trotskii, '"Yaponskii" vopros', *Evropa v Voine*, p. 33.

39. 'Psikhologicheskie zagadki voiny', ibid., p. 247.

40. 'Na severo-zapad', ibid., p. 26.

41. '"Sed'moi pekhotnyi" v bel'giiskoi epopee', ibid., p. 61.

42. Ibid., p. 64.

43. Ibid., p. 71.

44. Ibid., p. 69.

45. Ibid., p. 74.

46. 'Krepost' ili transheya?', ibid., p. 195.

47. Ibid., p. 196. In the sentence preceding the beginning of this quote, 'The triumph of the trench is so obvious that not only specialists of militarism bow down before it but also – and this might appear as paradoxical at first sight – pacifists'. Deutscher mistranslated 'trench' as 'the French'. In his attempt to make sense of why Trotsky should have used 'the French' in this context Deutscher totally changed the meaning of Trotsky's article. He did this by relating 'the French' to the Maginot Line and inserting the words 'in defence' into his translation to make the passage concur with

his reading: 'In a sarcastic aside he [Trotsky – IDT] dismissed in advance the illusion of the Maginot Line as it was beginning to emerge from the French experience in World War I. "The triumph of the French [in defence] is so evident that not only military experts bow to it, but also ... pacifists"' (Deutscher, *The Prophet Armed*, p. 229).

48. 'Transheya', *Evropa v Voine*, p. 196.
49. Ibid., p. 197.
50. Ibid.
51. Ibid.
52. Ibid., pp. 200–2.
53. Ibid., p. 198.
54. Ibid., pp. 202–3.
55. 'Psikhologicheskie zagadki voiny', ibid., p. 245. The absence of the conscious control of events by individuals was also mentioned by Trotsky in 'Otkhodit epokha', *Gody velikago pereloma*, p. 148.
56. 'Psikhologicheskie zagadki voiny', *Evropa v Voine*, p. 245.
57. Broué, *Trotsky*, p. 147.

3 The Censor in Paris

1. I. Deutscher, *The Prophet Armed* (Oxford, 1954), p. 220. (An earlier version of this chapter appeared in *European History Quarterly*, 24(2), 1994.)
2. L. Trotskii, *Voina i Revolyutsiya*, I (Petrograd, 1922), p. 12.
3. L. Trotskii, *Moya zhizn*, Moscow, 1991, p. 237.
4. Ibid., p. 19.
5. cf. —, 'Klyuch k pozitsii', *Nashe Slovo*, 138 (15 June 1916), p. 1, and *Voina i Revolyutsiya*, I, p. 197. Cf. also, —, 'Voennyi krizis i politicheskaya perspektivy. II Porazheniya i revolyutsiya', *Nashe Slovo*, 179 (1 September 1915), p. 1 and Trotskii, *Voina i Revolyutsiya*, I, p. 249.
6. Ibid. In this and in subsequent quotations text in square brackets did not appear in *Nashe Slovo*.
7. —, 'Klyuch k pozitsii'.
8. Cf. ibid., and Trotskii, *Voina i Revolyutsiya*, I, p. 197.
9. Cf. —, 'God voiny', *Nashe Slovo*, 156 (4 August 1915), p. 1, and L. Trotskii, *Voina i Revolyutsiya*, II, Moscow, 1924, p. 93.
10. —, 'God voiny'.
11. Cf. N. Trotskii, 'Nekriticheskii otsenka kriticheskoi epokhi. II Legenda "bor'by za demokratiyu"', *Nashe Slovo*, 35 (10 March 1915), p. 1, and Trotskii,*Voina i Revolyutsiya*, I, p. 316.
12. Cf. —, 'So slavyanskim aktsentom i ulybkoi na slavyanskikh gubakh', *Nashe Slovo*, 121 (24 May 1916), p. 1, and L. Trotskii, *Sochineniya, Evrope v Voine*, IX (Moscow, 1927), p. 168.
13. Trotskii, *Voina i Revolyutsiya*, II, p. 321.
14. Cf. —, 'Voennyya tainy i politicheskiya misterii', *Nashe Slovo*, 217 (17 October 1915), p. 1, and Trotskii, *Voina i Revolyutsiya*, I, p. 169.
15. Cf. —, 'Ironicheskii shchelchok istorii', *Nashe Slovo*, 73 (26 March 1916), p. 1, and Trotskii, *Sochineniya*, IX, p. 165.
16. Cf. N.T., 'Vremya nynche takovskoe', *Nashe Slovo*, 54 (1 April 1915), p. 1,

and Trotskii, *Voina i Revolyutsiya*, II, p. 314.

17. Cf. —, 'K Dublinskim itogam', *Nashe Slovo*, 154 (4 July 1916), p. 1, and Trotskii, *Voina i Revolyutsiya*, I, p. 193.

18. Cf. —, 'Voennyi krizis i polticheskiya persektivy. I. Prichiny krizisa', *Nashe Slovo*, 174 (26 August 1915), p. 1, and Trotskii, *Voina i Revolyutsiya*, I, p. 246; and N.T., 'Vpechatleniya i obobshcheniya g. Milyukova', *Nashe Slovo*, 193 (23 August 1916), p. 1, and Trotskii, *Voina i Revolyutsiya*, II, p. 288.

19. Cf. —, 'Konvent rasteryannosti i bezsiliya', *Nashe Slovo*, 167 (18 August 1915), p. 1, and Trotskii, *Voina i Revolyutsiya*, I, p. 240.

20. —, 'Konvent rasteryannosti i bezsiliya'.

21. Cf. —, 'Proekt deklaratsii', *Nashe Slovo*' 182 (8 August 1916), p. 1, and Trotskii, *Voina i Revolyutsiya*, II, pp. 216–17. Cf. also —, 'Frantsuzskii i nemetskii sotsial-patriotizm', *Nashe Slovo*, 212 (14 September 1916), p. 1, and Trotskii, *Voina i Revolyutsiya*, II, p. 226.

22. —, 'Vtorya tsimmerval'dskaya konferentsiya', *Nashe Slovo*, 111 (12 May 1916), pp. 1–2.

23. Cf. N.T., 'Vpechatleniya i obobshcheniya g. Milyukova', *Nashe Slovo*, 194 (24 August 1916), p. 1, and Trotskii, *Voina i Revolyutsiya*, I, p. 290.

24. Cf. —, 'V atmosphere neustoichivnosti i rastleniya', *Nashe Slovo*, 207 (8 September 1916), p. 1, and Trotskii, *Voina i Revolyutsiya*, I, pp. 209–10.

25. —, 'Voennyi krizis i politicheskiya perspektivy'.

26. —, 'Ona byla, konferentsiya v Tsimmerval'de!', *Nashe Slovo*, 218 (19 October 1915), p. 1.

27. See, for example, N.T., 'Nashi gruppirovki [iz zapisnoi knizhki]', *Nashe Slovo*, 209 (6 October 1915), p. 1; N.T., 'Nemetskaya S-D oppozitsiya [iz zapisnoi knizhki]', *Nashe Slovo*, 210, (7 October 1915), p. 1; N.T., 'Rossiskaya sektsiya internatsionalistov [iz zapisnoi knizhki]', *Nashe Slovo*, 212 (9 October 1915), p. 1; and N.T., 'Osnovnye tezisy [iz zapisnoi knizhki]', *Nashe Slovo*, 215 (13 October 1915), p. 1, and 216 (14 October 1915), p. 1.

28. Cf. —, 'Vtoroi novyi god', *Nashe Slovo*, 1 (1 January 1916), p. 1, and Trotskii, *Voina i Revolyutsiya*, II, p. 100.

29. Al'fa, 'Est eshche tsenzura v Parizhe', *Nashe Slovo*, 43 (20 February 1916), p. 1.

30. —, 'Novyi tsenzurnyi rezhim', *Nashe Slovo*, 212 (14 September 1916), p. 1.

31. Cf. —, 'Pervoe maya', *Nashe Slovo*, 102 (1 May 1916), p. 1, and Trotskii, *Voina i Revolyutsiya*, II, pp. 102–4.

32. Al'fa, 'Na nachalakh vzaimnosti', *Nashe Slovo*, 276 (28 December 1915), p. 2.

33. Al'fa, 'Zakon mekhaniki', *Nashe Slovo*, 114 (16 May 1916), p. 3.

34. Ibid.

35. —, 'Etapy', *Nashe Slovo*, 156, (6 July 1916), p. 1.

36. —, 'O chem molchit frantsuzskaya press. K sud'be Pol'shii', *Nashe Slovo*, 189 (18 August 1916) p. 1.

37. —, 'Stavka na sil'nykh', *Nashe Slovo*, 204, (5 September 1916), p. 1.

38. N. Trotskii, 'Nekriticheskii otsenka kriticheskoi epokhi. III. Politicheskie vyvod', *Nashe Slovo*, 41 (17 March 1915), p. 1; T, [no title], *Nashe Slovo*, 102 (1 June 1915), p. 2; and Al'fa, [no title], *Nashe Slovo*, 46 (24 February 1916), p. 1.

39. Cf. N. Trotskii, 'Osnovnye voprosy. I. Bor'ba za vlast', *Nashe Slovo*, No. 217 (17 October 1915), pp. 2–3,a nd L. Trotskii, *Itogi i perspektivy* (Moscow, 1919), Ch. 10.

4 Lenin and the Bolsheviks

1. K. Marx, *Surveys from Exile*, trans. B. Fowkes (Harmondsworth, 1973), p. 146. (An earlier version of this chapter appeared in *Slavonic and East European Review*, 72(1), 1994.)
2. This is most notable in accounts characteristic of Stalinist historiography. See, for example, A. N. Atsarkin and A. T. Barulina, *Bor'ba Bolshevikov za osushchestvlenie leninskoi programmy po voprosam voina, mir i revolyutsii* (Moscow, 1963); E. D. Chermenskii, *Rossiya v period imperialistichekoi voiny. Vtoraya revolyutsiya v Rossii (1914-Mart 1917)* (Moscow, 1957); P. A. Satyukov, *Bolshevistskaya pechat v period imperialisticheskoi voiny i vtoroi revolyutsii v Rossii* (Moscow, 1951); S. V. Shestakov, *Istoriografiya deyatel'nosti bol'shevistskoi partii v period pervoi mirovoi voiny i fevral'skoi revolyutsii* (Moscow, 1977); and V. V. Zaplatkin, *Bor'ba V. I. Lenina protiv 'Imperialisticheskogo ekonomizma'* (Moscow, 1967).
3. See, for example, I. Deutscher, *The Prophet Armed* (Oxford, 1954), pp. 218ff.
4. For the re-emergence of Trotsky studies in the Soviet Union under Gorbachev and post-USSR, see I. D. Thatcher, 'Recent Soviet Writings on Leon Trotsky', *Coexistence*, 27 (1990), pp. 141–67, 'Soviet Writings on Leon Trotsky: An Update', *Coexistence*, 29 (1992), pp. 73–96, and 'Trotsky Studies After the Crash: A Brief Note', *Europe-Asia Studies*, 48(3) (1996), pp. 481–6.
5. See, for example, T. Cliff, *Trotsky. Towards October* (London, 1989); *Trotsky. The Sword of the Revolution* (London, 1990) and *Trotsky: Fighting the Rising Stalinist Bureaucracy* (London, 1991); K. Mavrikis, *On Trotskyism* (London, 1976). For an outline of approaches to Trotsky see M. Cox, 'Trotsky and His Interpreters; or, Will the Real Leon Trotsky Please Stand Up?', *Russian Review*, 51 (January 1992), pp. 84–102, and David S. Law, 'Studies on Trotsky', *Journal of Communist Studies*, 2 (March 1986), pp. 83–90.
6. See, for example, D. Hallas, *Trotsky's Marxism* (London, 1979); I. Howe, *Trotsky* (Hove, Sussex, 1978); R. Segal, *The Tragedy of Leon Trotsky* (Harmondsworth, 1983); and R. S. Wistrich, *Trotsky* (London, 1979).
7. B. Pearce, 'Lenin versus Trotsky on "Revolutionary Defeatism"', *Study Group on the Russian Revolution Sbornik*, 13 (1987), pp. 16–30.
8. For an analysis of the impact of the censor's cuts on Trotsky's Paris journalism of 1914–16, see Chapter 3 of this work.
9. For an account of Trotsky's involvement in *Bor'ba*, see I. D. Thatcher, 'Trotsky and Bor'ba', *Historical Journal*, 37(1) (1994), pp. 113–25, and I. D. Thatcher, '*Bor'ba*: A Workers' Journal in St. Petersburg on the Eve of World War One', *English Historical Review*, 113(450) (1998), pp. 99–116.
10. N. Trotskii, 'Nash politicheskii lozung', *Nashe Slovo*, 22 (23 February 1915), p. 1.

11. N. Trotskii, 'Nash politicheskii lozung', *Golos*, 108 (17 January 1915), p. 1.
12. Ibid.
13. N. Trotskii, 'Nash politicheskii lozung', *Golos*, 106 (15 January 1915), p. 1.
14. N. Trotskii, 'Nash politicheskii lozung', *Nashe Slovo*, 23 (24 February 1915), p. 1.
15. N. Trotskii, 'Nash politicheskii lozung', *Golos*, 108, p. 2.
16. N. Trotskii, 'Nash politicheskii lozung', *Nashe Slovo*, 23, p. 1.
17. Ibid.
18. Ibid.
19. 'Voina i Rossiskaya Sotsial'demokratiya', *Sotsial'Demokrat*, 33 (1 November 1914), p. 1.
20. Ibid.
21. Ibid.
22. Ibid.
23. Ibid.
24. Ibid.
25. Ibid.
26. Ibid.
27. —, 'Konferentsiya zagranichnykh sektsii RSDRP', *Sotsial'Demokrat*, 40 (29 March 1915), p. 2. The five points were as follows: (1) the unconditional refusal to vote for war credits and immediate withdrawal from bourgeois governments; (2) complete abandonment of the policy of 'civil peace'; (3) the creation of illegal organisations where governments and the bourgeoisie declare a state of emergency and remove constitutional rights; (4) to support the brotherhood of soldiers of warring nations in the trenches and in the theatre of war in general; (5) to support all types of revolutionary mass demonstrations in general.
28. Ibid.
29. Trotsky's printed remarks on Eintracht's resolution are not consistent. In the first of 1917 he says that Eintracht's Executive Committee penned the resolution and he just made a speech in support of it, whereas in his autobiography (1929) he claims authorship for himself. Cf. N. Trotskii, 'Za dva s polovinoi goda voiny v Evrope', *Novyi Mir*, 928 (6 March 1917), p. 4, and L. Trotskii, *Moya zhizn* (Moscow, 1991), pp. 233–4.
30. For the full text of Eintracht's resolution, see 'Der Krieg und die Aufgabe der Internationale', *Volksrecht*, 15 October 1914, pp. 1–2.
31. 'Material k referatu "Voine i Sotsial-Demokratii"', *Leninskii sbornik*, XIV (Moscow, 1930), p. 139.
32. Ibid.
33. Ibid.
34. Ibid., p. 142.
35. Ibid., p. 139.
36. Ibid., p. 140.
37. Ya. G. Temkin, *Lenin i mezhdunarodnaya sotsial-demokratiya* (Moscow, 1968), p. 115.
38. *Leninskii sbornik*, XVII (Moscow, 1931), p. 198.
39. Ibid., p. 195.
40. Ibid.
41. V. I. Lenin, 'A. G. Shlyapnikovu', *Polnoe sobranie sochinenii*, XLIX (Moscow,

1978), p. 64. At the same time one should note that Trotsky himself was still wary of Lenin's 'machinations.' Thus, for example, in an undated letter to Radek, which was obviously written after *Nashe Slovo* had received Lenin's theses on the London Conference, Trotsky said: 'You asked me about Lenin's politics. Here is my opinion. To begin with Lenin attempted to unite with Martov against the non-fractionalists and the liquidationists. When he again became convinced that Martov is bound too tightly to his fraction he attempted, through *Nashe Slovo*, to unite with the non-fractionalists against Martov ... We will relate to all Lenin's steps thus: isolate ourselves completely from all those motives of a 'fractional character' which guide him and concentrate exclusively on his political steps. So we warmly welcomed his declaration, including huge chunks of it in our declaration, and we will act in a similarly in the future ... we will not participate in organisational games for a preventive struggle against possible opponents, and especially for the artificial fabrication of these opponents': RTsKhIDNI, F. 325, O. 1, D. 394.

42. —, 'K materialam Londonskoi konferentsii', *Nashe Slovo*, 20 (20 February 1915), p. 1.
43. Ibid.
44. —, 'K materialam Londonskoi konferentsii', *Nashe Slovo*, 26 (27 February 1915), p. 1.
45. *Leninskii sbornik*, XVII, pp. 199–200.
46. —, 'K materialam Londonskoi konferentsii', *Nashe Slovo*, 30 (4 March 1915), p. 1.
47. Ibid.
48. —, 'K materialam Londonskoi konferentsii. K edinstvu deistvii', *Nashe Slovo*, 32 (6 March 1915), p. 1.
49. Ibid.
50. Ibid. This call for unity was also advanced in two articles by Voinov. See Voinov, 'Ob edinstve', *Nashe Slovo*, 32 (6 March 1915), p. 1 and *Nashe Slovo*, 33 (7 March 1915), p. 1.
51. —, 'Gde bol'shinstvo?', *Nashe Slovo*, 42 (18 March 1915), p. 1.
52. 'Pis'mo TsK RSDRP: Redaktsii Nashego Slova', *Leninskii sbornik*, XVII, pp. 201–3.
53. Ibid., p. 202.
54. Ibid.
55. Ibid., p. 203.
56. —, 'Po povodu Londonskoi Konferentsii', *Sotsial'Demokrat*, 40 (29 March 1915), p. 1.
57. Ibid.
58. Ibid.
59. Ibid.
60. 'Pis'mo Redaktsii Nashego Slova: TsK RSDRP', *Leninskii sbornik*, XVII, pp. 204–6.
61. Ibid., p. 205.
62. Ibid.
63. Ibid., p. 206.
64. Ibid., p. 204.
65. RTsKhIdNI, F. 325, O. 1, D. 394.

66. N. Trotskii, 'Otkrytoe pis'mo v pedaktsiyu zhurnala *Kommunist*', *Nashe Slovo*, 105 (4 June 1915), pp. 1–2.
67. *Kommunist*, Nos. 1–2 (August 1915), p. 3.
68. Trotskii, 'Otkrytoe pis'mo ...', p. 1.
69. Ibid.
70. Ibid.
71. Ibid., p. 2.
72. Ibid.
73. On 13 February 1915 Trotsky published a statement in which he corrected Larin for his assertion that Trotsky, along with Plekhanov and Aksel'rod, was responsible for the policy of the Organisational Committee. Trotsky announced that he did not carry any more responsibility for the Organisational Committee than for any other part of the party. He also said that he had not participated in publications of the Organisational Committee since 1913 and had twice refused to act as the Organisational Committee's delegate – first in the International Socialist Bureau and second at the London Conference (N. Trotskii, 'Zayavlenie', *Nashe Slovo*, 14 (13 February 1915), p. 1). Twelve days later *Nashe Slovo* published several amendments to Trotsky's statement, submitted by the Organisational Committee. Their letter claimed that Larin's confusion of where to place Trotsky organisationally was understandable in view of that fact that Trotsky himself had not declared his opposition to the August Bloc, including the group *Bor'ba*. Furthermore, the Organisational Committee pointed out that they had never invited Trotsky to carry their mandate to the London Conference. A certain comrade had asked Trotsky, but on his own initiative (Zagranichnyi Sekretariat O.K., 'Pis'mo v Redaktsiyu', *Nashe Slovo*, 24 (25 February 1915), p. 2).

Trotsky never directly answered the Organisational Committee's queries and therefore the question of his exact allegiances remained open. This is not the interpretation followed by Deutscher. For Deutscher, Trotsky's statement amounted to a 'repudiation of the August Bloc ... [his] first step on the road that was to lead him to the Bolshevik Party' (Deutscher, *The Prophet Armed*, p. 219). Deutscher's view has since been copied by T. Cliff – right down to repeating Deutscher's mistake in dating the statement 14 February 1915. See Cliff, *Trotsky: Towards October*, p. 193. However, on other occasions Trotsky pointed out that he did not bear full responsibility for the views expressed by *Nashe Slovo* – but Deutscher never concluded from this that Trotsky had broken with *Nashe Slovo*. See, for example, *Nashe Slovo*, 106 (6 May 1916), p. 2. Here Trotsky denied Larin's assertion that *Nashe Slovo* was published by Trotsky. He also added to his anti-Larin comments of 13 February 1915: 'Readers should note that whatever Larin says needs verifying.' N. Trotskii, 'Nuzhdatsya v proverke', *Nashe Slovo*, 106 (6 May 1916).
74. Witness Lenin's desires to have a frequently issued publication during the negotiations to set up *Kommunist*. See, for example, the resolution 'TsO i novaya gazette', *KPSS v rezolyutsiyakh i ressheniyakh s'ezdov, konferentsii i plenumov TsK* (Moscow, 1983), p. 474.
75. G. Zinov'ev, 'Rossiskaya sotsial-demokratiya i Russkii sotsial-shovinizm', *Kommunist*, 1–2 (August 1915), pp. 102–54.

76. Ibid., p. 146. From Lenin's letters to Zinoviev of July 1915 we learn that the editorial board did vote on whether to approach Trotsky: V. I. Lenin, *Polnoe sobranie sochinenii*, XLIX, pp. 86–9. Lenin and Zinoviev voted against but were obviously defeated. The notes to volume XLIX of Lenin's *Collected Works* claim that Pyatkov and Bosh sent the invitation to Trotsky: ibid., p. 501, no 100. Zinoviev had wanted to mention these disputes within the editorial board in an article for *Kommunist*, but Lenin insisted that he cut this information: 'Guests have convinced me that to speak of our disagreements in the editorial board of *Kommunist* (that you and I voted against Trotsky) in press is not worth it. They are right. Expunge!!': ibid., pp. 87–8. Hence the possibility remains that Zinoviev constructed the experiment theory *post factum*.

77. —, 'Nasha pozitsiya', *Nashe Slovo*, 89 (15 May 1915), p. 1; 100 (29 May 1915), pp. 1–2; 106 (5 June 1915), p. 1; 107 (6 June 1915), p. 1; 146 (23 July 1915), p. 1; and 147 (24 July 1915), p. 1. In a letter of 13 May 1915 Trotsky informed Radek: 'The day after tomorrow there begins in *Nashe Slovo* a series of articles under the heading of "Our Position". These articles, written by me, will appear as editorials. They reject both Lenin's barbarous splitting and the social-patriot's and Aksel'rod's political concealment': RTsKhIDNI, F. 325, O. 1, D. 394.

78. —, 'Nasha pozitsiya', 100, p. 1.

79. —, 'Nasha pozitsiya', 106, p. 1.

80. Ibid.

81. —, 'Nasha pozitsiya', 146 and 147.

82. —, 'Nasha pozitsiya', 146, p. 1. This was the first time that Trotsky differentiated *Nashe Slovo* from the August Bloc. Previously, he had maintained that sections of the August Bloc – specifically the members of the group *Bor'ba*, considered by Trotsky to be an independent organisation, but according to the Organisational Committee part of the August Bloc (see n. 73 above) – were supporters of *Nashe Slovo*. See N. Trotskii, 'Diversii', *Nashe Slovo*, 137 (11 July 1915), p. 2.

83. —, 'Nasha pozitsiya', 147, p. 1.

84. Zinov'ev, 'Rossiskaya sotsial-demokratiya i Russkii sotsial-shovinizm', p. 141.

85. Ibid., p. 144.

86. Trotsky stated this view in 'Nasha pozitsiya', No. 89, p. 1.

87. Zinov'ev, 'Rossiskaya sotsial-demokratiya ...', p. 145.

88. Ibid., p. 146. Lenin carefully edited Zinoviev's articles to ensure that they conveyed a sufficiently anti-Trotsky message. Thus, for example, in his notes to Zinoviev's 'Pacifism or Marxism' Lenin changed the phrase 'one demand is lawless' as it 'smells of a concession to Trotsky', and added a sentence which said that 'Trotsky and the O[rganisational] C[ommittee] set themselves up as Popes': *Leninskii sbornik*, XXXIX (Moscow, 1980), p. 149.

89. —, 'O porazhenii svoego pravitel'stva v imperialistskoi voine', *Sotsial'Demokrat*, 43 (26 July 1915), p. 1.

90. Ibid.

91. Ibid.

92. Ibid.

93. —, 'O polozhenii del v Rossiiskoi Sots-Dem-Tii', *Sotsial'Demokrat*, 43 (26 July 1915), pp. 1–2.

94. Ibid., p. 1. Here Lenin had I. Bezrabotnyii and Anton Gla'skii in mind: see 'K organizatsionnomu voprosu', *Nashe Slovo*, 107 (6 June 1915), pp. 1–2. Deutscher suggests that Manuilskii, Lozovskii and Lunacharskii were the 'almost Bolsheviks' on *Nashe Slovo* (see Deutscher, *The Prophet Armed*, p. 224). Trotsky polemicised with Lozovskii on two occasions in *Nashe Slovo*. In April 1916 they clashed over the appropriate response to Camille Huysmans's attempts to convoke a meeting of the International Socialist Bureau in the Hague. Lozovskii insisted that Zimmerwaldists should attend. After all, he pointed out, Zimmerwald had not declared itself a Third International, but had the goal of winning existing organisations from within. He therefore recommended a list of demands to be taken to the Hague by Zimmerwaldists with the aim of achieving their aims; in the event of non-attendance, he claimed Huysmans would be able to declare the Zimmerwaldists 'splitters' and the International Socialist Bureau, a mighty organisation, his own. Trotsky, on the other hand, thought the main duty of revolutionary internationalists consisted of clearly counterposing Zimmerwald to Hague so that the proletariat could make a choice between the two. He preferred to leave the issue of tactics aside until it became clear whether Huysmans's plans would get off the ground or not. By declaring his hand ahead of time, Trotsky thought Lozovskii was confusing the proletariat. See A. Lozovskii, 'Tsimmervald i Gaaga', *Nashe Slovo*, 96 (22 April 1916), pp. 1–2, and —, 'Dva printsipa. Po povodu stati' t. A. Lozovskago', *Nashe Slovo*, 97 (23 April 1916), p. 1. Deutscher manages to misrepresent Lozovskii's and Trotsky's views on this matter: see Deutscher, *The Prophet Armed*, p. 235. Then, in August 1916, Lozovskii and Trotsky argued over *Nashe Slovo's* anti-Longuetist resolution to the *Comité pour la Reprise des Relations Internationales*. See —, 'V komitete dlya vosstanovleniya internats svyazei', *Nashe Slovo*, 188 (17 August 1916), p. 1; A. Lozovskii, 'Po povodu odnoi deklaratsii', *Nashe Slovo*, 189 (18 August 1916), p. 1; and 'Ot Redaktsii', ibid., pp. 1–2.

95. —, 'Voennyi krizis i politicheskaya perspektivy. II. Porazheniya i revolyutsiya', *Nashe Slovo*, 179 (1 September 1915), p. 1; 180 (2 September 1915), p. 1.

96. Ibid., 179, p. 1.

97. Ibid., 180, p. 1.

98. N.T., 'Nashi gruppirovki [iz zapisnoi knizhki]', *Nashe Slovo*, 209 (6 October 1915), p. 1.

99. Ibid.

100. Ibid.

101. Ibid.

102. Ibid.

103. N.T., 'Rossiskaya sektsiya internatsionalistov [iz zapisnoi knizhki]', *Nashe Slovo*, 212 (9 October 1915), p. 1.

104. Ibid. It is obvious that Trotsky was referring to the fact that the Central Committee produced their publications in neutral Switzerland.

105. N.T., 'Osnovnye tezisy [iz zapisnoi knizhki]', *Nashe Slovo*, 215 (13 October 1915), p. 1; 216 (14 October 1915), p. 1.

106. Ibid., 215, p. 1.

107. Ibid.

108. —, 'Mezhdunarodnaya sotsialisticheskaya konferentsiya v tsimmerval'de', *Sotsial'Demokrat*, 45–6 (11 October 1915), p. 1.

109. See, for example, —, 'Pervyi shag', ibid., p. 2; —, 'Pervaya mezhduranod-naya konferentsiya', ibid., pp. 2–3.

110. —, 'Nashe russkie tozhe-internatsionalisti na internatsional'noi konfer-entsii', ibid., p. 4.

111. Ibid.

112. —, 'Voina i revolyutsionnyi krizis v Rossii', ibid., pp. 1–2.

113. —, 'Voennyi krizis i politicheskaya perspectivy. III. Sotsial'naya sily Rossiskoi revolyutsii', *Nashe Slovo*, 181 (3 September 1915), p. 1; —, 'Voennyi krizis i politicheskaya perspectivy. IV. Natsional'nyi ili internat-sional'nyi kurs'?', *Nashe Slovo*, 182 (4 September 1915), p. 1.

114. N.T., 'K Tsimmerval'dskoi konferentsii. III', *Nashe Slovo*, 232 (5 November 1915), p. 2.

115. N.T., 'K Tsimmerval'dskoi konferentsii. IV', *Nashe Slovo*, 244 (19 November 1915), p. 1.

116. Ibid.

117. N. Trotskii, 'Osnovnye voprosy', *Nashe Slovo*, 217 (17 October 1915), pp. 2–3.

118. —, 'O dvukh liniyakh revolyutsii', *Sotsial'Demokrat*, 48 (20 November 1915), p. 1.

119. Ibid.

120. N. Trotskii, 'Pod bremenem ob'ektivizma', *Nashe Slovo*, 248 (24 November 1915), pp. 1–2; 249 (25 November 1915), pp. 1–2.

121. Ibid., No. 248, 24 November 1915, p. 1.

122. Ibid., p. 2.

123. RTsKhIDNI, F. 325, O. 1, D. 444.

124. L. Sinclair, *Trotsky: A Bibliography* (Aldershot, 1989), p. 72.

125. RTsKhIDNI, F. 325, O. 1, D. 444.

126. Ibid.

127. For a good analysis of the events surrounding the election of worker representatives to the War-Industries Committees, see Robert B. McKean, *St Petersburg Between the Revolutions* (New Haven, CT, and London), 1990, pp. 380–5.

128. —, 'Nasha pobeda', *Sotsial'Demokrat*, 48 (20 November 1915), p. 2.

129. —, 'Fakti i vyvody (eshche o petrogradskikh vyborakh)', *Nashe Slovo*, 270 (19 December 1915), p. 1.

130. N. Trotskii, 'Programma mira. 1. Nuzhna-li programma mira?', *Nashe Slovo*, 24 (29 January 1916), p. 1.

131. Ibid.

132. G. Zinov'ev and N. Lenin, *Sotsializm i voina* (Geneva, 1915), p. 40.

133. N. Trotskii, 'Programma mira. IV. Soedinennye shtaty Evropy', *Nashe Slovo*, 29 (4 February 1916), p. 2.

134. Ibid.

135. Ibid.

136. —, 'O lozunge soedinennykh shtatov Evropy', *Sotsial'Demokrat*, 44 (23 August 1915), p. 2.

137. Ibid.
138. N. Trotskii, 'Programma mira. V. Pozitsiya *"Sotsialdemokrata"'*, *Nashe Slovo*, 86 (11 April 1916), pp. 1–2; 87 (12 April 1916), pp. 1–2.
139. Ibid., 86, p. 2.
140. Ibid.
141. Ibid., 87, p. 1.
142. Ibid.
143. Ibid.
144. —, 'O lozunge soedinennykh shtatov Evropy'.
145. N. Trotskii, 'Programma mira . . . ', *Nashe Slovo*, 87, p. 2.
146. Ibid.
147. L. J. van Rossum, 'Ein unverffentlichter brief Trockijs von anfang 1916', *International Review of Social History*, 14 (1969), p. 256.
148. Ibid., p. 258.
149. Ibid.
150. Ibid., p. 257. For further evidence of Trotsky's view of *Vorbote* as a Leninist fractional publication, see his letter to Radek in RTsKhIDNI, F. 325, O. 1, D. 394, and his correspondence with D. B. Ryazanov, ibid., F. 325, O. 1, D. 396 and F. 325, O. 1, D. 399. Lenin was probably quite satisfied that Trotsky had declined Holst's offer of cooperation. After all, in a letter to Holst of 8 March 1916 he had outlined his differences with Trotsky regarding unity with Chkheidze (V. I. Lenin, *Polnoe Sobranie Sochinenii*, XLIX, pp. 191–2); while in a letter to I. F. Armand of 15 January 1916 he exclaimed that 'Trotsky has lost one more ally!!' (ibid., p. 174). Indeed, Lenin had consistently stressed his opposition to Trotsky on a number of issues in his personal correspondence from the beginning of the war onwards. See, for example, 'A. G. Shlyapnikovu' (28 November 1914, ibid., pp. 36–7); 'G. Gorteru' (5 May 1915, ibid., pp. 74–5); 'G. E. Zinov'evu' (After 11 July 1915, ibid., pp. 91–3); 'D. Vainkopu' (after 24 July 1915, ibid., pp. 104–6); 'A. M. Kollantai' (August 1915, ibid., pp. 117–18); 'A. G. Shlyapnikovu' (23 August 1915, ibid., pp. 132–34; 'A. G. Shlapnikovu' (September 1915, ibid., pp. 141–42); 'G. E. Zinov'evu' (August 1916, ibid., pp. 288–9); 'A. G. Shlyapnikovu' (after 3 October 1916, ibid., pp. 298–302); and 'A. M. Kollantai' (17 March 1917, pp. 401–3). See also 'A. Shlyapnikovu' (January 1915, *Leninskii sbornik*, 2, Moscow, 1914, p. 216); 'A. Kollantai' (July 1915, ibid., p. 231); and 'A. Kollantai' (summer 1915, ibid., p. 235).
151. —, 'Est-li svoye liniya u O.K. i u fraktsii Chkheidze?', *Sotsial'Demokrat*, 50 (18 February 1916), p. 2.
152. —, 'Nasha Dumskaya fraktsiya', *Nashe Slovo*, 77 (31 March 1916), p. 1.
153. Ibid.
154. —, 'Nasha Dumskaya fraktsiya. 1. revolyutsionnaya i passivno-vyzhidatel'naya politika', *Nashe Slovo*, 94 (20 April 1916), p. 1. However, this did not mean that Trotsky saw himself as now sharing Lenin's view of the Duma fraction. Thus, for example, in the second instalment of 'Our Duma Fraction' Trotsky defended *Nashe Slovo* from Martov's accusation that 'the fraction has gained one more enemy which does not balk at using Leninist methods to struggle against it': cited in —, 'Nasha Dumskaya fraktsiya. 2. "druz'ya" i "vragi" dumskoi fraktsii',

Nashe Slovo, 95 (21 April 1916), pp. 1–2.

155. —, 'Poezdka deputata Chkheidze', *Nashe Slovo*, 203 (3 September 1916), pp. 1–2. See also, —, 'K poezdke deputata Chkheidze', *Nachalo*, 29 (3 November 1916), p. 1.

156. N. Lenin 'Fraktsiya Chkheidze i eya rol', *Sbornik' Sotsial'Demokrata*, 2 (December 1916), p. 69.

157. V. I. Lenin, 'A. Kollontai', *Leninskii sbornik*, II, p. 282. See also Lenin's letter to Armand of 17 February 1917 (V. I. Lenin, *Polnoe sobranie sochinenii*, XLIX, p. 390). From Lenin's letter to Armand of 22 January 1917 we learn that Trotsky had written to Lenin. Trotsky never referred to this letter in his later writings. We do, however, know Lenin's feelings: 'Trotsky sent a stupid letter: we will not publish or answer him' (V. I. Lenin, ibid., p. 374). In his autobiography Trotsky tried to discredit Kollantai's letter to Lenin thus: 'In the New York period nothing was revolutionary enough for her. She corresponded with Lenin. Interpreting facts and ideas through the prism of her then ultra-leftism Kollantai sent Lenin information from America, in particular about my activities. In Lenin's letters of reply one can come across echoes of this consciously mischievous information' (L. Trotskii, *Moya zhizn*, pp. 265–6).

158. *Leninskii sbornik*, IV (Moscow, 1925), p. 303.

159. L. Trotskii, *Voina i Revolyutsiya*, I (Petrograd, 1922), pp. 7–29.

160. Ibid., pp. 25–6.

161. Ibid., p. 25.

162. N. I. Bukharin, *K Voprosu O Trotskizme* (Moscow, 1925), p. 53. Thus notable by their absence were: 'Nash politicheskii lozung'; 'Otkrytoe pis'mo v redaktsiyu zhurnala *Kommunist*'; 'Nasha pozitsiya'; 'Diversii'; 'Rossiskaya sektsiya internatsionalov [iz zapisnoi knizhki]'; 'K Tsimmerval'dskoi konferentsii. III'; 'Pod bremenem ob'ektivizma'; 'Programma mira. V. Pozitsiya *Sotsialdemokrata*'; and 'Nash Dumskaya fraktsiya' (no. 77).

163. L. Trotskii, 'Vyvody', *Voina i Revolyutsiya*, II (Moscow, 1924), pp. 55–9.

164. N.T., 'Vpechatleniya [iz zapisnoi knizhki]', *Nashe Slovo*, 207 (3 October 1915), p. 1; 'Nashi gruppirovki [iz zapisnoi knizhki]', *Nashe Slovo*, No. 209.

165. L. Trotskii, 'Vyrody', p. 55. Cf. also N.T., 'Osnovy tezisy [iz zapisnoi knizhki]', no. 215, and *Voina i Revolyutsiya*, II, p. 49. In the latter text Trotsky cut the sentence in square brackets from the original: 'in *Sotsial-Demokrat's* project, as in all of its platform, the slogan of peace figured not as the main cry of the proletariat at the present moment, mobilising against militarism and chauvinism, but as a semi retreat of pure revolutionary spirit to pacifist human fruit. [This is one of the features which gave its position a sectionist-grotesque character.]' Also omitted was the footnote in which Trotsky had criticised the Leninists for inconsistency in their understanding of pacifism.

166. Ibid., p. 62.

167. G. Zinov'ev, *Sochineniya*, V (Moscow, 1924), pp. 105–211.

168. Ibid., p. 211 n. 17.

169. L. Trotskii, *Sochineniya*, III, pt. 1 (Moscow, n.d.), pp. xi–lxvii.

170. See, for example, L. Kamenev, 'Leninizm ili Trotskizm', in L. D. Trotskii, *Uroki Oktyabrya* (St Petersburg), 1991, p. 187; I. Stalin, 'Trotskizm ili

Leninizm', ibid., p. 206; G. Zinov'ev, 'Bol'shevizm ili Trotskizm?', ibid., p. 213; and E. Kviring, 'Lenin, zagovorshchichestvo, Oktyabr', ibid., p. 269.

171. L. Kamenev, 'Leninizm ili Trotskizm', pp. 148–51; N. Bukharin, 'Kak ne nuzhno pisat' istoriyu Oktyabrya?', in L. Trotskii, *Uroki Oktyabrya*, pp. 313–18. Trotsky responded to the charge that he opposed Lenin during World War One in a letter of 27 October 1927 to IstPart. This source became well known in the West when Trotsky included it in *The Stalin School of Falsification*. In the letter, without mentioning that he had altered some of the original articles, he pointed to the collection *Voina i Revolyutsiya* as evidence of his 'Leninism' during World War One: 'The reviews of *War and Revolution* in all of the party press – Russian and foreign – a dozen and a thousand times showed that looking at my work during the war as a whole, one has to admit and understand that my differences with Lenin had a secondary character, and that my basic line was revolutionary which all the time brought me closer to Bolshevism, not only in words but also in reality': L. Trotskii, *Stalinskaya Shkola Fal'sifikatsii* (Moscow, 1990), p. 15. Trotsky even cited cases from the early process of the dressing-up of past disputes to serve the then current political purpose of presenting a united Bolshevik face as genuine accounts of the past. See, for instance, his quote of the following extract from the notes to volume 14 of the first (1921) edition of Lenin's collected works, 'From the beginning of the imperialist war [Trotskii] occupied a clear internationalist position', in L. Trotskii, *Stalinskaya shkola fal'sifikatsii*, p. 15.

172. L. Trotskii, *Moya zhizn*, pp. 244–5.

173. Ibid., p. 318; L. Trotskii, *Istoriya Russkoi Revolyutsiya*, I (Berlin, 1931), p. 522. In his 1927 letter to IstPart he was not so bold: 'I participated together with Bolsheviks on the editorial board of *Novyi Mir*, where I gave a Leninist evaluation of the first stages of the February Revolution': L. Trotskii, *Stalinskaya Shkola Fal'sifikatsii*, p. 14. Trotsky's claim of the identity of his and Lenin's analyses is in fact quite spurious. To cite just a few examples: for Trotsky the February Revolution had resulted in a shift of power to an evil imperialist bourgeoisie, whereas for Lenin Russia had become the freest country out of all the warring nations; Trotsky spoke of the need to create a workers' government, whereas Lenin emphasised the role of the peasantry and so on. For an account of the polemical underpinnings of Trotsky's *Istoriya*, see James D. White, 'Trotsky's *History of the Russian Revolution*', *Journal of Trotsky Studies*, 1 (1993), pp. 1–18.

174. A. V. Pantsov, '"Demon revolyutsii" ili proletarskii revolyutsioner?', *Politicheskie issledovaniya*, 1 (1991), p. 91.

5 Martov and the Mensheviks

1. For example in a letter of 19 August 1914 Martov congratulated Aksel'rod for writing a letter in French because, 'only letters written in French have a chance of getting into Switzerland' (*Pis'ma P. B. Aksel'roda i Yu. O. Martova*, Berlin, 1924, p. 298). (An earlier version of this chapter appeared in *Revolutionary Russia*, 9(2), 1996.)

2. Ibid., p. 299.
3. Ibid., p. 300.
4. Ibid., p. 303.
5. Ibid.
6. Ibid., p. 306. Deutscher makes the mistake of calling *Golos* 'Martov's newspaper': I. Deutscher, *The Prophet Armed* (Oxford, 1954), p. 216.
7. This summary of Martov's views was constructed from the following: 'Otkrytoe pis'mo L. Martova k Gustava Erve', *Golos*, 12 (25 September 1914), p. 1; L.M., 'Mir!', *Golos*, 19 (3 October 1914), p. 1; L. Martov, 'K pozitsii angliskikh sotsialistov', *Golos*, 21 (6 October 1914), p. 1; L.M., 'Miologiya "poslednei voiny"', *Golos*, 22 (8 October 1914), , p. 1; L.M., 'Umer "Vorwaerts"', *Golos*, 23 (9 October 1914), pp. 1–2; L.M., 'Promyshlenniki i voina', *Golos*, 34 (22 October 1914), p. 1; L. Martov, 'A Marksa ostav'te v pokoe ...', *Golos*, 35 (23 October 1914), p. 1; L.M., 'Voina i Ital'yanskie sotsialisty', *Golos*, 37 (25 October 1914), p. 1; L. Martov, 'Sryvayut ...!', *Golos*, 40 (29 October 1914), p. 1; L. Martov, 'Voina i t. Plekhanov', *Golos*, 41 (30 October 1914), pp. 1–2; and L.M., 'V dobryi chas'!', *Golos*, 43 (1 November 1914), p. 1.
8. —, 'Polozhenie i zadachi sotsialisticheskago internatsionala', *Sotsial'Demokrat*, 33 (1 November 1914), p. 2. It is interesting to note that in Soviet books on this period historians mention only the positive side of Lenin's evaluation of Martov. See, for example, Ya. G. Temkin, *Lenin i mezhdunarodnaya sotsial-demokratiya* (Moscow, 1968), pp. 41–2. See also P. Pomper, *Lenin, Trotsky and Stalin* (New York, 1990), p. 241.
9. Deutscher, *The Prophet Armed*, p. 216. Deutscher most likely overestimated Trotsky's enthusiasm for a bloc with Martov. After all, in the entry of 26 August 1914 in the diary he kept in Zurich Trotsky penned the following critique of Martov's explanation of Social-Democracy's recent 'capitulation': 'at a general meeting of Russian Social-Democrats the Menshevik M[artov] read a report about the International during the war. His attempt to explain the capitulation of Social-Democracy as an unexpected and accidental step brought forth by an all-general "panic" was to the highest degree untenable ... In other words: since an all-general panic reigned the Social-Democrats also panicked. This explanation is simply pleonasm ... a whole series of other forces acted and acts: governments, diplomats, general staffs, banks, bourgeois parties and the bourgeois press. In the chaos of mobilisation and war all of these forces conduct their policy which flows out of their interests and relies on all of their preparatory work': L. Trotskii, *Voina i Revolyutsiya*, I (Petrograd, 1922), pp. 65–6.
10. Cited in —, 'Polozhenie i zadachi sotsialiticheskago internatsionala'.
11. Temkin, *Lenin i mezhdunarodnaya sotsial-demokratiya*, p. 40.
12. 'S. Peterburg', *Sotsial'Demokrat*, 34 (5 December 1914), p. 2.
13. 'Ot' redaktsii', *Sotsial'Demokrat*, 34 (5 December 1914), p. 2.
14. Raf. Grigor'ev, 'P. B. Aksel'rod ob internatsionale i voine', *Golos*, 86 (22 December 1914), p. 1; and Raf. Grigor'ev, 'P. B. Aksel'rod ob internatsionale i voine. (okonchanie)', *Golos*, 87 (23 December 1914), p. 1.
15. L. Martov, 'O moem mnimom "odinodestve". (Pis'mo v redaktsiyu)', *Golos*, 87 (23 December 1914), p. 2.

16. The full list of names was as follows: P. B. Aksel'rod, Astrov, I. Bezrabotnyi [Manuilsky – IDT] , I. Ber, Vasil'ev, A. Voinov [Lunacharsky – IDT], Volonter (M. Pavlovich), L. Vladimirov, A. Gal'skii, Raf. Grigor'ev, K. Zalevskii [Zalewski – IDT], Kanaev, I. Klimov, A. Kolontai, A. Lozovskii, V. Maiskii, V. Mandel'berg, L. Martov, Martynov, Ya. Master, M. N. P-skii [Pokrovskii – IDT] , N. Trotskii, Ttsanev, G. Ts-ich, and many others: *Golos*, 63 (25 November 1914), p. 1.

17. *Pis'ma P. B. Aksel'roda i Yu. O. Martova*, p. 309. In his account of these disputes Deutscher makes two factual errors. First, he claims that Lenin thought that Martov's *and* Aksel'rod's 'internationalism' did not concur with the rest of the Menshevik fraction's social-chauvinism when, in actual fact, Lenin said that Martov stood alone. Second, without saying that Martov's reference to Zinov'ev was made in connection with the dispute between Martov and Trotsky over the reviewer for Trotsky's pamphlet, Deutscher concludes that 'Martov resorted to a well-tested stratagem: he tried to "frighten" Trotsky (as Martov himself put it), telling him that if he were to break with the Mensheviks he would place himself at the mercy of the Bolsheviks and "deliver himself into the hands of Grisha Zinoviev", now Lenin's chief assistant in Switzerland. But the bogy was not as effective as it used to be; and Martov related that he had to approach Trotsky with smooth diplomacy and to treat him "like a little china statuette"': *The Prophet Armed*, p. 218. Deutscher's confusion on this point is really quite remarkable.

18. See, for example, ibid., p. 224; I. Getzler, *Martov* (Cambridge, 1967), p. 141.

19. *Pis'ma P. B. Aksel'roda i Yu. O. Martova*, p. 310. For a brief account of the background to and proceedings of the Copenhagen Conference see, for example, M. Fainsod, *International Socialism and the World War* (New York, 1973), pp. 46–7. For *Golos*'s statement to the Copenhagen Conference, see —, 'Sotsialisticheskoi konferentsii v Kopengagene. Ot' redaktsii i sotrudnikov "Golosa"', *Golos*, 100 (8 January 1915), pp. 1–2.

20. The three points of Martov's programme were as follows: '1) to agitate for peace against 'war to the finish'; 2) against the "national bloc"; 3) a categorical declaration on the necessity to continue the struggle of international socialism against tsarist reaction': *Pis'ma Aksel'roda i Matova*, p. 315. Martov did not succeed in receiving an invitation to attend the London Conference. For the various declarations on this event and *Nashe Slovo*'s attempts to build a united response from the various sections of the RSDLP see the previous chapter.

21. *Pis'ma Aksel'roda i Martova*, pp. 315–16.

22. Ibid., p. 319.

23. For Martov's rejection of the chauvinist line published in *Nasha Zarya*, 7–9 (1914), see L. Martov, 'Zayavlenie', *Nashe Slovo*, 1 (29 January 1915), p. 1. For Martov's dilemmas over whether to publish Dan's letter or not, see his letters to Dan of 9 February and 11 March 1915 in *Pis'ma Aksel'roda i Martova*, pp. 320ff.

24. Ibid., p. 321.

25. N. Trotskii, 'Zayavlenie', *Nashe Slovo*, 14 (13 February 1915), p. 1. For the debates which surrounded this statement, see n. 73 of the previous

chapter. The extent to which Trotsky remained unconvinced by Martov's anti-*Nasha Zarya* statement can be gauged from his letter to Radek of 6 February 1915. Here he stated that Martov would not be able to break with the semi-social-patriotic Organisational Committee which, in turn, could not break with the social-patriotic *Nasha Zarya*. See RTsKhIDNI, F. 325, O. 1, D. 394.

26. N. Trotskii, 'Nekriticheskaya otsenka kriticheskoi epokhi. I. Slabost ili neuverennaya v sebe sila?', *Nashe Slovo*, 28 (1 March 1915), p. 1.

27. N. Trotskii, 'Nekriticheskaya otsenka kriticheskoi epokhi. II Legenda "bor'by za demokratiyu"', *Nashe Slovo*, 35 (10 March 1915), p. 1.

28. The chronology of this dispute was as follows. First, Izvol'skaya praised Parabellum (Radek) for arguing that internationalists in German social-democracy should not split from the SPD but win the organisation from within: I. Izvol'skaya, 'Germanskaya oppozitsiya o raskole', *Nashe Slovo*, 75 (27 April 1915), p. 1. Radek then submitted a 'Necessary Addition' to Izvol'skaya's piece, in which he stated that while his views had been presented in an objective manner, he hoped that Izvol'skaya herself would follow his advice and adopt a more irreconcilable stance against social-patriots in Menshevik ranks: see Parabellum, 'Neobkhodimoe dopolnenie', *Nashe Slovo*, 84 (8 May 1915), p. 2. In his (delayed) reply Martov claimed that Menshevik social-patriots had been condemned in a sufficiently clear and open way. After all, he said, the former literary group *Nasha Zarya* and An had been censured by the Organisational Committee and its Foreign Secretariat for social-patriotism: see L. Martov', 'Napadenie tov. Parabelluma. (Pis'mo v redaktsiyu)', *Nashe Slovo*, 87 (12 May 1915), p. 2.

29. *Pis'ma Aksel'roda i Martova*, p. 334.

30. —, 'Rezolyutsiya, prinyataya sobraniem redaktsii i kollegi Parizhskikh sotrudnikov "Nashego Slova"', *Nashe Slovo*, 85 (9 May 1915), p. 1.

31. —, 'Iz besedy s P. B. Aksel'rodom'. O nashikh raznoglasiyakh', *Nashe Slovo*, 87 (12 May 1915), p. 1.

32. A., 'Iz besedy s P. B. Aksel'rodom'. O nashikh raznoglasiyakh. II.', *Nashe Slovo*, 90 (16 May 1915), p. 2.

33. 'Ot Redaktsii', *Nashe Slovo*, 90 (16 May 1915), p. 2.

34. —, 'Nasha Pozitsiya. I Raspad i pererozhdenie starikh gruppirovok v sotsializme', *Nashe Slovo*, 89 (15 May 1915), p. 1.

35. —, 'Nasha Pozitsiya. II Noviya gruppirovoki v sotsializme', *Nashe Slovo*, 100 (29 May 1915), p. 1.

36. P. Aksel'rod and S. Semkovskii, 'Mezhdunarodnomu Sotsialisticheskomu Byuro', *Izvestiya zagranichnago sekretariata organizatsionnago komiteta*, 1 (22 February 1915), p. 1.

37. For *Nasha Zarya*'s view on the war see 'Kopengagenskoi konferentsii', *Izvestiya zagranichnago sekretariata organizatsionnago komiteta*, 1 (22 February 1915), p. 1.

38. —, 'Nasha Pozitsiya. III Raskol i edinstvo (okonchanie tret'ei stat'i)', *Nashe Slovo*, 107 (6 June 1915), p. 1.

39. 'Demagogiya i mezhevatel'stvo', *Izvestiya zagranichnago sekretariata organizatsionnago komiteta*, 2 (14 June 1915), p. 4. Also cited in *Pis'ma Aksel'roda i Martova*, p. 339.

40. Ibid., p. 342.
41. Ibid., pp. 337, 339.
42. Gaf. Gri'gorev, 'Pis'mo v redaktsiyu', *Nashe Slovo*, 137 (11 July 1915), p. 2.
43. 'Ot redaktsii', *Nashe Slovo*, 137 (11 July 1915), p. 2.
44. N. Trotskii, 'Diversii', *Nashe Slovo*, 137 (11 July 1915), p. 2.
45. L. Martov, 'Po povodu odnoi polemiki. (Pis'mo v redaktsiyu)', *Nashe Slovo*, 137 (11 July 1915), pp. 2–3.
46. —, 'Rezolyutsiya, prinyataya sobraniem redaktsii i kollegi Parizhskikh sotrudnikov "Nashego Slova"'.
47. 'Ot redaktsii', *Nashe Slovo*, 137 (11 July 1915), p. 3.
48. *Pis'ma Aksel'roda i Martova*, p. 344.
49. L. Martov, 'Pis'mo v redaktsiyu', *Nashe Slovo*, 144 (21 July 1915), p. 2.
50. —, 'Rezolyutsiya, prinyataya sobraniem redaktsii i kollegii Parizhskikh sotrudnikov "Nashego Slova"'.
51. *Pis'ma Aksel'roda i Martova*, p. 344.
52. —, 'Nasha pozitsiya. 4. Nashi fraktsii i zadachi russkikh internatsionalistov (okonchanie)', *Nashe Slovo*, 147 (24 July 1915), p. 1.
53. Getzler, *Martov*, p. 141.
54. Alfred Rosmer, 'Trotsky in Paris During World War I', *New International*, September–October 1950, p. 269.
55. 'Now Trotskii uses the news only just received by him that Kollantai warmly supports *Kommunist* against us, concluding from this: among the Mensheviks there are elements who, even more than *Nashe Slovo*, support "splitters" ... Uritskii's and Zurabov's involvement in Parvus's epic will be very useful to humble Trotsky's arrogance': *Pis'ma Aksel'roda i Martova*, pp. 344–5.
56. Ibid., p. 347.
57. N. Trotskii, 'Nash politicheskii lozung', *Nashe Slovo*, 22 (23 February 1915), p. 1; N. Trotskii, 'Nash politicheskii lozung (okonchanie)', *Nashe Slovo*, 23 (24 February 1915), p. 1.
58. —, '"Porochnyi krug"', *Nashe Slovo*, 7 (5 February 1915), p. 1.
59. —, 'Nasha Pozitsiya. II Noviya gruppirovoki ... '
60. A. Martynov, 'Ot abstraktsii k konkretnoi deistvitel'nosti. II. Lozung "Soedinennykh' shtatov Evropy"', *Nashe Slovo*, 192 (16 September 1915), p. 2.
61. —, 'Nash politicheskii lozung'.
62. A. Martynov, 'Ot abstraktsii k konkretnoi deistvitel'nosti. III. Lozung "ni pobedy, ni prazheniya!"', *Nashe Slovo*, 193 (17 September 1915), p. 1.
63. N.T., 'Rossiskaya sektsiya internatsionalistov. (iz zapisnoi knizhki)', *Nashe Slovo*, 212 (9 October 1915), p. 1.
64. P. Aksel'rod, 'K konferentsii v tsimmerval'de. 1. Pis'mo v redaktsiyu', *Nashe Slovo*, 225 (27 October 1915), p. 1.
65. N.T., 'K konferentsii v tsimmerval'de. 2. Otvet P. B. Aksel'rodu', *Nashe Slovo*, 225 (27 October 1915), p. 2.
66. A. Lozovskii, 'Vorpos tt. Volonteru i Veshnevu', *Nashe Slovo*, 169 (20 August 1915), p. 2.
67. Ibid.
68. A. Lozovskii, 'Sovmestimo-li? (Dva voprosa t. Volonteru)', *Nashe Slovo*, 188 (11 September 1915), p. 2.

69. L. Martov, 'Pis'mo v redaktsiyu', *Nashe Slovo*, 235 (9 November 1915), p. 2.

70. —, 'O sovmestnykh vystupleniyakh s sots-patriotami. (Po povodu "Pis'ma t. Martova")', *Nashe Slovo*, 236 (10 November 1915), p. 2.

71. L. Martov, 'Po povodu moikh "sovmestnykh vystuplenii"', *Nashe Slovo*, 263 (11 December 1915), p. 2.

72. —, 'Sotrudnichestvo s sotsial-patriotami. (Otvet t. Martavu)', *Nashe Slovo*, 264 (12 December 1915), p. 2.

73. L. Martov, 'Slishkom mnogo sub'ektivizma. (Po povodu konferentsii)', *Nashe Slovo*, 247 (23 November 1915), p. 2. For Trotsky's original outline of the three groups at Zimmerwald see N.T., 'Nashi gruppirovki [iz zapisnoi knizhki]', *Nashe Slovo*, 209 (6 October 1915), p. 1. In this article Trotsky claimed that he had illustrated that there were three groups at Zimmerwald, whereas Aksel'rod incorrectly perceived only two.

74. N. Trotskii, 'Pod bremenem ob'ektivizma. I', *Nashe Slovo*, 248 (24 November 1915), p. 1.

75. N. Trotskii, 'Pod bremenem ob'ektivizma. II', *Nashe Slovo*, 249 (25 November 1915), p. 2.

76. L. Martov, 'V sherengu! (tsimmerval'dskaya konferentsiya i gruppirovki na nei)', *Nashe Slovo*, 4 (6 January 1916), pp. 1–2; L. Martov, 'V sherengu! (tsimmerval'dskaya konferentsiya i gruppirovki na nei) (okonchanie)', *Nashe Slovo*, 5 (7 January 1916), pp. 1–2.

77. N.T., 'Vokrug Tsimmerval'da. (popovodu stat'i t. Martova)', *Nashe Slovo*, 10 (13 January 1916), p. 1. Trotsky did, however, summarise how his evaluation of the groups which had emerged at Zimmerwald clashed with Martov's in N. Trotskii, 'Programma mira. VI. Patsifistskoe i revolyutsionnoe otnoshenie k' programma mira', *Nashe Slovo*, 88 (13 April 1916), pp. 1–2. In this article Trotsky rejected Martov's assertion that at Zimmerwald it was agreed that the struggle against the war was only the starting-point of a renewal of class conflict.

78. N. Trotskii, 'Programma Mira. II "Mir bez anneksii" i status quo ante', *Nashe Slovo*, 25 (30 January 1916), p. 2.

79. N. Trotskii, 'Programma Mira. IV Soedinennye Shtaty Evropy', *Nashe Slovo*, 29 (4 February 1916), pp. 1–2.

80. N. Trotskii, 'Programma Mira. V Pozitsiya "Sotsialdemokrata"', *Nashe Slovo*, 86 (11 April 1916), p. 2.

81. See, for example, —, 'Fakty i vyvody. (eshche o petrogradskikh vyborakh)', *Nashe Slovo*, 270 (19 December 1915), p. 1; —, 'Politicheskie shtreikbrekhery: Novye "vybory" v voenno-promyshlennyi Komitet', *Nashe Slovo*, 277 (29 December 1915), p. 1 ; and —, 'Tsimmerval'd ili gvozdevshchina?', *Nashe Slovo*, 11 (14 January 1916), p. 1.

82. A. Martynov, 'Patrioticheskaya epopeya', *Izvestiya zagranichnago sekretariata organizatsionnago komiteta*, 3 (5 February 1916), p. 4.

83. S. Semkovskii, 'Voenno-promyshlennyya komitety i taktika', *Izvestiya zagranichnago sekretariata organizatsionnago komiteta*, 3 (5 February 1916), p. 6.

84. —, 'Sotsial-patriotizm v Rossii. I Ikh "pobeda"', *Nashe Slovo*, 34 (10 February 1916), p. 1; —, 'Sotsial-patriotizm v Rossii. I Ikh "pobeda" (okonchanie)', *Nashe Slovo*, 35 (11 February 1916), p. 1; —, 'Sotsial-patriotizm v

Rossii. II "Timy gor'kikh istin nam dorzhe nas vozvyshayushchii obman"', *Nashe Slovo*, 53 (3 March 1916), pp. 1–2; —, 'Sotsial-patriotizm v Rossii. III "Voenno-promyshlennye" sots-dem-ty i ikh gruppirovki', *Nashe Slovo*, 54 (4 March 1916), p. 1; —, 'Sotsial-patriotizm v Rossii. IV Klass i partiya, massy i vozhdi', *Nashe Slovo*, 62 (14 March 1916), p. 1; —, 'Sotsial-patriotizm v Rossii. V Neobkhodimo izolirovat sotsialpatrioticheskii shtab'', *Nashe Slovo*, 63 (15 March 1916), p. 1.

85. —, 'Sotsial-patriotizm ... II "Timy ... '

86. —, 'Sotsial-patriotizm ... V Neobkhodimo ... '

87. L. Martov, 'To, chto est', *Nashe Slovo*, 84 (8 April 1916), pp. 1–2.

88. Martov is here referring to: —, 'Rabochie i voenno-promyshlenniye komitety. (Pis'mo iz Peterburga)', *Sotsial'Demokrat*, 50 (18 February 1916), pp. 1–2.

89. Trotsky is here referring to: —, 'Vesti iz Rossii', *Nashe Slovo*, 7 (9 January 1916), p. 2; and M. Boretskii, 'Iz besed s Plekhanovtrem iz Rossii', *Nashe Slovo*, 47 (25 February 1916), pp. 1–2.

90. Trotsky is here referring to: —, 'K voprosu o nashikh gruppirovkakh', *Nashe Slovo*, 68 (21 March 1916), p. 1.

91. —, 'Logika plokhogo polozheniya. (Otvet' t. Martovu)', *Nashe Slovo*, 85 (9 April 1916), p. 2.

92. L.M., 'Zayalenie tov. Martova', *Nashe Slovo*, 93 (19 April 1916), p. 1. For the original statement, see L. Martov, 'Zayavlenie', *Izvestiya zagranichnago sekretariata organizatsionnago komiteta*, 4 (10 April 1916), p. 2.

93. —, 'Po povodu "zayavlenie" tov. Martova', *Nashe Slovo*, 93 (19 April 1916), p. 2.

94. See 'Pis'mo iz Rossii', *Izvestiya zagranichnago sekretariata organizatsionnago komiteta*, 4 (10 April 1916), p. 2.

95. —, 'Bez sterzhnya', *Nashe Slovo*, 104 (4 May 1916), p. 1.

96. 'Peterburgskie i moskovskie men'sheviki o voine', *Izvestiya zagranichnago sekretariata organizatsionnago komiteta*, 5 (10 June 1916), pp. 2–3; 'Deklaratsiya initsiativnoi gruppy', ibid., p. 3.

97. —, 'Korennoe raskhozhdenie. I. Politicheskiya osnovy voenno-promyshlennago "internatsionalizma"', *Nashe Slovo*, 165 (19 July 1916), p. 1; —, 'Korennoe raskhozhdenie. II. Dve isklyuchayushchiya drug druga takticheskiya linii', *Nashe Slovo*, 166 (20 July 1916), p. 1.

98. —, 'Korennoe raskhozhdenie ...', 166.

99. Ibid.

100. For an English translation of this draft manifesto see O. H. Gankin and H. H. Fisher, *The Bolsheviks and the World War* (Stanford, CA, 1940), pp. 429–33.

101. —, 'Dva litsa', *Nashe Slovo*, 174 (29 July 1916), p. 1

6 Russian Social-Patriotism in Paris

1. *Voina: sbornik statei* (Paris, 1915), p. 4.

2. The members of *Prizyv*'s editorial board were Avksent'ev, Bunakov, Voronov, Lyubimov and Plekhanov. Sixty issues of the newspaper appeared from 1 October 1915 to 31 March 1917.

3. G. Aleksinskii, 'Voina i sotsializm', *Golos*, 55, 15 November 1914, p. 1; 56 (17 November 1914), p. 1; 57 (18 November 1914), p. 1; and 58 (19 November 1914), p. 1.
4. Aleksinskii, 'Voina i sotsializm', *Golos*, 58.
5. L. Trotskii, *Voina i Revolyutsiya*, I, (Petrograd, 1922), p. 141. Extracts from Trotsky's brochure appeared in *Golos*. See N. Trotskii, 'Voina i Internatsional', *Golos*, 59 (20 November 1914), p. 1; 'Voina i Internatsional', *Golos*, (21 November 1914), p. 1; and 'Voina i Internatsional II', *Golos*, 79 (13 December 1914), p. 1.
6. N. Trotskii, 'Neobkhodimaya popravka', *Golos*, 63 (25 November 1914), p. 1.
7. Ibid.
8. N.K., 'Vozhdi S-D o voine', *Golos*, 31 (18 October 1914), p. 1; N.K., 'Vozhdi S-D o voine', *Golos*, 32 (20 October 1914), p. 1.
9. N.K., 'Vozhdi S-D o voine', *Golos*, 31.
10. Ibid.
11. N.K., 'Vozhdi S-D o voine', *Golos*, 32. Lenin's critique of Plekhanov's views was summarised in N.K., 'Vozhdi S-D o voine', *Golos*, 33 (21 October 1914), p. 1. For a summary of Lenin's pamphlet *The Proletariat and the War* see N.K., 'Vozhdi Russkoi S-D o voine', *Golos*, 37 (25 October 1914), p. 1 and 'Vozhdi Russkoi S-D o voine', *Golos*, 38 (27 October 1914), p. 1.
12. 'Pis'mo Plekhanova', *Golos*, 37, 25 October 1914, pp. 1–2.
13. Ibid., p. 1.
14. N. Trotskii, 'Pechal'nyi dokument. G. Plekhanov o voine', *Golos*, 93 (30 December 1914), pp. 1–2.
15. Ibid.
16. Ibid.
17. Ibid.
18. Ibid.
19. Iks', 'Khronika. Referat N. Trotskago', *Novosti*, 195 (23 March 1915), p. 2.
20. N.T., 'Vremya nynche takovskoe', *Nashe Slovo*, 54 (1 April 1915), p. 1.
21. —, 'Voennyya zametki. K sdache Przhemyshlya', *Nashe Slovo*, 51 (28 March 1915), p. 2.
22. N. T., 'Vremya nynche takovskoe'.
23. 'Pis'mo v redaktsiyu', *Novosti*, 203 (3 April 1915), p. 2.
24. N. T., 'Nekhorosho-s!', *Nashe Slovo*, 60 (9 April 1915), p. 2.
25. G. Aleksinskii, 'Mnimye internatsionalisti', *Novosti*, 210 (13 April 1915), p. 1.
26. Al'fa, 'Porazhenchestvo i iskazhenchestvo', *Nashe Slovo*, 66 (16 April 1915), p. 2. This was not the end of this dispute. Four days later Aleksinskii, writing in *Novosti*, produced a quote from *Golos* of 30 October 1914 as evidence of defeatism in the *Nashe Slovo* camp. At the same time he noted Al'fa's rejection of defeatism 'with joy', but claimed 'an individual rejection does not deprive me of the right to look at the current [*Nashe Slovo*] tendency as "defeatist", for "defeatism" ... is the essence of the leading exponents of this direction [*Nashe Slovo*]': G. Aleksinskii, '"Porazhentsi" i "Otrechentsi"', *Novosti*, 216 (20 April 1915), p. 2. In the aptly named 'It Continues' Martov objected to Aleksinskii's use of his

Golos article. He claimed that in his contribution of October 1914 he was repeating an idea he had held since 1907: that only through a successful aggressive war could 'official Russia avoid revolution and gain for itself the possibility of a "Prussian–German" path of development'. This was why he desired Russia to be 'unsuccessful' in the war. Martov wrote that this was not the same as defeatism. After all, *Golos* and *Nashe Slovo* were quite clear that, 'from the point of view of the interests of democracy one should desire the "failure" of the imperialist aspirations of all countries and not the "defeat" of any one of them': L. Martov, 'Prodolzhaet', *Nashe Slovo*, 72 (23 April 1915), pp. 1–2. The last word, however, belonged to Aleksinskii. In 'Two Words' he welcomed Martov's denunciation of defeatism and said that he was prepared to take any amount of abuse from Martov as long as the latter at the same time rejected defeatism: 'The great social utility of these public rejections of defeatism will entail a small harm which causes – not me but himself – Martov to lower himself to petty wrangling': G. Aleksinskii, 'Dva Slovo', *Novosti*, 222 (27 April 1915), p. 1.

27. N. Trotskii, 'Sytinskii "malyi" o Rakovskom', *Nashe Slovo*, 67 (17 April 1915), p. 1.

28. Ibid.

29. G. Aleksinskii, 'Pis'mo v redaktsiyu', *Nashe Slovo*, 74 (25 April 1915), p. 2; —, 'Klevetnikam!', ibid., pp. 1–2.

30. Ibid.

31. Ibid.

32. N. Trotskii, 'Otkrytoe pis'mo t. Plekhanovu', *Nashe Slovo*, 142 (18 July 1915), pp. 1–2.

33. G. Aleksinskii, 'S kem bol'shinstvo', *Voina: sbornik statei*, pp. 97–106.

34. Ibid., p. 102. Antid Oto was, of course, the pseudonym used by Trotsky for his articles in *Kievskaya Mysl*. For an analysis of Trotsky's articles penned for the Ukrainian newspaper during World War One, see Chapter 2 above.

35. Trotskii, 'Otkrytoe pis'mo t. Plekhanovu', p. 1.

36. Aleksinskii, 'S kem bol'shinstvo', p. 102.

37. Trotskii, 'Otkrytoe pis'mo t. Plekhanovu', p. 2.

38. Ibid.

39. —, 'Rakovskii o russkikh sots-patriotakh', *Nashe Slovo*, 204 (30 September 1915), p. 1.

40. Al'fa, 'Les Russes D'Abord!', *Nashe Slovo*, 210 (7 October 1915), p. 2.

41. A, 'Slovo za Prizyvom', *Nashe Slovo*, 224 (26 October 1915).

42. —, 'Ostav'te nas v pokoe', *Nashe Slovo*, 216 (14 October 1915), p. 1.

43. Ibid.

44. Ibid.

45. Ibid.

46. Ibid.

47. Ibid.

48. Postoronnii, 'Neveroyatno! (Pis'mo v redaktsiyu)', *Nashe Slovo*, 239 (13 November 1915), p. 2.

49. Postoronnii, 'Itak?', *Nashe Slovo*, 277 (29 December 1915), p. 2.

50. Al'fa, 'Ikh literatura. Vmesto novogodnyago obzora', *Nashe Slovo*, 1 (1 January 1916), p. 2.

51. K. Marx, *The First International and After*, ed. David Fernbach (Harmondsworth, 1974), p. 81.
52. G. Plekhanov, 'Eshche o voine', *Voina: sbornik statei*, p. 23.
53. Al'fa, 'Ikh literatura'.
54. Ibid.
55. Ibid.
56. Ibid.
57. Ibid. In this same article other members of *Prizyv*'s editorial board (Avksent'ev, Voronov, Argunov and Bunakov) were labelled Gogolian 'Tyapkin-Lyapkin' characters. Trotsky said one had to avoid polemicising with L. Deich, a Russian social-patriot living in America, since he would only remind *Nashe Slovo* that he had mastered and rejected the theory of surplus value while it was still having its nappies changed.
58. Postoronnii, 'Eto nedorazumenie!', *Nashe Slovo*, 26 (1 February 1916), p. 2.
59. G. Plekhanov, 'Oboran strany, reaktsiya i interesy trudyashchagosya naseleniya', *Prizyv*, 19 (5 February 1916), pp. 1–2.
60. Ibid., p. 1.
61. Ibid., p. 2.
62. Al'fa, 'Plekhanov o Khvostove', *Nashe Slovo*, 35 (11 February 1916), p. 2.
63. V. Buslaev, 'Zhivaya Rossiya', *Prizyv*, 24 (11 March 1916), p. 1.
64. Ibid.
65. Ibid., p. 2.
66. Ibid.
67. —, 'Ironicheskii shchslchok istorii', *Nashe Slovo*, 73 (26 March 1916), p. 1.
68. Ibid.
69. Ibid.
70. Ibid. In 'To the End' Trotsky's polemics with *Prizyv* had centred around a different social class in Russia, the peasantry. Here Trotsky's main focus of criticism was a report in *The Times* which gave an account of the prosperity then being enjoyed by the Russian peasant. A similar claim about the condition of the Russian countryside had also been made by Prince Trubetskii in his analysis of why Russia's victory in the war was guaranteed. Trotsky mentioned that Trubetskii, as well as Khvostov and *Prizyv*, shared the British correspondent's views. Thus Trotsky attempted to discredit the social-patriotic publication along with representatives of Russia's ruling classes. In actual fact, Aleksinskii had disputed Trubetskii's views as leading to complacency, whereas one had to mobilise the people to win what was a people's war. For the various articles see: G. Aleksinskii, 'Zalog pobedy', *Prizyv*, 19 (5 February 1916), pp. 3–4; —, 'The Temper of Russia', *The Times*, 12 February 1916, p. 5; Al'fa, 'Zhuskobu', *Nashe Slovo*, 40 (17 February 1916), p. 2. For further reports of the less than ideal state prevailing in Russian villages at that time, see, —, 'Shokolad upletayut', *Nashe Slovo*, 36 (12 February 1916), p. 2, and —, 'Kuda uzh tut shokolad', *Nashe Slovo*, 37 (13 February 1916), p. 2.
71. Al'fa, 'Fantastika. Pervomaiskiya razmyshleniya.', *Nashe Slovo*, 102 (1 May 1916).
72. Ibid.
73. See, for example, G. Plekhanov, 'Sotsialisty i golosovaniye voennykh

kreditov', *Prizyv*, 17 (22 January 1916), p. 6.
74. Al'fa, 'Dve velichiny., porozn ravnye tret'ei ... ', *Nashe Slovo*, 114 (16 May 1916), p. 4.
75. See, for example, G. Plekhanov, 'Internationalisty, da tolko s drugoi storony', *Prizyv*, 21 (19 February 1916), p. 4.
76. —, 'Pochemu ne nazvali Plekhanova', *Nashe Slovo*, 119 (21 May 1916), p. 2.
77. Redaktsiya Prizyva, 'Al'bert Toma v tsarskom sele', *Prizyv*, 33 (13 May 1916), pp. 1–2.
78. —, 'Perepolokh v redaktsii Prizyva', *Nashe Slovo*, 116 (18 May 1916), p. 2.
79. —, 'Pochmeu ne nazvali Plekhanova'
80. Ibid.
81. Ibid.
82. Ibid.
83. V. Voronov, 'Front prorvan', *Prizyv*, 38 (17 June 1916), pp. 1–2.
84. Ibid., p. 2.
85. —, 'Argument ot kopyta', *Nashe Slovo*, 150 (29 June 1916), p. 1.
86. Ibid.
87. —, 'Prigovor nad Aleksinskim', *Nashe Slovo*, 208 (9 September 1916), pp. 1–2.
88. N. T., 'Istoriya s moral'yu', *Nashe Slovo*, 187 (13 August 1916), p. 1.
89. Ibid.
90. Ibid.
91. —, 'Neudobstva novoi professii', *Nashe Slovo*, 154 (4 July 1916), p. 2.
92. D. S., 'Osedomiteli', *Prizyv*, 46 (12 August 1916), p. 8.
93. —, 'Vandervel'd, Nashe Slovo and Vorwärts', *Nashe Slovo*, 192 (22 August 1916), p. 1.
94. 'Tri prigovora', *Nashe Slovo*, 208 (9 September 1916), p. 2.
95. —, 'Prizyv i ego Aleksinskii', *Nashe Slovo*, 209 (10 September 1916), p. 2.
96. Ibid.
97. Ibid.
98. Ibid.
99. —, 'Ale ksinskii goPrizyv', *Nashe Slovo*, 210 (12 September 1916), p. 2.
100. Ibid.
101. Ibid.

7 Russian Politics

1. Dmitrii Volkogonov, *Trotskii. Politicheskii portret*, I (Moscow, 1992), p. 96.
2. For an exposition and explanation of the various turns in Milyukov's approach to foreign policy from 1913 to the immediate outbreak of war, see T. Riha, *A Russian European: Paul Miliukov in Russian Politics* (Notre Dame, 1969), pp. 205–18.
3. For an account of why the liberals issued a patriotic response to the war, see R. Pearson, *The Russian Moderates and the Crisis of Tsarism 1914–17* (London, 1977), pp. 16–19.
4. N. Trotskii, 'Gregus po demokraticheskomu spisku', *Golos*, 76 (10 December 1914), pp. 1–2.

5. Ibid., p. 1.
6. Ibid.
7. Ibid., p. 2.
8. —, 'Politika "tyla"', *Nashe Slovo*, 145 (22 July 1915), p. 1.
9. Ibid.
10. —, 'Konvent rasteryannosti i bessiliya', *Nashe Slovo*, 167 (18 August 1915), p. 1.
11. Ibid.
12. Ibid.
13. —, 'Sobytiya idut svoim cheredom', *Nashe Slovo*, 10 (13 January 1916), p. 1.
14. The declaration of the Progressive Bloc was as follows: 'The undersigned are representatives of groups within the State Duma and the State Council. We believe that only a powerful, stable and active government can lead the homeland to victory. Such a government has to depend upon the trust of the people and be able to organise the active cooperation of all citizens. We have unanimously concluded that the important and urgent task of the formation of such a government cannot be realised without the following conditions:

1. The formation of a united government from figures who have the people's trust and who agree to uphold the law to fulfil a certain programme in the coming period.

2. The decisive change in the conduct of government. In particular:

a. Government based on the rule of law.

b. The removal of dual-power, military and civil, in non-military matters.

c. The renewal of local government administration.

d. A rational and thorough policy directed at domestic harmony. Specifically:

1. For an enlightened monarchy the ending of legal proceedings for purely political and religious crimes which should not be criminal offences; an amnesty for those imprisoned for these crimes and the lowering of sentences for those remaining condemned for political and religious crimes, excluding spies and traitors;

2. The return of political and religious exiles;

3. An end to religious persecution;

4. The resolution of the Russo-Polish question, in particular: abolition of residence restrictions; Polish autonomy; the reexamination of the laws on Polish land ownership;

5. Abolition of anti-Jewish legislation, in particular, abolition of the settlements, educational reform, the abolition of restrictions to election into professions, and the restoration of the Jewish press;

6. Concessions to Finland, including a more just administration and the end of persecution;

7. The restoration of the little Russian press, the urgent examination of the matter of the Galician residents held under guard and exiled. The liberation of those subject to persecution when innocent;

8. Trade Union and political rights, including the legalisation of underground parties and the restoration of the workers' press;

9. Emergency legislation on:

a: national defence, supplying the army, security for the wounded, arranging participation for refugees and of other matters directly related to the war;

b: organising the country for victory and supporting civil harmony: equal rights for the peasants, the introduction of district councils, changing the town law of 1890, the introduction of council institutions in the regions, Siberia, Archangel, the Don, the Caucasus and so on, laws on cooperatives, laws on holidays for trade workers, improvement of conditions for post-telegraph workers, guarantee of rights for land and town congresses and unions, a law on inspections, the introduction of civil courts in those districts where their introduction was halted for financial reasons, the passing of a law in which the carrying-out of the above-mentioned programme is guaranteed.

This programme is signed by: from the Progressive Group of Nationalists – Sir V. Bobrinskii, from the Centre fraction – V. L'vov, from Land-Octobrists – I. Dmitryukov, from the group Union of 17 October – S. Shidlovskii, from the Progressive fraction – I. Efremov, from the fraction People's Freedom, P. Milyukov, from the group of members of the State Council, V. Meller-Zakomel'skii, D. Grimm.' (Translated from L. Trotskii, *Sochineniya*, VIII (Moscow, 1927), pp. 383–5.) For an analysis of the events leading to the formation of the Progressive Bloc and of its ultimate failure, see Pearson, *The Russian Moderates*, pp. 39–64.

15. —, 'Sobytiya idut' ...
16. Ibid.
17. For an account of Milyukov's activities during his visit to Russia's allies, see Riha, *A Russian European*, pp. 250–4, and Pearson, *The Russian Moderates*, pp. 92–3.
18. —, 'So slavyanskim aktsentom i ulybkoi na slavynskikh gubakh', *Nashe Slovo*, 121 (24 May 1916), p. 1.
19. Ibid.
20. —, 'Razochovaniya i bespokoistva', *Nashe Slovo*, 143 (21 June 1916), p. 1.
21. —, 'Uroki poslednei dumskoi sessii', *Nashe Slovo*, 161 (12 July 1916), p. 1.
22. Ibid. For an account of peasant and Jewish dissatisfaction with the politics of the Progressive Bloc, see Pearson, *The Russian Moderates*, pp. 94–6.
23. N.T., 'Vpechatleniya i obobshcheniya g. Milyukova. 1. Pobeda i svoboda', *Nashe Slovo*, 193 (23 August 1916), p. 1, and N.T., 'Vpechatleniya i obobshcheniya g. Milyukova. 2. Tsimmerval'dtsy i longetisty', *Nashe Slovo*, 194 (24 August 1916), p. 1.
24. N.T., 'Vpechatleniya i obobshcheniya g. Milyukova. 1. Pobeda i svoboda'. Trotsky is referring to the following statement made by Milyukov during a debate in the Duma on 4 March 1916: 'I cannot be sure that the government will lead us to defeat. We are afraid of it and wish to prevent it. But I know that a revolution in Russia will, without fail, lead us to defeat, and no wonder our enemy so desires it. Were I told that organising Russia for victory meant organising it for revolution I would say: better leave her, for the duration of the war, as she was, unorganised.' (Cited in Riha, *A Russian European*, p. 248.)

25. N.T., 'Vpechatleniya i obobshcheniya g. Milyukova. 2. Tsimmerval'dtsy i longetisty'
26. Ibid.
27. —, '"Bor'ba za vlast'": Progressivno-kadetskaya Moskva i ministerstvo Shtyumera', *Nashe Slovo*, 197 (27 August 1916), p. 1.
28. See, for example, L. Trotskii, *Voina i Revolyutsiya* (Petrograd, 1922), p. 76.
29. —, 'Va-bank', *Nashe Slovo*, 77 (29 April 1915), p. 1.
30. Al'fa., 'Pervyi shag sdelan', *Nashe Slovo*, 122 (24 June 1915), p. 2.
31. Ibid.
32. For the details of this crisis and the events leading to Khvostov's appointment, see R. Pipes, *The Russian Revolution, 1899–1919* (London, 1990), pp. 223–8.
33. —, 'Khvostov!', *Nashe Slovo*, 227 (29 October 1915), p. 1. For a further unflattering account of Khvostov, see —, 'Svoim poryadkom', *Nashe Slovo*, 232 (5 November 1915), p. 1. Trotsky claimed that the fantastical nature of Russia's domestic affairs reached new heights under Khvostov, to the extent that only a combination of Shchedrin, Poe and Poprishchin could adequately describe Khvostov's rule. See —, 'Otechestvennoe ... ', *Nashe Slovo*, 89 (14 April 1916), p. 1, and Al'fa, 'Fantastika. Pervomaiskiy razmyshleniya', *Nashe Slovo*, 102 (1 May 1916), pp. 2–3.
34. —, 'Ravnenie po Makarovu', *Nashe Slovo*, 172 (27 July 1916), p. 1.
35. —, 'Dve telegrammy', *Nashe Slovo*, 173 (28 July 1916), p. 1.
36. En, 'Rodnyya teni', *Nachalo*, 1 (30 September 1916), p. 1.
37. Ibid.
38. Ibid.
39. —, 'Iz'yan v tverdom kurse', *Nachalo*, 11 (12 October 1916), p. 1.
40. —, 'Voennayi krizis i politicheskiya perspectivy. III. Sotsial'nya sily rossiiskoi revolyutsii', *Nashe Slovo*, 181 (3 September 1915), p. 1.
41. —, 'Voennayi krizis i politicheskiya perspectivy. IV. Natsional'nyi ili internatsional'nyi kurs?', *Nashe Slovo*, 182 (4 September 1915), p. 1.
42. For an excellent account of the events leading to the formation of the War-Industries Committees, see Robert B. McKean, *St. Petersburg Between the Revolutions* (New Haven, 1990), pp. 430ff. For an exposition of the events surrounding the elections among the workers to the War-Industries Committees, see ibid., pp. 380ff.
43. —, 'Petrogradskii proletariat', *Nashe Slovo*, 229 (31 October 1915), p. 1.
44. —, 'Nuzhno sdelat vse vyvody', *Nashe Slovo*, 237 (11 November 1915), p. 1.
45. Ibid.
46. Ibid.
47. —, 'Politicheskie shtreikbrekhery. Novye "vybory" v voenno-promyshlennyi komitet', *Nashe Slovo*, 277 (29 December 1915), p. 1. Trotsky may not have received a full and accurate version of what happened at the meeting of electors. His account is similar, but differs in important respects to that given by Robert B. McKean. He informs us that at the first meeting of electors, held on 27 September 1915, the Bolsheviks 'smuggled in two of their leaders, Bogdatian-Bogdat'ev and Zalezhskii, using the mandates of two Putilov delegates without their permission': McKean, *St. Petersburg ...*, p. 383. When Gvozdev discovered the Bolshevik's foul play he petitioned the Central War-Industries Committee to arrange a second

electoral meeting, which took place on 29 November. However, the Bolsheviks decided to attend the meeting only to denounce it and then walk out. This they duly did and the 109 left behind 'proceeded to elect ten representatives to the TsVKP (all were Mensheviks) and six to the Petrograd War-Industries Committee (three Mensheviks and three SRs)': McKean, ibid., p. 384.

48. N.T., 'Sbornik "Samozashchita"', *Nashe Slovo*, 13 (16 January 1916), p. 2.
49. N.Trotskii,' "Samozashchita". I. "bude nuzhno"', *Nashe Slovo*, 58 (9 March 1916), pp. 1–2.
50. *Samozashchita. Marksistskii sbornik* (Petrograd, 1916), p. 57.
51. *Samozashchita* ..., 'Predislovie'; cited in Trotskii, '"Samozashchita". I ...', p. 1.
52. Ibid.
53. V.I. Zasulich, 'O voine', *Samozashchita* ..., pp. 1–4.
54. Trotskii, '"Samozashchita". I ...'
55. Zasulich, 'O voine', p. 1.
56. A.N. Potresov, 'O patriotizm i o mezhduranodnosti', *Samozashchita* ..., p. 21. Cited in Trotskii, '"Samozashchita". I ...', p. 2.
57. Potresov, 'O patriotizm i o mezhduranodnosti', pp. 6–7.
58. Ibid., pp. 11–13.
59. I. Kubikov, 'Rabochii klass i natsional'noe chuvstvo', *Samozashchita* ..., pp. 22–8.
60. P. Maslov, 'Ekonomicheskoe znachenie voiny dlya Rossii', *Samozashchita* ..., p. 32.
61. Ibid., p. 34.
62. Trotskii, '"Samozashchita". I ...', p. 2.
63. Maslov, 'Ekonmicheskoe znachenie ...', p. 35.
64. K. Dmitriev, 'Narodnoe khozyaistvo v nachale vtorogo goda voiny', *Samozashchita* ..., pp. 42–56.
65. Ibid., p. 52.
66. Ibid., p. 43.
67. Ibid., p. 56. Cited in Trotskii, '"Samozashchita". I ...', p. 2.
68. Trotskii, '"Samozashchita". I ...', p. 2. For the original text, see An, 'Marksizm i radikalizm', *Samozashchita* ..., p. 77.
69. Ibid.
70. An, 'Marksizm i radikalizm', p. 74.
71. Ibid., p. 77.
72. Ibid.
73. V. Vol'skii, 'Zametki po povodu voiny', *Samozashchita* ..., p. 83.
74. Trotskii, '"Samozashchita". I ...', p. 2. First cited in Vol'skii, 'Zametki po povodu ...', p. 88.
75. Ibid.
76. Vol'skii, 'Zametki po povodu ...', p. 89.
77. E. Maevskii, 'Tsenzovaya Rossiya i demokratiya', *Samozashchita* ..., p. 107.
78. Trotskii, op. cit.
79. Ibid. For the original text see Maevskii, 'Tsenzovaya Rossiya ...', p. 107.
80. Ibid. (emphasis original). For the original text, see V. Levitskii, 'Organizatsiya obshchestvennykh sil i zashchita strany', *Samozashchita* ..., p. 120.

81. A. P. Bibik, 'V plashche Gamleta', *Samozashchita* ... , p. 121.
82. Trotskii, '"Samozashchita". I ...'
83. Bibik, 'V plashche Gamleta', p. 126.
84. Trotskii, '"Samozashchita". I ...'
85. Ibid.
86. V. L'vov-Rogachevskii, 'Kak bylo togda', *Samozashchita* ..., pp. 128–41.
87. Ibid., p. 140.
88. Trotskii, '"Samozashchita". I ...', p. 2. For the original text, see L'vov-Rogachevskii, 'Kak bylo togda', p. 141.
89. Ibid.
90. Ibid.
91. Ibid.
92. N. Trotskii, '"Samozashchita". II. Na vyuchku k patriotizmu?', *Nashe Slovo*, 69 (22 March 1916), p. 1.
93. Ibid.
94. See n 58 above.
95. Trotskii, '"Samozashchita". II'
96. Ibid.
97. Ibid.
98. Ibid.
99. —, 'Nasha dumskaya fraktsiya I', *Nashe Slovo*, 77 (31 March 1916), p. 1.
100. Trotsky did not give an accurate account of *Prizyv's* view of Chkheidze. Thus N. N-ev quoted Chkheidze as saying that he would support the Progressive Bloc when it opposed the government and expose it when did not. N. N-ev urged Chkheidze to throw his total support behind the Progressive Bloc. After all, N-ev pointed out, the Progressive Bloc had declared that it would have no further dealings with the old regime: (N-ev,'K poslednei cherty', *Prizyv*, 26 (25 March 1916), pp. 1–2). In the next issue of *Prizyv* A. Lyubimov criticised Chkheidze's position thus: 'It is clear that Chkheidze recognises national tasks, that he does not believe in permanent or in social revolution for Russia and yet he does not recognise defence as a national task. This is the root of his confusion and in which all his contradictions lie': A. Lyubimov, 'Burzhuaznaya oppozitsiya i tsimmervald'skie putaniki', *Prizyv*, 27 (1 April 1916), p. 2.
101. —, 'Nasha dumskaya fraktsiya I'.
102. —, 'Nasha dumskaya fraktsiya II', *Nashe Slovo*, 78 (1 April 1916), p. 1.
103. —, 'Nasha dumskaya fraktsiya. I. Revolyutsionnaya i passivno-vyzhidatel'naya politika', *Nashe Slovo*, 94 (20 April 1916), p. 1.
104. —, 'Poezdka deputata Chkheidze', *Nashe Slovo*, 203 (3 September 1916), p. 2. See also —, 'K poezdke deputata Chkheidze', *Nachalo*, 29 (3 November 1916), p. 1.

8 European Social-Democracy

1. —, 'Eshche est na svete sotsial'demokraty', *Nashe Slovo*, 53 (31 March 1915), p. 1.
2. —, 'Oni – drugovo dukha', *Nashe Slovo*, 113 (13 June 1915), p. 1.
3. For an excellent exposition of Kautsky's views during World War One, see

Massimo Salvadori, *Karl Kautsky and the Socialist Revolution, 1880–1938* (London, 1979), esp. pp. 181ff.

4. 'Perspektivy mira. St. Karla Kautskago', *Golos*, 18 (2 October 1914), p. 1.
5. 'Perspektivy mira. St. Karla Kautskago (okonchanie)', *Golos*, 19 (3 October 1914), p. 2.
6. —, 'Kautskii o Plekhanove. I', *Nashe Slovo*, 116 (17 June 1915), p. 1.
7 Ibid.
8. Ibid.
9. —, 'Kautskii o Plekhanove. III', *Nashe Slovo*, 118 (19 June 1915), p. 1.
10. 'Vozzvanie nemetskikh internatsionalistov', *Nashe Slovo*, 104 (3 June 1915), p. 1.
11. Ibid.
12. Cited in A. Joseph Berlau, *The German Social Democratic Party 1914–1921* (New York, 1949), p. 75.
13. —, 'Nemetskaya oppozitsiya i nemetskaya diplomatiya', *Nashe Slovo*, 121 (23 June 1915), p. 1.
14. Cited in —, '"Levaya" i "tsentra" v nemetskoi sots-dem', *Nashe Slovo*, 137 (11 July 1915), p. 1.
15. Ibid.
16. Ibid.
17. Vl. Kosovskii, 'Kak vozstanovit internatsional', *Informatsionnyi Listok*, 8 (May 1915), p. 5.
18. Ibid., p. 6.
19. Ibid., p. 5.
20. 'Staromodnyi masschtab', *Nashe Slovo*, 95 (22 May 1915), p. 1.
21. Vl. Kosovskii, 'Pis'mo v redaktsiyu', *Nashe Slovo*, 137 (14 July 1915), p. 4.
22. —, 'Bez masshtaba', *Nashe Slovo*, 141 (17 July 1915), p. 1.
23. —, 'Gaaze-Ebert-David!', *Nashe Slovo*, 175 (27 August 1915), p. 1.
24. N.T., 'Nemetskaya S-D oppozitsiya (iz zapisnoi knizhki)', *Nashe Slovo*, 210 (7 October 1915), p. 1.
25. See Bukvoed, 'Mering o voine. II.', *Nashe Slovo*, 239 (13 November 1915), p. 1; 'Mering o voine (okonchanie vtoroi stat'i).', *Nashe Slovo*, 240 (14 November 1915), pp. 1–2; and 'Mering o voine. III', *Nashe Slovo*, 241 (16 November 1915), pp. 1–2.
26. Bukvoed, 'Mering o voine. I.', *Nashe Slovo*, 238 (12 November 1915), p. 2.
27. —, 'Gruppirovki v nemetskoi sots-dem. (Po povodu stat'i t. Bukvoeda)', *Nashe Slovo*, 242 (17 November 1915), p. 1.
28. —, 'Deklaratsiya dvadtsati', *Nashe Slovo*, 276 (28 December 1915), p. 1.
29. Cited in Peter Nettl, *Rosa Luxemburg* (Oxford, 1969), p. 395. Nettl's book contains an excellent chapter on Luxemburg's wartime activities.
30. Redaktsiya, 'Privet F. Meringu i R. Lyuksemburg!', *Nashe Slovo*, 53 (3 March 1916), p. 1.
31. Cited in Nettl, *Rosa Luxemburg*, p. 397. Nettl's work includes a copy of Rosa Luxemburg's appeal to Zimmerwald on pp. 392–4.
32. See, for example, Trotsky's analysis of Russian liberalism in his 'Open Letter to Professor P. N. Milyukov' (translated and edited by Ian D. Thatcher), *Revolutionary Russia*, 3 (2) (1990), pp. 224–38.
33. —, 'Novaya glava (K raskolu s-d fraktsii reikhstaga)', *Nashe Slovo*, 79 (2 April 1916), p. 1.

34 Cited in —, 'K. Kautskii ob Internatsionale', *Nashe Slovo*, 98 (26 April 1916), p. 1.

35. —, 'Kheglund i Libknekht', *Nashe Slovo*, 106 (6 May 1916), p. 1.

36. —, 'Karl Libknekht', *Nashe Slovo*, 152 (1 July 1916), p. 1.

37. —, 'Sredi germanskoi oppozitsii. Sektanstvo ili neobkhodimoe vyyasnenie', *Nashe Slovo*, 177 (2 August 1916), p. 1. Trotsky did, however, write several reports of the Reichkonferenz of the German Social-Democracy held in September 1916 for *Nashe Slovo's* successor, *Nachalo*. His analysis of this event followed the distinction between social-imperialists (Scheidemann), passive centre oppositionists (Haase) and revolutionary internationalists (Liebknecht) which he had established in earlier writings on German Social-Democracy (discussed above). For Trotsky's reports on the Reichkonferenz of September 1916, see —, 'Imperializm i sotsializm', *Nachalo*, 6 (6 October 1916); —, 'Imperializm i sotsializm' (Po povodu germanskoi s-d konferentsii) I', *Nachalo*, 15 (17 October 1916); —, 'Imperializm i sotsializm' (Po povodu germanskoi s-d konferentsii) II', *Nachalo*, 16 (18 October 1916); and —, 'Imperializm i sotsializm'. bor'ba za respubliku v Germanii', *Nachalo*, 21 (24 October 1916).

38. Cited in S. F. Kissin, *War and the Marxists* (London, 1988), p. 178.

39. —, 'V Austrii', *Nashe Slovo*, 119 (21 May 1916), p. 1.

40. —, 'Iz ideinoi zhizni Austriiskoi sots-dem', *Nashe Slovo*, 130 (4 June 1916), p. 1.

41. —, 'Kto iz nikh luchshe?', *Nashe Slovo*, 146 (24 June 1916), p. 1.

42. —, 'Frits Adler', *Nachalo*, 22 (25 October 1916), p. 1. In a short note to the 1924 edition of *Voina i Revolyutsiya*, in which this piece was reprinted, Trotsky took Adler's recent opposition to the Third International into account to reinterpret the Austrian assassin's intentions: 'He used his authority as a terrorist to hold-up the proletarian revolution': L. Trotskii, *Voina i Revolyutsiya*, II (Moscow, 1924), p. 293.

43. Cited in N. Trotskii, 'Pis'mo v Redaktsiyu "L'Humanité"', *Nashe Slovo*, 208 (5 October 1915), p. 1.

44. N. Trotskii, 'Parvus', *Nashe Slovo*, 15 (14 February 1915), p. 1.

45. —, 'Sushchnost krizisa', *Nashe Slovo*, 228 (30 October 1915), p. 1.

46. —, 'Bez programmy, bez perspektiv, bez kontrolya', *Nashe Slovo*, 233 (6 November 1915), p. 1.

47. —, 'Po adresu Longetistov', *Nashe Slovo*, 187 (13 August 1916), p. 1.

48. —, 'Proekt deklaratsii', *Nashe Slovo*, 182 (8 August 1916), p. 1.

49. —, 'V komitete dlya vosstanovleniya internats svyazei', *Nashe Slovo*, 188 (17 August 1916), p. 1.

50. A. Lozovskii, 'Po povodu odnoi deklaratsii', *Nashe Slovo*, 189 (18 August 1916), p. 1.

51. 'Ot Redaktsii', *Nashe Slovo*, 189 (18 August 1916), p. 2.

52. —, 'Frantsuzskii i nemetskii sotsial-patriotizm. chem sushchnost ppozitsii" longetistov?', *Nashe Slovo*, 212 (14 September 1916), p. 1.

53. —, 'Frantsuzskii i nemetskii sotsial-patriotizm'. II. Longetizm i nemetskoe "bol'shinstvo"', *Nashe Slovo*, 213 (15 September 1916), p. 1.

54. For a brief and useful account of the splits in British socialism during the war see Kissin, *War and the Marxists*, pp. 198–208.

55. —, 'K Dublinskim itogam', *Nashe Slovo*, 154 (4 July 1916), p. 1. See also

Trotsky's critique of Renaudel's sympathetic account of British action in Ireland in —, 'Clémence!', *Nashe Slovo*, 110 (11 May 1916), p. 1.

56. For an account of Chicherin's journalism from Britain, see, for example, Ian D. Thatcher, 'Representations of Scotland in *Nashe Slovo* during World War One: A Brief Note', *Scottish Historical Review* 78 (1999).

57. See, for example, 'Novaya Turtsiya', *Kievskaya Mysl*, 3 (3 January 1909); 'Balkanskii vopros i sotsial-demokratii', *Pravda*, 15 (1 August 1910); 'Nikola Pashich', *Kievskaya Mysl*, 349 (17 December 1912); 'Vokrug Voiny', *Kievskaya Mysl*, 295 (24 October 1912); 'Bolgariya i russkaya diplomatiya', *Dyen*, 38 (9 November 1912); and 'Bukharestskii mir', *Kievskaya Mysl*, 206 (28 July 1913).

58. N. Trotskii, 'Natsiya i khozyaistvo. I', *Nashe Slovo*, 130 (3 July 1915), p. 1.

59. —, 'Imperializm i natsional'naya ideya', *Nashe Slovo*, 82 (6 May 1915), p. 1.

60. N. T., 'Privet tov. Dobrodzhanu-Gerea', *Nashe Slovo*, 100 (29 May 1915), p. 3.

61. —, 'Na Balkanakh. II', *Nashe Slovo*, 143 (20 July, 1915), p. 1.

62. —, 'Bolgarskaya sots-dem i voina', *Nashe Slovo*, 214 (12 October 1915), p. 1.

63. —, 'Rakovskii o sotsial'-patriotakh', *Nashe Slovo*, 208 (5 October 1915), p. 1.

64. —, 'Khristyu Rakovskii', *Nashe Slovo*, 154 (4 July 1916), p. 1.

65. Dmitrii Volkogonov, *Trotskii. Politicheskii portret*, II (Moscow, 1992), p. 96.

9 From the Old World to the New: Spain and America

1. L. Trotskii, *Evropa v Voine* (Moscow, 1927), p. 267. (Part of this chapter appeared in an earlier form in *Historical Research*, 69, 1996.)

2. Ibid., p. 263.

3. Ibid., p. 265.

4. Ibid., pp. 271–2.

5. Ibid., pp. 289–90. At the same time Trotsky did favourably compare the friendly, attentive but lax regime of one of his Spanish police 'minders' with the professional attentiveness of the French secret police: see ibid., pp. 293–4).

6. 'Twenty Letters of Leon Trotsky', *The Socialist* (24 July 1919), p. 280.

7. Trotskii, *Evropa v Voine*, p. 312

8. Ibid., p. 305.

9. Trotsky wrote a satirical piece on the banning of *Nashe Slovo* under his new pseudonym of 'En' for *Nachalo*. See: En, 'Prestuplenie i nakazanie', *Nachalo*, 2 (1 October 1916), p. 1.

10. —, 'Privet druz'yam', *Nachalo*, 31 (5 November 1916), p. 1.

11. —, 'N. Trotskii v kadikse', *Nachalo*, 42 (18 November 1916), p. 1.

12. —, 'O tov. TROTSKOM', *Nachalo*, 52 (30 November 1916), p. 1.

13. Trotsky had written a critique of pacifism which appeared in *Nashe Slovo* of 1 and 2 of September 1916: —, 'Garantii mira. (K kharakteristike patsifizma) I.', *Nashe Slovo*, 201 (1 September 1916), pp. 1–2, and —, 'Garantii mira. (K kharakteristike patsifizma) II.', *Nashe Slovo*, 202 (2 September

1916), p. 1. Here he distinguished two varieties of pacifism: one, bourgeois, which argued that a lasting peace could be constructed on the basis of capitalism through international law; and another, socialist, which accepted that wars were a product of capitalist contradictions but thought it possible to regulate relations between imperialist countries through arbitration courts and disarmament programmes until the arrival of socialism. Trotsky rejected both bourgeois and socialist pacifism as 'utopian': 'no treaties and no arbitration courts can, however, stop the growth of the productive forces, their onslaught on the framework of the national state and the desire of the latter to widen the arena of exploitation for national capital with the help of militarism.' In conclusion Trotsky cited from a resolution of the Kienthal Conference which spoke of the illusions of pacifism and which insisted that peace could only be guaranteed through the establishment of socialism. For this resolution from Kienthal, see 'The Attitude of the Proletariat toward the Question of Peace. [Resolution of the Kienthal Conference]', Olga Hess Gankin and H. H. Fisher, *The Bolsheviks and the World War* (Stanford, 1940), pp. 421–4.

14. In his notebook in prison Trotsky speculated that it was French pressure on Spain, then dependent upon the Entente, which had led to his arrest. In turn, the demands of Tsarist diplomacy lay behind French actions. Trotsky thought that he was being held in prison to prepare his transfer to a Russian court and resolved to start a campaign in the press via Depré: see Trotskii, *Evropa v Voine*, pp. 279–80. In a letter to Depré of 29 November Trotsky claimed that Tsarist agents had planted copies of *Nashe Slovo* on Russian soldiers who had killed their colonel at Marsailles to justify his expulsion from France: see 'Twenty Letters of Leon Trotsky', *The Socialist* (31 July 1919), p. 288.

15. En, 'Ispanskiya "vpechatelniya". Pochti-arabskaya skazka', *Nachalo*, 54 (2 December 1916), p. 1.

16. For a copy of this letter, see *Evropa v Voine*, pp. 274–6.

17. This was also propagated by certain sections of the Spanish press. In a letter to Depré of 13 November Trotsky recommended that legal action be undertaken against the Spanish conservative paper *Accion* which had labelled Trotsky a 'terrorist': see 'Twenty Letters of Leon Trotsky', *The Socialist* (24 July 1919).

18. Ibid.

19. En, 'Ispanskiya "vpechatelniya"', p. 2.

20. Cited in —, 'Sotsialisticheskoe deistvie', *Nachalo*, 49 (26 November 1916), p. 1. In a letter of 9 December Trotsky speculated that his old enemy Aleksinskii was the author of the unsigned article in *L'Action Socialiste*: see 'Twenty Letters of Leon Trotsky', *The Socialist*, 7 August 1919, p. 296.

21. See, for example, —, 'Po povodu gnusnostei "Action Socialiste"', *Nachalo*, 59 (8 December 1916), p. 1; —, 'V zashchitu odnogo izganannika', *Nachalo*, 67 (17 December 1916), p. 1.

22. N. Trotskii, 'Vnusheniya "khefov", otkroveniya "akhentov"', *Nachalo*, 74 (27 December 1916), p. 1.

23. Vladimiorov sent a letter to *Nachalo* confirming Trotsky's version of events, claiming that other matters had prevented him from revealing the

falsity of *L'Action Socialiste*'s claims earlier. See L. Vladimirov, 'Pismo v Redaktsiyu', *Nachalo*, 75 (28 December 1916), p. 2.

24. See, for example, —, 'Tov. Trotskii v N'yu-Iorke', *Nachalo*, 108 (6 February 1917), p. 2; —, 'Tov. Trotskii v N'yu-Iorke', *Nachalo*, 116 (16 February 1916), p. 1. The latter piece was partially censored.

25. —, 'Trotskii vyslan iz ispanii, sobiraetsya v N'yu-Iorke', *Novyi Mir*, 851 (6 December 1916), p. 1.

26. —, 'Tov. Trotskii v N'yu-Iorke', *Novyi Mir*, 885 (15 January 1917), p. 1.

27. L. Trotskii, *Moya zhizn* (Moscow, 1991), p. 262.

28. N. Trotskii, 'Da zdravstvuet bor'ba!', *Novyi Mir*, 886 (16 January 1917), p. 4.

29. L. Trotskii, 'Pod znamenem sotsial'noi revolyutsii. (Rech na internatsional'nom n'yu-iorkskom "mitinge vstrechi" 25 Yanvarya 1917 g.)', *Voina i Revolyutsiya*, II (Moscow, 1924), p. 368.

30. N. Trotskii, 'Za dva s polovinoi goda voiny v Evrope (iz dnevnika). I. Serbskie terroristy i frantsuzskie "osvoboditeli" – Venskiya nastroeniya v pervyie dni voiny', *Novyi Mir*, 895 (26 January 1917), p. 4; N. Trotskii, 'Za dva ... II. Nastroeniya v avstriiskoi s-d – Viktor Adler – Ot'ezde v Tsyurikh', *Novyi Mir*, 903 (5 February 1917), p. 2; Lev N. Trotskii, 'Za dva ... III. "predatel'stvo nemtsev" – Plekhanov – Greilikh', *Novyi Mir*, 914 (17 February 1917), p. 4; Lev N. Trotskii, 'Za dva ... IV. Shveitsurskaya sotsialdemokratya – "Gryutli" – "Eintrakht" – Frits Platten – Nemetskaya broshyura   "Voina i Internatsional" – Sotsialisticheskaya pripiska k shtatu', *Novyi Mir*, 928 (6 March 1917), p. 4; Lev N. Trotskii, 'Za dva ... V. Pereezde vo Frantsie – Parizh – Viviani – Zhofre – Brian – Klemanso', *Novyi Mir*, 943 (22 March 1917), p. 4. Trotsky gave his version of how tsarist diplomacy had had him exiled from France in Lev N. Trotskii, 'Tsarizm na respublikanskoi pochve. I', *Novyi Mir*, 908 (10 February 1917), p. 4, and Lev N. Trotskii, 'Tsariam na respublikanskoi pochve. II', *Novyi Mir*, 909 (12 February 1917), p. 4.

31. In a subsequent note in *Novyi Mir* Trotsky said that he had received a letter in which he was asked why he had remained silent on Plekhanov's social-nationalism when he first learned of it from Rakovsky in 1913? In reply Trotsky pointed to the state of affairs in the pre-war era. In public Plekahnov either spoke the language of internationalism or said nothing at all. In such circumstances what basis would the public have had for believing Trotsky's revelations based on a personal conversation? It was Plekhanov's current post-war stance that made Trotsky's revelation possible: 'If now I considered it possible to cite these personal observations, it was only because they supplement Plekhanov's current public excesses and to a certain degree add to them a psychological explanation': Lev N. Trotskii, 'Na zaprosy chitatelei. O Plekhanove', *Novyi Mir*, 926 (3 March 1917), p. 4.

32. N. Trotskii, 'Vo frantsuzkom vagone. (Razgovory i razmyshleniya). I', *Novyi Mir*, 900 (1 February 1917), p. 3. Two days later Trotsky presented another depressing account of trench warfare when he reproduced the letter of a Russian volunteer serving in the French army: see Al'fa, 'Dokumenty voiny', *Novyi Mir*, 902 (3 February 1917), p. 4.

33. N. Trotskii, 'Vo frantsuzkom vagone. (Razgovory i razmyshleniya). II', *Novyi Mir*, 901 (2 February 1917), p. 4.

34. For an account of America's neutrality and the events which led it to enter the First World War, see, for example, John Whiteclay Chambers II, *The Tyranny of Change: America in the Progressive Era, 1900–1917* (New York, 1980), pp. 199–228.
35. N. Trotskii, 'Povtorenie proidennago', *Novyi Mir*, 905 (7 February 1917), p. 4.
36. N. Trotskii, 'V shkole voiny', *Novyi Mir*, 904 (6 February 1917), p. 4.
37. Lev N. Trotskii, 'Chto govoril International o zashchite otechestva?', *Novyi Mir*, 922 (27 February 1917), p. 4.
38. Lev N. Trotskii, 'Dva voyuyushchikh lagerya', *Novyi Mir*, 930 (8 March 1917), p. 4.
39. Trotsky also made this point in the article 'One Has to Choose the Way'. Here, however, he illustrated how social-patriotism leads to a rejection of revolutionary socialism not so much through the example of recent European experience, as through a comparison of social-patriotism with other movements (Christianity, the Reformation, liberalism and democracy) which had began as a protest on behalf of the oppressed and ended as tools of the oppressors. See Lev N. Trotskii, 'Nuzhno vybirat put', *Novyi Mir*, 919 (23 February 1917), p. 4.
40. Cited in —, 'Bol'shoe obyazatel'stvo. (Po povodu rezolyutsii mitinga v Karnegi Goll)', *Novyi Mir*, 906 (8 February 1917), p. 3. For Trotsky's response to the pacifist Hillquit's charge that Trotsky had no right to advise others to pursue revolutionary tactics since Trotsky himself had not been prepared to stay in Russia to do likewise, see 'Revolyutsionnyi tsenz Khilkvita. (Pis'mo v redaktsiyu "N.-Y. Volkszeitung")', Trotskii, *Voina i Revolyutsiya*, II, pp. 381–3.
41. Lev N. Trotskii, 'Karlu Tsetkin lushche im ostavit v pokoe. (Pis'mo v redaktsiyu)', *Novyi Mir*, 910 (13 February 1917), p. 4.
42. Anna Ingerman, 'Iz za chego shum tov. Trotskii?', *Novyi Mir*, 913 (16 February 1917), p. 3.
43. In *Novyi Mir* of 3 March 1917 Trotsky replied to a letter that he had received from Mary Ragoz. Ragoz asked Trotsky what assistance international socialists could afford the war wounded when, as far as she knew, there were only two doctors among the group of Russian socialists in America, and none among the Finish section. In light of this she wondered whether it would not be better to view the Red Cross as a neutral organisation, like a library or a tram. Trotsky stated that he was not proposing that internationalists should *replace* the Red Cross with their own body. He knew that the movement did not have the resources to achieve this, and even if it did the state would not permit this 'just as it does not give soldiers a free choice between state and private doctors'. As matters stood the Red Cross had as its aim healing the sick so as to ensure their speedy return to the front and this was why socialists could not participate in it. Socialists could aid the wounded by publicising soldiers' rights, maintaining ties with comrade soldiers, sending them books and tobacco; in this way preserving their *socialist* spirit: see Lev N. Trotskii, 'Na zaprosy chitatelei. O Krasnom Kreste', *Novyi Mir*, 926 (3 March 1917), p. 4.
44. L. Trotskii, 'A vse-taki Klaru Tsetkin naprasno trevozhite!', *Novyi Mir*, 913

(16 February 1917), p. 3.

45. For an exposition of the origins of the Council for National Defence, its Advisory Council and Gompers role in them, see B. Mandel, *Samuel Gompers* (Ohio, 1963), pp. 364ff.

46. —, 'Baran'ya konstitutsiya. (Konferentsiya Gompersa i Ko)', *Novyi Mir*, 936 (15 March 1917), p. 4.

47. For an account of the American Jewish workers' movement and *Forverts*'s place in it, see, for example, Arthur A. Goren, *New York Jews and the Quest for Community* (New York, 1970); Irving Howe, *The Immigrant Jews of New York* (London, 1976); and Nora Levin, *Jewish Socialist Movements, 1871–1917* (London, 1978).

48. Joseph Nedava, *Trotsky and the Jews* (Philadelphia, 1971), p. 26.

49. Lev N. Trotskii, 'Obshchei pochvy s "Forvertsom" U Nas Net', *Novyi Mir*, 928 (6 March 1917), p. 4 . On the following day Trotsky likened *Forverts*'s change from a pro- to an anti-German stance to the dilemma of a German bourgeois proprietor who until 3 February had published pro-German articles, but after this date found it expedient to argue for the American cause. See Al'fa, 'Kto otgadaet?', *Novyi Mir*, 929 (7 March 1917), p. 4.

50. On 9 March Trotsky reported that *Forverts* was claiming that somebody had mistranslated its editorial of 1 March for Trotsky. Trotsky's response is illustrated by the heading of his reply to *Forverts*: 'It's Untrue!'. See L.N.T., 'Nepravda!', *Novyi Mir*, 931 (9 March 1917), p. 3. Given Trotsky's Jewish origins, it may at first sight appear strange that he needed somebody to translate from Yiddish into Russian for him. However, from his autobiography we discover that Trotsky did not learn to speak Yiddish at home (his father spoke a mixture of Ukrainian/Russian), and he must have gained only the slightest knowledge of Hebrew from his brief period of study of the bible in Hebrew: see Trotskii, *Moya zhizn*, pp. 38, 54, 56. For an alternative view, i.e. that Trotsky knew Yiddish well and could easily communicate in it, see Nedava, *Trotsky and the Jews*, pp. 35–7. Here Nedava claims that Trotsky hid his knowledge of Yiddish when he came to write his autobiography since he wanted to stress that he was a citizen of the world: 'As he never considered himself a son of the Pale of Settlement, but rather a true citizen of the world, he naturally could not admit to ever having shown interest in learning the language of the Pale.'

51. —, 'Neobkhodimo ochishchenie riadov; rol "Forvertsa" v evreiskom rabochem dvizhenii', *Novyi Mir*, 935 (14 March 1917), p. 4.

52. Trotsky commented on Cahan's activities one more time in *Novyi Mir* when, to mark Cahan's speech at a meeting in Madison Square Garden, he argued that the editor of *Forverts* had no revolutionary credentials. He labelled Cahan's comment in *Forverts* that Russia was not ripe for a republic and his telegram of welcome to Milyukov as an 'impudent call to the Russian proletariat and an insult to the Russian revolution'. See —, 'G-n Kagan, kak istolkovatel russkoi revolyutsii pered rabochimi N'yu Iorka', *Novyi Mir*, 941 (20 March 1917), p. 4. When Trotsky came to write of his time in New York in his autobiography he did not mention his initial cooperation with *Forverts*, giving only a negative characterisation of the Jewish daily newspaper: Trotskii, *Moya zhizn*, p. 268.

53. Al'fa, 'Zatrudneniya chitatelya', *Novyi Mir*, 931 (9 March 1917), p. 4.

54. Al'fa, 'Obrabotka i pozolota', *Novyi Mir*, 937 (16 March 1917), p. 4.

55. Cited in Chambers, *The Tyranny of Change*, p. 221. In 'Through the Window' Trotsky described the scene, witnessed while staring out of *Novyi Mir's* office window, of an old man picking his way through a litter bin and selecting some mouldy bread, and wondered how President Wilson would explain how the old man's rights and dignity were being defended by the war: see Al'fa, 'U okna', *Novyi Mir*, 926 (3 March 1917), p. 3).

56. Lev N. Trotskii, 'Dlya chego Amerike voina?', *Novyi Mir*, 931 (9 March 1917), p. 4.

57. Trotskii, *Moya zhizn*, p. 263.

58. Al'fa, 'Zhvachka', *Novyi Mir*, 932 (10 March 1917), p. 4.

59. —, 'Voina i revolyutsii', *Novyi Mir*, 943 (22 March 1917), p. 4. In 'Sober Thoughts' Trotsky noted the mayor's inadequate response to the problem of rising prices brought about by the war crisis. He warned the mayor that when hungry mothers protest it is not only mayors who lose their jobs: See Al'fa, 'Trezvyya mysli', *Novyi Mir*, 928 (6 March 1917), p. 4.

60. —, 'Gotov'te soldat revolyutsii', *Novyi Mir*, 930 (8 March 1917), p. 4.

61. N. Trotskii, 'Uroki velikago goda. 9 yanvarya 1905 – 9 yanvarya 1917g', *Novyi Mir*, 890 (20 January 1917), p. 4.

62. Al'fa, 'Opyat otkryli dumu', *Novyi Mir*, 930 (8 March 1917), p. 4.

63. For an exposition of Trotsky's views on these issues as they developed from 1905 onwards, see Ian D. Thatcher, 'Uneven and Combined Development', *Revolutionary Russia*, 4(2) (1991), pp. 235–58.

64. Lev N. Trotskii, 'Dva litsa. (Vnutrenniya sily russkoi revolyutsii)', *Novyi Mir*, 938 (17 March 1917), p. 4 .

65. Lev N. Trotskii, 'Ot kogo i kak zashchishchat revolyutsiyu?', *Novyi Mir*, 942 (21 March 1917), p. 4 . For Trotsky's analysis of Europe on the verge of revolution, see also Lev N. Trotskii, 'Nespokoino v Evrope', *Novyi Mir*, 936 (15 March 1917), p. 4 and —, 'Pod znamenem kommuny', *Novyi Mir*, 938 (17 March 1917), p. 4. For further articles by Trotsky on Russia after the March revolution which were summarised but not directly quoted from in the main text of this chapter see, Lev N. Trotskii, 'U poroga revolyutsii', *Novyi Mir*, 934 (13 March 1917), p. 4; —, 'Revolyutsiya v Rossii', *Novyi Mir*, 937 (16 March 1917), p. 4; Lev N. Trotskii, 'Narostayushchii konflikt'. (Vnutrenniya sily revolyutsii)', *Novyi Mir*, 940 (19 March 1917), p. 4; and —, 'Voina ili mir? (Vnutrenniya sily revolyutsii)', *Novyi Mir*, 941 (20 March 1917), p. 4. For an account of how Trotsky attempted to use his 1917 articles in *Novyi Mir* to argue that only he and Lenin had shared the same analysis of the further development of the Russian revolution when he wrote his *Istoriya russkoi revolyutsii* (1931), see James D. White, 'Trotsky's *History of the Russian Revolution*', *Journal of Trotsky Studies*, 1 (1993), pp. 1–18.

66. *Novyi Mir* announced Trotsky's departure for Russia in —, 'Ot'ezd tovarishchii', *Novyi Mir*, 949 (28 March 1917), p. 1. For Trotsky's account of the difficulties he encountered at the Russian embassy in New York in obtaining a passport, see, Al'fa, 'V Russkom konsul'stve', *Novyi Mir*, 944 (23 March 1917), p. 4.

67. Giving lectures was also a convenient way of raising money. Draper says

that while in New York Trotsky gave 'no fewer than thirty-five lectures ... at ten dollars a lecture': T. Draper, *The Roots of American Communism* (New York, 1957), p. 77.

Conclusion

1. For this argument, see, for example, R. Pipes, *The Russian Revolution 1899–1919* (London 1990), p. 195.
2. For this argument, see, for example, I. Kershaw, *Hitler 1889–1936: Hubris* (London, 1998), p. 73.
3. Peter Gowan, 'The NATO Powers and the Balkan Tragedy', *New Left Review*, 234 (March/April 1999), p. 104.

Bibliography

As the notes to each chapter contain extensive references, the Bibliography is limited to the main items consulted.

Archive Materials

Rossiiskogo Tsentra Khraneniya i Izucheniya Dokumentov Noveishei Istorii (RTsKhIDNI), Moscow.

Published Books by L. D. Trotsky

Ot Fevralya do Oktyabr. Sochineniya, vol. III, pt. 1 (Moscow, nd).
Gody Velikogo Pereloma (Moscow, 1919).
Itogi i Perspektivy (Moscow, 1919).
Voina i Revolyutsiya, 2 vols (Moscow and Petrograd, 1922–4).
Evrope v Voine. Sochineniya, vol. IX (Moscow and Leningrad, 1927).
Istoriya Russkoi Revolyutsiya, vol. I (Berlin, 1931).
Stalinskaya Shkola Fal'sifikatsii (Moscow, 1990).
Uroki Oktyabrya (St Petersburg, 1991).
Moya Zhizn (Moscow, 1991).
The War and the International (n.p., 1971).
Le Guerre et la Révolution (Paris, 1974).

Published Books and Collections of Works by Other Russian Social Democrats

Samozashchita. Marksistskii sbornik (Petrograd, 1916).
Voina: sbornik statei (Paris, 1915).
V.V. Adoratskii, V.V. Molotov and M.A. Savel'ev (eds), *Leninskii sbornik*, vols XIV, XVII (Moscow, 1930, 1931).
N.I. Bukharin, *K Voprosu o Trotskizme* (Moscow, 1925).
F. Dan, B. Nikolaevskii and L. Tsederbaum-Dan (eds), *Pis'ma P.B. Aksel'roda i Yu.O. Martova* (Berlin, 1924).
A.G. Egorov (ed.), *Leninskii sbornik*, vol. XXXIX (Moscow, 1980).
L.B. Kamenev (ed.), *Leninskii sbornik*, vols II, IV (Moscow, 1924, 1925).
V.I. Lenin, *Polnoe sobranie sochinenii*, 55 vols (Moscow, 1971–80).
L. Martov, *Protiv voiny! Sbornik statei* (Moscow, 1917).
G.V. Plekhanov, *O voine* 5th Edition (Petrograd, n.d.).
G.V. Plekhanov, *Voprosy voiny i sotsializma* (Petrograd, 1917).
G. Zinov'ev & N. Lenin, *Sotsializma i voina* (Geneva, 1915).
G. Zinov'ev, *Sochineniya*, vol. V (Moscow, 1924).

255

Published Documents

E. Egorov and K.M. Bogolyubova (eds), *KPSS v Rezolyutsiyakh i Ressheniyakh S'ezdov, Konferentsii i Plenumov*, vol. I (Moscow, 1983).

O.H. Gankin and H.H. Fisher (eds), *The Bolsheviks and the World War* (Stanford, 1940).

J. Riddle (ed.), *Lenin's Struggle for a Revolutionary International* (New York, 1984).

Journals and Newspapers

Golos
Informatsionnyi Listok Zagranichnoi Organizatsii Bunda
Izvestiya Zagranichnago Sekretariata Organizatsionnago Komiteta
Kommunist
Nachalo
Nashe Slovo
Novosti
Novyi Mir
Prizyv
Sbornik Sotsial'Demokrata
Sotsial'Demokrat
The Times

Other Sources

A.N. Atsarkin and A.T. Barulina, *Bor'ba Bolshevikov za osushchestvlenie leninskoi programmy po voprosam voina, mir i revolyutsii* (Moscow, 1963).

A.J. Berlau, *The German Social Democratic Party, 1914–1921* (New York, 1949).

P. Broué, *Trotsky* (Paris, 1988).

J. Carmichael, *Trotsky: An Appreciation of his Life and Thought* (London, 1975).

J.W. Chambers II, *The Tyranny of Change: America in the Progressive Era, 1900–1917* (New York, 1980).

E.D. Chermenskii, *Rossiya v period imperialisticheskoi voiny. Vtoraya revolyutsiya v Rossii (1914–Mart 1917)* (Moscow, 1957).

T. Cliff, *Trotsky 1879–1917: Towards October* (London, 1989).

T. Cliff, *Trotsky: The Sword of the Revolution* (London, 1990).

T. Cliff, *Trotsky: Fighting the Rising Stalinist Bureaucracy* (London, 1991).

I. Deutscher, *The Prophet Armed* (Oxford, 1954).

T. Draper, *The Roots of American Communism* (New York, 1957).

V.S. Dyakin, *Russkaya burzhuaziya i tsarizm v gody pervoi mirovoi voiny 1914–1917* (Leningrad, 1967).

M. Fainsod, *International Socialism and the World War* (New York, 1973).

I. Getzler, *Martov* (London, 1967).

A.A. Goren, *New York Jews and the Quest for Community* (New York, 1970).

Yu.V. Got'e, 'Moi zametki', *Voprosy istorii*, 11 (1991), pp. 150–77.

D. Hallas, *Trotsky's Marxism* (London, 1979).

I. Howe, *The Immigrant Jews of New York: 1881 to the Present* (London, 1976).

I. Howe, *Trotsky* (Sussex, 1978).

S.F. Kissin, *War and the Marxists: Socialist Theory and Practice in Capitalist Wars* (London, 1988).

B. Knei-Paz, *The Social and Political Thought of Leon Trotsky* (Oxford, 1978).

R.B. McKean, *St Petersburg Between the Revolutions* (New Haven and London, 1978).

B. Mandel, *Samuel Gompers: A Bibliography* (Ohio, 1963).

K. Marx, *Preface to a Contribution to a Critique of Political Economy* (Moscow, 1970).

K. Marx, *Surveys from Exile* (Harmondsworth, 1973).

K. Marx, *The First International and After* (Harmondsworth, 1974).

K. Mavrikis, *On Trotskyism* (London, 1976).

S. Miller and H. Potthoff, *A History of German Social Democracy* (New York, 1983).

J. Nedava, *Trotsky and the Jews* (Philadelphia, 1972).

P. Nettl, *Rosa Luxemburg* (Oxford, 1969).

A.V. Pantsov, '"Demon revolyutsii" ili proletarskii revolyutsioner?', *Politicheskie issledovanniya*, 1 (1991), pp. 88–94.

B. Pearce, 'Lenin versus Trotsky on "Revolutionary Defeatism"', *Study Group on the Russian Revolution Sbornik*, 13 (1987), pp. 16–30.

R. Pearson, *The Russian Moderates and the Crisis of Tsarism 1914–1917* (London, 1977).

R. Pipes, *The Russian Revolution 1899–1919* (London, 1990).

P. Pomper, *Lenin, Trotsky and Stalin* (New York, 1990).

T. Riha, *A Russian European: Paul Miliukov in Russian Politics* (Notre Dame, 1969).

A. Rosmer, 'Trotsky in Paris During World War One', *New International*, September–October 1950, pp. 263–78.

L.J. van Rossum, 'Ein unverffentlichter brief Trockijs von anfang 1916', *International Review of Social History*, 14 (1969), pp. 251–66.

M. Salvadori, *Karl Kautsky and the Socialist Revolution, 1880–1938* (London, 1979).

P.A. Satyukov, *Bolshevistskaya pechat v period imperialisticheskoi voiny i vtoroi revolyutsii v Rossii* (Moscow, 1951).

C.E. Schorske, *German Social Democracy, 1905–1917* (Cambridge, Mass., 1955).

R. Segal, *The Tragedy of Leon Trotsky* (Harmondsworth, 1983).

S.V. Shestakov, *Istoriografiya deyatel'nosti bol'shevistskoi partii v period pervoi mirovoi voiny I fevral'skoi revolyutsii* (Moscow, 1977).

L. Sinclair, *Trotsky: A Bibliography* (Aldershot, 1989).

Ya.G. Temkin, *Lenin i mezhdunarodnaya sotsial-demokratiya 1914–1917* (Moscow, 1968).

D. Volkogonov, *Trotskii. Politicheskoi portret*, vol. I (Moscow, 1992).

R. Wistrich, *Trotsky: Fate of a Revolutionary* (London, 1979).

E. Zaleski, *Mouvements ouvriers et socialistes (chronologie et bibliographie): La Russie*, vol. II (Paris, 1956).

V.V. Zaplatkin, *Bor'ba V.I. Lenina protiv 'Imperialisticheskogo ekonomizma'* (Moscow, 1967).

Index

258

DATE DUE
